UNDERSTANDING
BALANCE
SHEETS

Other related books include:

Understanding Income Statements by Franklin J. Plewa, Jr., and
George T. Friedlob

Understanding Cash Flow by Franklin J. Plewa, Jr., and
George T. Friedlob

Understanding Return on Investment by George T. Friedlob and
Franklin J. Plewa, Jr.

How to Read a Financial Report by John A. Tracy

UNDERSTANDING BALANCE SHEETS

George T. Friedlob
Franklin J. Plewa, Jr.

JOHN WILEY & SONS, INC.
New York • Chichester • Brisbane • Toronto • Singapore

Copyright © 1996 by George T. Friedlob and Franklin J. Plewa, Jr.
Published by John Wiley & Sons, Inc.

Library of Congress Cataloging-in-Publication Data:

ISBN 0-471-13075-3

Printed in the United States of America

10 9 8 7 6 5 4 3 2 1

Preface

*T*his book can be used by readers who have little or no accounting knowledge. No assumptions are made regarding readers' educational background, but some exposure to business will facilitate a quicker grasp of the relevance of some of the material.

The creation and use of accounting information are emphasized, to give the reader a broad, general understanding of the elements of the balance sheet, the related disclosures contained in an annual report, and the methods used to analyze a company's balance sheet. Although the focus is on the balance sheet, exploration of its significance must be viewed in light of all the information presented in a company's annual report.

The book's objectives are to:

1. Present the general conventions and principles that govern financial accounting and reporting.

2. Explain how accounting data are created, accumulated, and used in the development of financial statements.

3. Illustrate how information contained in the balance sheet often reflects a company's choices of methods and techniques of reporting.

4. Link a company's choice of accounting methods and techniques to its balance sheet presentation and to readers' analysis and use of the information the balance sheet contains.

Chapters 1 through 3 present a discussion of general-purpose financial statements and generally accepted accounting principles. Chapters 4 through 6 discuss the *current assets* section of the balance sheet, focusing on cash, short-term investments, receivables, notes receivable, and inventories. Investments, plant assets, natural resources, intangibles, and other noncurrent assets are examined in Chapters 7 through 11, and a comprehensive review of depreciation methods is offered in Chapter 8.

Chapter 12 covers *current liabilities* and how they create spontaneous financing when businesses grow. The time value of money, used to value many long-term liabilities, is the topic of Chapter 13. Long-term liabilities themselves are discussed in Chapters 14 and 15, and stockholders' equity is presented in Chapter 16.

The disclosures relating to the balance sheet and an explanation of the audit opinion are covered in Chapter 17. Financial leverage and operating leverage are discussed in Chapters 18 and 19 respectively. The final chapter details the analysis of the balance sheet through the use of ratios.

Extensive excerpts from actual public company annual reports are included to illustrate the text discussion and to highlight important points. The book is a working reference for understanding a company's balance sheet in the context of its annual report.

GEORGE T. FRIEDLOB
FRANKLIN J. PLEWA, JR.

Clemson, South Carolina
Pocatello, Idaho
March 1996

Acknowledgments

*W*e wish to express our heartfelt gratitude to our families. Their support and suggestions have made this book possible. In particular, we thank our wives for creating an atmosphere in which we could let the creative juices flow at any hour, day or night.

G.T.F.
F.J.P.

Contents

1

ACCOUNTING AND THE BALANCE SHEET

*A*ccounting is thousands of years old. The earliest accounting records, found in ruins of ancient Babylon, Assyria, and Sumeria, date back more than 7,000 years. Scribes recorded business transactions on clay tablets, in wedge-shaped cuneiform writing. Accounting evolved, improving over the years and advancing as business advanced. Primitive people, using agricultural and pastoral accounting methods, recorded the growth of crops and herds. Because there is a natural season to farming and herding, it is easy to count and determine profit after the crops are harvested or the young animals weaned.

Later, when Columbus, Magellan, and others traveled the world in search of wealth, accounting focused on determining the profit earned by particular ventures. Queen Isabella gave Columbus ships and supplies for his voyages. Upon his return, accountants compared the worth of the ships and new-world booty to the cost of the initial provisions. The difference was profit.

1

EXHIBIT 1–1
Pastoral Accounting

Balance sheet/Owner's wealth
Beginning of spring:
  100 sheep

Profit = 20 sheep

Balance sheet/Owner's wealth
End of summer:
  120 sheep

Because of the natural beginning and end of ventures and of agricultural and pastoral activities, balance sheets for those activities were easy to prepare. Profit was the growth in the owners' wealth between balance sheets. If a shepherd took 100 sheep into a high meadow in early spring and returned in August with 120 sheep, the profit was 20 sheep (Exhibit 1–1). If a farmer planted 50 shekels worth of seed and later harvested grain worth 1,000 shekels, the profit was 950 shekels (Exhibit 1–2).

Accounting and Modern Business

Modern business ventures do not have a convenient beginning and end. Plants operate continually, year after year. Trucks make deliveries,

EXHIBIT 1–2
Agricultural Accounting

Balance sheet/Owner's wealth		Balance sheet/Owner's wealth	
Beginning of summer:		End of summer:	
Land	2,000 shekels	Land	2,000 shekels
Seed	50 shekels	Grain	1,000 shekels
Total	2,050 shekels	Total	3,000 shekels

Profit = 950 shekels

---

merchants open their doors, and, in the absence of failure, business goes on indefinitely. Balance sheets, which were once pictures of a business at rest at the start or finish of a venture, are now action photographs of an entity in motion. Plants do not shut down, trucks are not garaged, merchants do not close their doors so accountants can measure wealth or debt on balance sheet dates.

Accountants must break business activity into artificial periods (quarters and years) because investors are not content to wait until a long-term "venture" is over to learn of its success or failure. Accountants must divine the values in the balance sheets and the profit between balance sheet dates, in a dynamic environment where nothing ever stands still and the best measures available are often only estimates. If equipment wears out over 20 years, how much wear should be expensed each year? Some customer accounts will not be collected, but a business can't predict which ones. How much should be charged off as bad debts?

Interestingly, accountants do a pretty accurate job, even in today's uncertain world—mostly because their profession had thousands of years to develop a system and has spent over 200 years perfecting the procedures in use today. Two years after Columbus discovered America, another Italian, Luca Bartolomes Pacioli, wrote a book (*Summa de Arithmetica, Geometria, Proportioni et Proportionalita*) that described the method used by Venetian merchants to record business transactions. (The book also contained the first published explanation of the concept of negative numbers and used negative numbers in recording business activities—exciting, cutting-edge technology in the 15th century!)[1] The *Summa* provided the sense and rationale for the modern accounting methods that followed.

The Language of Business

Accounting is called the language of business because it is the vehicle for reporting financial information about a company to many different groups

---

[1] Michael E. Scorgie, "Early Arithmetics and Accounting Histories: A Comment," *Abacus,* Vol. 27, No. 1, March 1991, pp. 78–79.

of people. Accounting that concentrates on reporting to people inside the company is called managerial accounting and is used to provide information to employees, managers, owner-managers, and auditors. Managerial accounting is concerned primarily with providing a basis for making management and operating decisions.

Accounting that provides the information used by people outside the company is called financial accounting. Financial accounting provides information to groups including present and potential stockholders, creditors such as banks or vendors, financial analysts, economists, and government agencies. Because these users have different needs, the presentation of financial accounting information is very structured and subject to many more rules than managerial accounting. Each user group must satisfy its needs from the same publicly available quarterly or annual reports, so it is essential that the content and form of presentation of financial information are clearly understood.

The body of rules that governs financial accounting is called generally accepted accounting principles, or GAAP. The GAAP are derived from custom and tradition and from the pronouncements of the Financial Accounting Standards Board (FASB) and the Securities and Exchange Commission (SEC). The Internal Revenue Service (IRS) requires companies to use a modified version of GAAP-based reporting.

The Balance Sheet

Pacioli's Venetian method is based on a simple relationship: economic resources can be described in terms of their sources, and the dollar amount of economic resources must equal the dollar amount of their sources.

$$\text{Resources} = \text{Their Sources}$$

The resources owned by a company are called *assets*. The two sources of a company's assets are debt and owners' investment. The dollar amount of assets owned must equal the dollar amount of debt and owners' investment.

$$\text{Assets} = \text{Debts} + \text{Owners' Investment}$$

The accounting terms for debt and owners' investment are *liabilities* and *owners' equity*. Equity means property rights, and owners' equity in the balance sheet includes the owners' direct investment in the company and all reinvestments of company earnings not distributed to owners. This relationship is called the balance sheet equation.

$$\text{Assets} = \text{Liabilities} + \text{Owners' Equity}$$

This equation provides a system of internal checks on the accounting system because each transaction must affect the balance sheet equation in two ways if the equation is to be kept in balance. Because of this function, modern accounting is known as the double-entry system.

To illustrate, assume Baxter Company is started with a $50,000 investment by owners who receive shares of stock. Because the accounts are arranged in an equation, the birth of the company must be shown as affecting both the asset cash and owners' equity. If both effects are not recorded, or if they are recorded incorrectly, the equation will not balance.

$$\text{Assets} = \text{Liabilities} + \text{Owners' Equity}$$

Cash		Common Stock
$50,000 =	0 +	$50,000

Assume that Baxter Company borrows $80,000 from a bank. Assets are increased when cash is received, and the liability of the bank note is recorded.

Assets =	Liabilities	+ Owners' Equity
Cash	Note to Bank	Common Stock
$ 50,000 =	0 +	$50,000
+ 80,000 =	$80,000 +	0
$130,000 =	$80,000 +	$50,000

Next, Baxter purchases a truck for $40,000 cash. Again, two accounts are affected, only this time they are both asset accounts: Cash and Truck.

Cash is decreased by $40,000, and the Truck account is increased by $40,000. (Accountants frequently use parentheses to indicate negative numbers. We use this technique to record this transaction.)

Assets		=	Liabilities	+ Owners' Equity
Cash	Truck		Note to Bank	Common Stock
$130,000		=	$80,000 +	$50,000
(40,000)	$40,000			
$ 90,000	+ $40,000 =		$80,000 +	$50,000

The balance sheet is also called the Statement of Financial Position. It describes a company's financial position by showing the company's assets, liabilities, and owners' equity at a particular point in time (often, December 31). Exhibit 1–3 shows the balances in the accounts of Wal-Mart Stores as of January 31, 1994, and compares them to the balances a year earlier.[2]

Profit Earned Between Balance Sheet Dates

Owners' equity is increased by owners' investments in the company and is decreased by owners' withdrawals of funds from the company (by means of declaring and paying dividends, if the company is incorporated). But a business is formed to create a profit and increase the owners' wealth. Individual business transactions that increase owners' equity (owners' wealth) are called revenues. Individual business transactions that decrease owners' equity (owners' wealth) are called expenses. The excess of revenues over expenses is profit. Exhibit 1–4 summarizes the basic changes in owners' equity.

---

[2] Throughout the book, notes accompanying displayed balance sheets or other financial reports are not reproduced unless specifically noted.

EXHIBIT 1–3
Wal-Mart Stores, Inc., and Subsidiaries, Consolidated Balance Sheet

(Amounts in thousands) January 31,	1994	1993
Assets		
Current assets:		
Cash and cash equivalents	$ 20,115	$ 12,363
Receivables	689,987	524,555
Recoverable costs from sale/leaseback	208,236	312,016
Inventories:		
At replacement cost	11,483,119	9,779,981
Less LIFO reserve	469,413	511,672
LIFO	11,013,706	9,268,309
Prepaid expenses and other	182,558	80,347
Total current assets	12,114,602	10,197,590
Property, plant, and equipment, at cost:		
Land	2,740,883	1,692,510
Buildings and improvements	6,818,479	4,641,009
Fixtures and equipment	3,980,674	3,417,230
Transportation equipment	259,537	111,151
	13,799,573	9,861,900
Less accumulated depreciation	2,172,808	1,607,623
Net property, plant, and equipment	11,626,765	8,254,277
Property under capital leases	2,058,588	1,986,104
Less accumulated amortization	509,987	447,500
Net property under capital leases	1,548,601	1,538,604
Other Assets and Deferred Charges	1,150,796	574,616
Total assets	$26,440,764	$20,565,087
Liabilities and Shareholders' Equity		
Current liabilities:		
Commercial paper	$ 1,575,029	$ 1,588,825
Accounts payable	4,103,878	3,873,331
Accrued liabilities	1,473,198	1,042,108
Accrued federal and state income taxes	183,031	190,620
Long-term debt due within one year	19,658	13,849
Obligations under capital leases due within one year	51,429	45,553
Total current liabilities	7,406,223	6,754,286
Long-Term Debt	6,155,894	3,072,835
Long-Term Obligations Under Capital Leases	1,804,300	1,772,152
Deferred Income Taxes	321,909	206,634
Shareholders' equity:		
Preferred stock ($.10 par value; 100,000 shares authorized, none issued)		
Common stock ($.10 par value; 5,500,000 shares authorized, 2,298,769 and 2,299,638 issued and outstanding in 1994 and 1993, respectively)	229,877	229,964
Capital in excess of par value	535,639	526,647
Retained earnings	9,986,922	8,002,569
Total shareholders' equity	10,752,438	8,759,180
Total liabilities and shareholders' equity	$26,440,764	$20,565,087

EXHIBIT 1-4

Events That Cause Increases or Decreases in Owners' Equity

Owners' equity is increased by:
  Revenues earned
  Investment by owners

Owners' equity is decreased by:
  Expenses incurred
  Dividends paid to owners

When revenues and expenses are included, our original equation expands to five accounts.

$$\text{Assets} = \text{Liabilities} + \text{Owners' Equity} + \text{Revenues} - \text{Expenses}$$

The relationship among the accounts has grown more complex, but the equation now contains all the categories of accounts that accountants ever use. There are no others.

To illustrate the way revenues and expenses affect the balance sheet, assume Baxter makes a delivery with its truck and receives $1,000 cash in payment for this service. The Cash and Revenue accounts are each increased $1,000, thereby increasing total Assets and Owners' Equity.

Assets		=	Liabilities	+	Owners' Equity	+	Revenue
Cash	Truck		Note to Bank		Common Stock		
$90,000 +	$40,000 =		$80,000	+	$50,000		
1,000						+	$1,000
$91,000 +	$40,000 =		$80,000	+	$50,000	+	$1,000

The truck driver is paid $50 in wages, and $200 for gasoline was charged on the company credit card. These two events affect the accounts as follows.

Assets		= Liabilities		+ Owners' Equity	+ Revenue	− Expenses	
Cash	Truck	Note to Bank	Credit Card			Wages	Gasoline
$91,000 +	$40,000 =	$80,000	+	$50,000	+ $1,000		
($ 50)		+	$200			$50	$200
$90,950 +	$40,000 =	$80,000 +	$200 +	$50,000	+ $1,000 −	$50 −	$200

Do the assets still equal the liabilities plus owners' equity? Yes, assets of $130,950 equal liabilities of $80,200 plus owners' equity of $50,750.

$$\text{Assets} = \text{Liabilities} + \text{Owners' Equity}$$
$$\$130,950 = \$80,200 + \$50,750$$

Notice that the owners' equity is increased by the $1,000 revenue and decreased by the $250 of wages and gasoline expense. Net income—or profit—is determined by including these changes.

Revenue	$1,000
Less expenses:	
Gasoline	$ 200
Wages	50
Net income	$ 750

The Matching Principle and Accrual Accounting

Note that, in determining income, the gasoline is an expense even though no cash has been paid. All expenses and revenues must be recognized when the revenues are earned and the expenses are incurred, regardless of when cash actually changes hands. This important concept, called the **matching principle**, states that revenues should be recognized in the period they are earned, and expenses should be matched against the revenues they helped to generate. Thus, the cost of gasoline is not expensed when it is bought or when it is paid for, but when it is used in Baxter's delivery operation to generate revenues. This method, a contrast to cash accounting, is called accrual accounting.

Baxter must account for the fact that the truck will eventually wear out. This expense is called depreciation and is estimated by one of several methods described later. For now, let's assume the truck is expected to last for 100,000 miles, at which time it will be worthless. The depreciation

EXHIBIT 1–5
Ending Balance Sheet and Final Income Statement for Baxter Company

Baxter Company
Statement of Financial Position
As of December 31, 2000

Assets		*Liabilities*	
Current assets:		Current liabilities:	
Cash	$ 90,950	Account payable	$ 200
Long-Lived assets:		Noncurrent liabilities:	
Truck (net of depreciation)	39,600	Note payable to bank	80,000
		Total liabilities	$ 80,200
		Owners' Equity	
		Owners' equity	50,350
		Total liabilities and	
Total assets	$130,550	owners' equity	$130,550

Baxter Company
Income Statement
For the year ended December 31, 2000

Revenue	$1,000
Less expenses:	
Depreciation	$ 400
Gasoline	200
Wages	50
Net income	$ 350

rate per mile is thus $.40 ($40,000/100,000 miles). If the truck is driven 1,000 miles while making the delivery, the depreciation expense is $400 ($.40 × 1,000 miles). The depreciation decreases the Truck account and decreases the Owners' Equity account.

Assets			= Liabilities		+ Owner's Equity	+ Revenue	− Expenses		
Cash	Truck	Note to Bank	Credit Card				Wages	Gasoline	Depreciation
$90,950	+ $40,000 =	$80,000	+ $200	+ $50,000 +	$1,000 +		$50		
	(400)							$200	$400
$90,950	+ $39,600 =	$80,000	+ $200	+ $50,000 +	$1,000 −		$50 −	$200 −	$400

Exhibit 1–5 contains Baxter's ending balance sheet and its final income statement, including expenses for wages, gasoline, and depreciation. Baxter's balance sheet—and the balance sheet in Exhibit 1–3—classify assets, liabilities, and owners' equity into groupings that financial statement readers find useful; for example, the amounts of a company's current (or short-term) assets are compared with its current (or short-term) debt.

"Current" in financial statements' nomenclature means one year or one operating cycle, whichever is longer. A company's operating cycle is the length of time required to go from cash to cash: to purchase inventory, sell it, and collect from the customer. Each of these categories is discussed later in the book.

2

UNDERSTANDING THE
BALANCE SHEET

*T*o understand a completed balance sheet, one must first understand the principles that accountants follow in its construction. These principles help make the balance sheet useful, because they enable financial statement readers worldwide to interpret and rely on the information presented. Accounting principles are much like natural laws: they determine how different economic events impact the balance sheet, just as natural laws determine how physical events impact the world around us. The moon stays in orbit around the earth because of natural laws of gravity, centrifugal force, mass, distance, and so on. A machine is entered on a balance sheet as an asset and given a certain dollar amount because of accounting principles of future benefit, historical cost, the unit of measurement, cost depreciation, and so on.

Many generally accepted accounting principles (GAAP) are derived from prevailing practice; others are determined by the standard-setting bodies of the Financial Accounting Standards Board (FASB) and the Securities and Exchange Commission (SEC). Underlying all GAAP, however, are a few basic principles that establish the foundation and limits for the deliberations of the FASB and the SEC. The first of these underlying principles, that of economic and accounting entities, is discussed in this chapter. The remainder of the basic principles are covered in Chapter 3. Principles based on prevailing practice and the pronouncements of the FASB and the SEC are covered in Chapter 4 and subsequent chapters.

Economic and Accounting Entities

An accounting entity is an activity for which separate records are kept. Financial statements can be prepared for each accounting entity. For example, in accounting for the personal affairs of an individual, accountants separate them from the person's business affairs. If Mary owns Mary's Cleaners, her accountant would keep separate records for the two entities, Mary as an individual and Mary's business. If Mary also owns a shoe repair shop, another set of records would be maintained for that business. Accounting entities are often separate economic entities.

Legal Form

Accountants do not follow legal form in determining an accounting entity. Only corporations and trusts have legal existence apart from their owners, but separate records will be kept for Mary's personal affairs and each of her two businesses regardless of whether they are incorporated. Mary, Mary's Cleaners, and Mary's Shoe Repair are separate economic entities. If no separate records are kept, Mary will not be able to determine whether the businesses have been profitable or what is owned by each entity.

Consolidated Balance Sheets

In contrast to Mary's situation, where greater meaning is achieved by accounting for each entity separately, most published balance sheets are not for a single company; instead, they present the consolidated financial position of a number of companies related by common ownership.

Suppose a *parent* company purchases the majority of the stock of one or more *subsidiary* companies. For example, a manufacturer might decide that it can be more profitable if it owns a company that produces the raw materials it needs. Sun Company, producer of Sunco gasoline, owns oil wells, pipelines, chemical manufacturing facilities, and retail gasoline stations. Sun's description of its strategic direction is reproduced in Exhibit 2–1.

Bankers often believe that, compared to smaller banks, bigger banks can serve customers better and create larger profits. At this writing, Chase Manhattan and Chemical Banking Corporation have announced plans to combine in the biggest bank merger yet (the Associated Press values it at $10 billion). The five biggest bank mergers in the 1990s are listed in Exhibit 2–2.

A parent company and its subsidiaries are separate legal entities and separate accounting entities for which separate accounting records are maintained and separate financial statements are issued. But because the stockholders of the parent also control (through the parent) the subsidiaries, the combined companies are treated as a single economic entity, and financial statements are prepared as if they were a single accounting entity.

Substance over Form

Financial statement readers must see the financial statements of the combined entity (parent and subsidiaries) if they are to understand the activities of the company and its economic implications. The requirement that a parent and its subsidiaries publish consolidated financial statements is an application of the concept of **substance over form**. The parent and its

EXHIBIT 2–1
Sun Company Management's Statement of Strategic Direction

Strategic Direction

In October 1992, the Company announced a new strategic direction for Sun. This strategy focuses on investing in Sun's core domestic refining and marketing businesses. Sun will also invest opportunistically in international oil and gas production activities in the U.K. North Sea, if returns on such investments are expected to exceed the Company's cost of capital for such projects. In addition, Sun will continue to exit non-productive/non-strategic businesses and improve productivity. During 1994, the Company continued to implement this plan through the following strategic initiatives:

- Sun acquired a 177,000 barrel-per-day refinery in Philadelphia ("Girard Point"), related inventory and certain pipeline interests from Chevron U.S.A. Inc. ("Chevron").

- Sun continued a major program ("Branded for Success") to upgrade and modernize its retail service station network and convert its existing Atlantic® gasoline outlets to Sunoco® and converts its Sunoco Food Market® convenience stores to APlus®.

- Sun completed a project ("Northeast Aromatics and Cyclohexane Project") to expand benzene extraction capacity and construct a 34-million-gallon-per-year cyclohexane plant at its Marcus Hook refinery.

- Sun constructed a pipeline connecting its Philadelphia and Marcus Hook facilities, which should be operational in the first quarter of 1995.

- Sun acquired an interest in Block 3/8a (Ninian and Columba fields) in the U.K. North Sea, which is expected to produce over 10 thousand net barrels daily of crude oil during 1995.

In 1995, Sun expects to reduce the level of capital spending on growth projects as it fully integrates the above noted projects into its asset base. This decrease is consistent with the Company's 1995 goal of maintaining its total debt (excluding borrowings at Suncor Inc., the Company's 55-percent-owned Canadian integrated oil company) at approximately the year-end 1994 level.

EXHIBIT 2–2
The Five Biggest Bank Mergers of the 1990s

1. Chase Manhattan and Chemical Banking Corporation, August 1995, valued at $10 billion
2. First Union and First Fidelity, June 1995, valued at $5.4 billion
3. First Chicago Corporation and NBD Bancorp, July 1995, valued at $5.3 billion
4. BankAmerican Corporation and Security Pacific, August 1991, valued at $4.7 billion
5. NCNB Corporation and C&S Sovran, July 1991, valued at $4.5 billion

Source: Associated Press, August 29, 1995. Prices are based on the prices announced by the banks themselves or by the investment firm involved.

subsidiaries are, in substance, one economic entity, regardless of their separate legal forms.

The Mechanics of Balance Sheet Consolidation

Suppose Triple-A Company purchases 100 percent of the stock of Lazy Z Company. The fair market values of both companies are the same as the accounting values in their balance sheets (the investment in Lazy Z common stock is already included in the following asset total for Triple-A).

Triple-A	Assets	= Liabilities	+ Owners' Equity
	$500,000 =	$300,000 +	$200,000
Lazy Z	Assets	= Liabilities	+ Owners' Equity
	$200,000 =	$150,000 +	$50,000

Because Triple-A purchased all the Lazy Z stock, Triple-A now owns all of the Lazy Z owners' equity ($50,000). When the financial statements

EXHIBIT 2–3
Sun Company, Consolidated Balance Sheet

(Millions of Dollars) At December 31,	1994	1993
Assets		
Current assets:		
Cash and cash equivalents	$ 117	$ 118
Accounts and notes receivable, net of allowances of		
$12 in 1994 and $11 in 1993	655	572
Inventories (Note 8)	613	464
Deferred income taxes (Note 6)	123	123
Total current assets	1,508	1,277
Investment in Coal Operations Held for Sale (Note 2)	51	113
Investment in Real Estate Operations Held for Sale		
(Note 2)	123	134
Long-Term Receivables and Investments (Note 9)	143	217
Properties, Plants, and Equipment, net (Note 10)	4,348	3,831
Deferred Charges and Other Assets	292	328
Total assets	$6,465	$5,900
Liabilities and Stockholders' Equity		
Current liabilities:		
Accounts payable	$ 776	$ 641
Accrued liabilities (Note 14)	540	487
Short-term borrowings (Note 11)	221	110
Current portion of long-term debt (Note 12)	99	26
Taxes payable	279	241
Total current liabilities	1,915	1,505
Long-Term Debt (Note 12)	1,073	726
Retirement Benefit Liabilities (Note 13)	515	523
Deferred Income Taxes (Note 6)	301	369
Other Deferred Credits and Liabilities (Note 14)	429	421
Commitments and Contingent Liabilities (Note 14)		
Minority Interest	369	372
Stockholders' Equity (Notes 15 and 16)		
Common stock, par value $1 per share		
Authorized—200,000,000 shares; Issued, 1994—		
129,521,449 shares; Issued, 1993—129,312,		
735 shares	130	129
Capital in excess of par value	1,309	1,303
Cumulative foreign currency translation adjustment	(89)	(62)
Earnings employed in the business	1,534	1,636
	2,884	3,006
Less common stock held in treasury, at cost		
1994—22,583,733 shares; 1993—22,629,825 shares	1,021	1,022
Total stockholders' equity	1,863	1,984
Total liabilities and stockholders' equity	$6,465	$5,900

of the two companies are combined in consolidated financial statements, Triple-A must remove the $50,000 investment in Lazy Z and replace it with the individual assets and liabilities of Lazy Z. Notice that the total owners' equity of Triple-A is not changed by the consolidation.

	Assets	= Liabilities	+ Owners' Equity
Triple-A before consolidation	$500,000	= $300,000 +	$200,000
Less: Investment in Lazy Z	(50,000)		
Plus: Assets and Liabilities of Lazy Z	200,000	150,000	
Triple-A Consolidated Balance Sheet	$650,000	= $450,000 +	$200,000

Exhibit 2–3 shows the consolidated balance sheet of Sun Company, as it appeared in its 1994 annual report.

3

BASIC ACCOUNTING PRINCIPLES

*L*ike Chapter 2, this chapter is concerned with the basic principles that establish the foundation for all other standards. The principle governing the basic business economic and accounting entity is discussed in Chapter 2. The principles discussed in this chapter are included in Exhibit 3–1.

Periodicity

Resuming the example in Chapter 2, profit is best determined by comparing Mary's investment when she began each of her businesses to the worth of her interest in the business when it is finally sold or otherwise disposed of. We see in Chapter 1 how well this method worked for ancient accountants, when businesses were based on agriculture or herding, or on distinct ventures with definite beginnings and endings. But waiting until the end of a company's life does not satisfy the needs of investors and creditors.

EXHIBIT 3-1
The Principles on Which Accounting Is Based

Entity
Periodicity
Unit of Measure
Historical Cost
Revenue Recognition
Conservatism
Going Concern
Materiality
Matching

Modern business must be divided into artificial time periods (years, quarters, or months) to measure a company's profit or loss in a meaningful way.

Unit of Measure

In the United States, amounts on financial statements are in nominal dollars. A nominal dollar is a dollar that arises from an exchange transaction (as buying or selling) and is not adjusted for inflation.

For nonmonetary exchanges, such as when a company gives shares of its common stock in exchange for a parcel of land, the land received must be recorded, and placed on the balance sheet, at an amount of nominal dollars equal to the market value of the transaction. The transaction market value is determined from the value of either the stock or the land, whichever can be determined most objectively. If the stock, for example, is traded on an exchange at the time it is given up, its value is more objective than an appraisal of the land. But if the stock is in a closed corporation and not actively traded, an appraisal of the value of the land is more objective than an arbitrary value assigned to the stock.

Historical Cost

Assets and liabilities are recorded in the accounting records (and appear on the balance sheet) at their original acquisition cost, called historical cost. With little exception, there is no attempt to show assets at their "value." Land that cost $300,000 but which is appraised to sell at $1,000,000 is shown at its $300,000 acquisition cost. Inventory that the company expects to sell for twice its original cost is still shown at its original cost.

Historical cost is used for two reasons. First, it is the most objective measure available. Appraisals, estimates of selling prices, and other alternative measures of "value" are all, to some extent, subjective. Historical cost, established in an arm's-length exchange, is the most objective measure available.

Second, a primary purpose of accounting is to measure the extent to which managers are able to increase the wealth of the company's owners. That increase is measured as the revenue inflow achieved minus the cost necessary to achieve it. If an item of inventory, originally bought for $100, is sold for $200 at a time when it costs $150 to replace the inventory item, the profit is $100: a revenue of $200 minus the $100 cost of inventory sold. (An analysis of the gain will disclose that half the gain is an inflation gain, caused by the increasing replacement cost of the inventory, and half is an operating gain.)

Revenue Recognition

Assume that, in January, Red Company manufactures a Gizmo for $100 that it knows it can sell for $150. Red sells the Gizmo for $150 in February, gives the customer 30-day terms, and is paid in March. When does Red recognize the revenue: at the date of production, sale, or collection of cash?

The general rule says, Red should recognize revenue and an increase in owners' equity when two conditions are satisfied:

1. The earnings process is complete.
2. There is a reliable measure of the worth of the goods or services sold.

Generally, these conditions are satisfied at the point of sale when the Gizmo is manufactured, the earnings process is complete, and Red knows it will receive $150 in 30 days. Red should recognize $150 in revenue and place a $150 asset Account Receivable on the balance sheet.

But there are exceptions. If Red is selling in a market where collection of receivables is often in doubt, the revenue should not be recognized until the cash is collected. Likewise, if Red is manufacturing a commodity that is readily salable at a fixed, known price (perhaps a precious metal or an agricultural product), Red may be justified in recognizing revenue and a receivable when production is complete.

By satisfying the conditions in the general rule, these two examples justify revenue recognition at a point other than the point of sale. But there is another exception, based solely on utility rather than the general rule. If Red is manufacturing submarines for the Navy, or building skyscrapers, or engaging in other projects that may take several years to complete, Red may use long-term contract accounting and recognize a portion of revenue each period, based on the company's estimated progress on the project. This exception is allowed so that stockholders and creditors can receive periodic information on a company's earnings and financial condition. The estimated information is more useful than no information at all.

Conservatism

Conservatism results in a pessimistic measurement bias. Conservatism is a holdover from a time when banks were the primary users of balance sheets. Under a conservative approach, accountants prefer to undervalue assets, overvalue liabilities, and understate net income. But neither understatement nor overstatement is desirable. Conservatism is now limited to situations where there is uncertainty as to the amount of a transaction. In these situations, conservatism tells accountants to "anticipate all losses"—recording them before they actually occur, if their occurrence is likely—and to "delay all gains"—recording them only when they have actually occurred.

Going Concern

Accountants assume that, in the absence of evidence to the contrary, a company will continue in business as a going concern for the foreseeable future. Such a going concern must preserve historical costs, carrying them forward and expensing them against the income they help generate. The going concern assumption is one reason accountants carry over the historical cost values of assets, liabilities, and owners' equity from one year to the next.

Also, accounting theorists feel that market prices reflect the sale price of a company, rather than its value as a continuing entity. Financial statements are intended to provide information about the company's performance and financial position as a going concern, rather than to assess its worth in a liquidation.

As an example, consider a local bakery. If the bakery's balance sheet showed the ovens, pans, display racks, and other assets at the price each would be expected to bring if sold, the value of the assets would be much lower than the value of the assets when collected together and operated as a business. Assets have a much greater value as part of an integrated, functioning business system than they do when sold as separate items. (Coincidentally, when there *is* evidence that a company will not continue in business, the information most useful to financial statement readers is the market or liquidation value of the assets, liabilities, and owners' equity—and that is what accountants put on the financial statements.)

Materiality

In all of life, we give a great deal of attention to important matters that make a difference to us, and less attention to those things that are inconsequential. Likewise, in accounting, some items deserve a great deal of attention and should be prominently disclosed to financial statement readers, and others are immaterial.

In our lives, we use many different standards to determine what is important; in financial statement presentation, materiality is determined by whether an item could make a difference to a reader of the financial statements. If the item will not make a difference, it is immaterial. If it will, it is material. Materiality is determined by the effect of an item on the financial statements taken as a whole, not by the impact on a single account. Sometimes, however, similar items that are immaterial may have a material effect when they are combined. For example, the purchase of a computer costing $10,000 is not generally material to a large company such as AT&T. It makes no difference to readers of the financial statements whether AT&T records the computer as an expense or as an asset. But the effect of recording all the computers purchased by AT&T each year as expenses instead of assets probably would have a material effect on both the income statement (by overstating expenses) and the balance sheet (by understating assets).

Matching (and Accrual Accounting)

The matching principle directs accountants to measure revenues when they are earned, and expenses when they are incurred, regardless of when the related cash flow occurs. This concept is discussed for revenues in our explanation of revenue recognition.

Expenses are matched to the period they benefit *and* to the revenue they help generate. The timing of charges to expenses is more complex than the timing of revenue recognition. Basically, an expenditure results in an asset if it creates a future benefit, and in an expense if it produces no future benefit. Accountants spend a great deal of their time recording the costs of assets when expenditures are made (as for the purchase of buildings, trucks, or inventory) and then transferring these costs to expense accounts as the future benefit is used up (the building and truck are worn out, the inventory is sold).

Technically, three rules determine when a cost becomes an expense:

1. Cause and effect.
2. Systematic and rational allocation.
3. Immediate charge.

Cause and Effect

This rule requires that costs directly associated with producing a certain revenue be expensed in the period in which the revenue is earned. The cost of commissions paid to salespersons is an excellent example of this rule— there is a direct association between the work of the salesperson to earn the commission and the revenue generated by the sales of the product.

Systematic and Rational Allocation

The benefit of some costs is consumed over long periods of time. For example, money spent on a building or a truck benefits the company for years. For items such as these, there is no direct association between the consuming of the benefit (and the cost) and the earning of revenue. Because of this, the cost of these items is expensed in a systematic and rational way over the time period believed to be benefited.

Immediate Charge

Some costs do not create a long-term benefit (as buildings and trucks do), yet they have no direct association to any revenue (as sales commissions do). These costs are charged off as expenses immediately.

For example, in a manufacturing company, the cost of the accounting department is necessary to run the business, but has neither long-term benefit nor a direct association to any revenue produced. This cost is thus expensed immediately.

4

CURRENT ASSETS: CASH AND SHORT-TERM INVESTMENTS

*T*his chapter discusses *cash* and *short-term investments*. *Accounts receivable* and *short-term notes receivable* arising from credit sales and prepaid expenses are examined in Chapter 5. *Inventory* is discussed in Chapter 6. These five accounts are the most common current assets on a company's balance sheet.

The consolidated balance sheet from the 1994 annual report of the Atlantic Richfield Company (ARCO) is presented in Exhibit 4–1. Note the components of ARCO's current assets, which are almost 28 percent of ARCO's total assets. Current assets are always listed in order of liquidity or ease of realization in cash.

EXHIBIT 4–1
Atlantic Richfield Company, Consolidated Balance Sheet

	December 31,	
Millions	1994	1993
Assets		
Current assets:		
Cash and cash equivalents	$ 1,394	$ 1,458
Short-term investments	2,991	2,289
Accounts receivable	1,446	1,333
Inventories	797	914
Prepaid expenses and other current assets	185	237
Total current assets	6,813	6,231
Investments and long-term receivables:		
Investments accounted for on the equity method	348	266
Other investments and long-term receivables	297	221
	645	487
Fixed assets:		
Property, plant, and equipment	32,248	31,494
Less accumulated depreciation, depletion, and amortization	16,526	15,628
	15,722	15,866
Deferred charges and other assets	1,383	1,310
Total assets	$24,563	$23,894
Liabilities and Stockholders' Equity		
Current liabilities:		
Notes payable	$ 1,478	$ 1,510
Accounts payable	986	1,091
Long-term debt due within one year	630	165
Taxes payable, including excise taxes	253	272
Accrued interest	183	190
Other	958	1,107
Total current liabilities	4,488	4,335

EXHIBIT 4-1 (Continued)

Millions	December 31, 1994	1993
Long-term debt	7,198	7,089
Deferred income taxes	2,721	2,779
Other deferred liabilities and credits	3,471	3,177
Minority interest	407	387
Stockholders' equity:		
Preference stocks	1	1
Common stock, $2.50 par value; shares issued 160,800,137 (1994), 160,746,125 (1993); shares outstanding 160,753,966 (1994), 159,953,960 (1993)	402	402
Capital in excess of par value of stock	647	661
Retained earnings	5,342	5,308
Foreign currency translation	(51)	(133)
Pension liability adjustment	(20)	(29)
Treasury stock, at cost	(5)	(83)
Net unrealized loss on investments	(38)	—
Total stockholders' equity	6,278	6,127
Total liabilities and stockholders' equity	$24,563	$23,894

The Company follows the successful efforts method of accounting for oil and gas producing activities.

Cash

Cash is one of a company's most important assets because it is the most liquid asset. A company's business cycle is a cash-to-cash cycle; that is, a company spends cash to purchase or manufacture goods or offer services, sells the goods or provides the promised services, and ultimately collects cash from the sale. Payments for operating expenses, dividends, and purchases of assets (such as inventory, supplies, or plant and equipment) are all eventually paid for with cash. Company obligations must be paid, and stockholders must be rewarded. Sufficient cash must be generated to cover all of its payments if a company is to survive.

The amount of cash reported on a balance sheet is the amount of cash available to a company as of that date. Cash on hand includes currency, coins, and undeposited customer checks. Cash in the bank includes checking accounts and savings or time deposit accounts. These amounts are generally totaled and shown as a single amount on the balance sheet. Because cash is the most liquid asset, it is listed first in the current asset section of the balance sheet.

In its 1994 annual report, Humana Inc., a provider of managed health care services, included this note regarding its Cash account:

2. Summary of Significant Accounting Policies

• • •

Cash and Cash Equivalents
Cash and cash equivalents include cash, money market funds, commercial paper, and certain U.S. Government securities with an original maturity of three months or less.

Cash is the most active account in a company's ledger because everything a company does affects cash in some way. Because cash is easy to transport and readily converted into goods or services, accounting for cash requires great care and is subject to many business controls. And because most companies engage in a large number of cash transactions, the opportunity for theft or negligence is great. Cash is easier to misappropriate than a company's other assets, such as inventory or equipment. For that reason, safeguarding cash and establishing a rigorous system of internal control over cash are paramount concerns.

The Petty Cash Fund

In many companies, it is convenient to have small amounts of cash on hand to pay for minor expenditures such as postage, freight, supplies, or stamps. To meet these costs, companies establish petty cash funds.

A petty cash fund is established by writing a check for a small amount, perhaps $150. A petty cash custodian cashes the check and is then responsible for maintaining the fund. A petty cash voucher—a form of receipt showing the date, amount, and reason for the expenditure—is prepared by the custodian each time cash is disbursed from the fund. Approval for the expenditure is evidenced by the signature of the custodian, and the voucher is signed by the person receiving the cash.

From time to time, the petty cash fund must be replenished. After the vouchers have been inspected for completeness and accuracy, a check is drawn for the amount of the vouchers, and the fund is restored to its initial balance.

Short-Term Investments

Because idle cash is not productive, companies may place their cash in short-term investments such as treasury bills, certificates of deposit, bonds, common and preferred stock, and debt instruments. Management invests in short-term investments all cash not needed for daily operations and to increase its return on investment. Short-term investments are classified as current assets on the balance sheet if they are readily marketable and management intends to convert them into cash in a short period of time (usually one year). Exhibit 4–2 shows the current asset section of the UAL Corporation's balance sheet from its 1994 annual report. UAL is a holding company whose primary subsidiary is United Airlines. The related note disclosure pertaining to cash and short-term investments read as follows:

(1) Summary of Significant Accounting Policies

• • •

Cash and Cash Equivalents and Short-Term Investments—Cash in excess of operating requirements is invested in short-term, highly liquid, income-producing investments. Investments with an original maturity of three months or less on their acquisition date are classified as cash and cash equivalents. Other investments are classified as short-term investments.

EXHIBIT 4–2
UAL Corporation, Excerpt from Statement of
Consolidated Financial Position

(In Millions)	December 31,	
Assets	1994	1993
Current assets:		
Cash and cash equivalents	$ 500	$ 437
Short-term investments	1,032	1,391
Receivables, less allowance for doubtful		
accounts (1994—$22; 1993—$22)	889	1,095
Aircraft fuel, spare parts and supplies, less		
obsolescence allowance (1994—$44;		
1993—$70)	285	278
Refundable income taxes	—	26
Deferred income taxes	151	124
Prepaid expenses	335	362
	$3,192	$3,713

All short-term investments are recorded at their acquisition cost, plus additional costs such as brokerage fees. Short-term investments in common or preferred stock can result in dividend revenue to a company. When dividends are declared, the company normally creates an account called Dividends Receivable for the amount of the dividends to be received. The account is a current asset, but is normally not shown separately in published financial statements. The amount is combined with other current accounts and presented in the current asset section of the balance sheet as Other Current Assets.

If a company purchases bonds as a short-term investment, interest accrues on the bonds, meaning that as time goes by, the company earns interest on its investment. The interest is earned because the company has loaned money to the seller of the bonds, who in turn has the use of that money. An account titled Interest Receivable appears in the current asset section of the balance sheet, or, more commonly, is combined and shown as Other Current Assets. Interest revenue appears on the income statement for the current period.

The market price of many short-term investments is subject to constant fluctuation, reflecting changes in market conditions. Generally accepted accounting principles (GAAP) do not call for the recognition of changes in the market values of short-term investments such as certificates of deposit, bonds, or treasury bills; however, they do call for the recognition of changes on certain marketable equity securities (common and preferred stocks) and debt securities (bonds).

Equity Securities

Equity securities are of two types: trading securities and available-for-sale (AFS) securities. Securities are classified as trading if they are purchased and held principally to be sold in a short period of time: by buying and selling frequently, the company hopes to generate profits from short-term price differences. These securities are always current assets and are reported at fair value with unrealized holding gains or losses reported as a component of net income. A holding gain or loss is the change in fair value of a security from one period to another. For example, assume a company purchases 1,000 shares of Company A for $2 per share in December of the current year. In preparing its financial statements for the year ending on December 31, the company determines that the fair value of Company A's stock is $3 per share. The company then has a holding gain of $1,000 [($3 − $2) × 1,000 shares]. The short-term investment in Company A's stock will be shown in the current assets section of the balance sheet at $3,000, and the $1,000 holding gain will appear in its income statement.

Equity securities not classified as trading are, by default, available-for-sale securities. Although AFS securities are marketable, their classification as current or noncurrent depends on management's intent. AFS equity securities are also reported at fair value; however, any holding gains or losses appear as a separate component of stockholders' equity rather than as a component of net income.

Debt Securities

Debt securities are classified as held-to-maturity (HTM) securities, trading securities, or available-for-sale securities. HTM securities are purchased by a company with the intent and ability to hold those securities until they mature. (There is no HTM classification for equity securities because generally they do not mature.) HTM securities are not adjusted to fair value and are accounted for at cost. AFS and trading debt securities are reported and accounted for in the same manner as AFS and trading equity securities.

Exhibit 4–3 is an excerpt from the balance sheet and footnote disclosure relating to investments for CoreStates Financial Corp and Subsidiaries.

EXHIBIT 4–3
CoreStates Financial Corp and Subsidiaries,
Excerpt from Consolidated Balance Sheet

(in thousands) December 31,	1994	1993
Assets		
Cash and due from banks (Note 4)	$ 2,262,512	$ 2,521,676
Time deposits, principally Eurodollars	1,750,458	1,319,457
Investment securities held-to-maturity (market value: 1994—$2,423,830; 1993—$2,257,513) (Note 5)	2,454,584	2,228,560
Investment securities available-for-sale (Note 5)	426,047	1,370,606
Total loans, net of unearned discounts of $146,305 in 1994 and $151,994 in 1993 (Note 6)	20,526,216	19,776,258
Less: Allowance for loan losses (Note 7)	(500,631)	(450,823)
Net loans	20,025,585	19,325,435
Federal funds sold and securities purchased under agreements to resell	731,820	161,527
Trading account securities	1,206	6,393
Due from customers on acceptances	342,211	332,234
Premises and equipment (Note 8)	423,832	410,022
Other assets (Note 20)	906,881	758,707
Total assets	$29,325,136	$28,434,617

1. Summary of Significant Accounting Policies

• • •

Investment securities   Held-to-maturity securities are carried at cost adjusted for amortization of premiums and accretion of discounts, both computed on the interest method. Held-to-maturity securities primarily consist of debt securities. The Corporation has both the ability and positive intent to hold these securities until maturity. Trading account securities are carried at market values. Gains on trading account securities include both realized and unrealized gains and losses on the portfolio.

Debt securities not classified as held-to-maturity or trading and marketable equity securities are classified as available-for-sale. Available-for-sale securities are carried at fair value, with unrealized gains and losses, net of tax, reported as a component of shareholders' equity. The accumulated net unrealized gain on available-for-sale securities included in retained earnings was $11,354 at December 31, 1994.

The adjusted cost of a specific certificate sold is the basis for determining realized securities gains and losses as included in the consolidated statement of income in "non-interest income".

Interest and dividends on investment securities are recognized as income when earned.

The concept behind this accounting treatment is discussed in greater detail in Chapter 7, *Noncurrent Assets: Investments.*

5

CURRENT ASSETS: RECEIVABLES AND PREPAIDS

This chapter covers accounts receivable, short-term notes receivable, nontrade receivables, and prepaid expenses. Inventory is discussed in Chapter 6. In discussing accounts receivable, we focus on adjustments to that account arising from uncollectible accounts.

The assets section of the consolidated balance sheet from the 1994 annual report of Phillips Petroleum Company is presented in Exhibit 5–1. Accounts and notes receivable comprise 59 percent of Phillips' total current assets. Prepaid expenses are normally a much smaller percentage of total current assets.

The 1994 current assets section of the balance sheet for W. W. Grainger, Inc., and Subsidiaries is shown in Exhibit 5–2. This company is a leading nationwide distributor of maintenance, repair, and operating supplies, and related information, to commercial, contractor, and institutional customers.

EXHIBIT 5–1
Phillips Petroleum Company, Assets Section of
Consolidated Balance Sheet

At December 31,	Millions of Dollars	
	1994	1993
Assets		
Cash and cash equivalents	$ 193	$ 119
Accounts and notes receivable		
(less allowances: 1994—$20; 1993—$14)	1,462	1,398
Inventories	527	538
Deferred income taxes	186	170
Prepaid expenses and other current assets	97	118
Total Current Assets	2,465	2,343
Investments and long-term receivables	708	544
Properties, plants, and equipment (net)	8,042	7,961
Deferred income taxes	122	98
Deferred charges	99	89
Total	$11,436	$11,035

Note that Grainger's prepaid expenses are approximately 1½ percent of total current assets.

Accounts Receivable

Goods or services sold on credit create accounts receivable from customers, sometimes referred to as trade receivables. They are customarily expected to be collected by the company within 30 to 60 days and are normally the most significant type of claim to assets held by a company.

A company normally has many credit customers and must maintain a separate account for each one. A customer account is a record of the amount of purchases, the amounts collected, and the current balance owed. The accounts receivable amount appearing in the financial statements is the

EXHIBIT 5–2
W. W. Grainger, Inc., and Subsidiaries,
Consolidated Balance Sheet

(In thousands of dollars)

	December 31,		
	1994	1993	1992
Assets			
Current assets:			
Cash and cash equivalents	$ 15,292	$ 2,572	$ 44,809
Accounts receivable, less allowances for doubtful accounts of $15,333 for 1994, $13,573 for 1993, and $13,810 for 1992	345,793	299,856	265,410
Inventories	519,966	466,214	432,233
Prepaid expenses	14,233	10,832	11,856
Deferred income tax benefits	68,362	44,408	39,958
Total current assets	$963,646	$823,882	$794,266

total amount due from all the individual customers. In accounting jargon, this account is called an accounts receivable control account, and an individual account is called an accounts receivable subsidiary account. At any time, the balance appearing in the control account must equal the sum of all the individual customer subsidiary accounts. To ensure that this happens, the amount of every credit sale (which increases accounts receivable) must be used to adjust both the amount of the accounts receivable appearing in the balance sheet (control account) and the proper individual customer subsidiary account. Likewise, the amount of each payment is used to reduce both the accounts receivable control account and the individual customer subsidiary account.

Uncollectible Accounts

Company managers know that some customers who receive credit will not pay and that, ultimately, the amount collected will differ from the amount of the original credit sales. This difference is an expense, and it reduces earnings and the carrying value of accounts receivable. Based on experience and the current economic climate, companies can accurately estimate the total dollar amount of uncollectible accounts. The expense can only be estimated because there is no accurate way to predict which customer accounts will be uncollectible in the future. In measuring net income, companies match the expenses incurred (including uncollectible accounts expense) to the sales revenue generated for the period.

At year end, when the estimated amount of uncollectible accounts expense has been determined, the company increases its Uncollectible Accounts Expense (or Bad Debt Expense) account, and increases an account called Allowance for Uncollectible Accounts (or Allowance for Doubtful Accounts). The allowance account reduces the accounts receivable control account. The Allowance for Uncollectible Accounts account is a "contra account" in bookkeeping language, because it is subtracted from the Accounts Receivable in the asset section of the balance sheet. For example,

Accounts Receivable	$150,000
Less: Allowance for Uncollectible Accounts	(15,000)
	$135,000

The purpose of the Allowance for Uncollectible Accounts account is to value the accounts receivable shown on the balance sheet. Instead of reducing the accounts receivable, the company increases the allowance account to bring the balance in accounts receivable to its estimated amount. If the company were to reduce the accounts receivable control account, it would also have to reduce specific customer accounts; however, at the time of the adjustment, the company does not know which accounts will prove to be uncollectible and can only estimate an overall amount.

The purposes of estimating the amount of uncollectible accounts expense are: (1) to match the expense against the revenue generated, and (2) to report the Accounts Receivable account at its realizable value. Realizable value is the amount of the total accounts receivable that the company expects will ultimately be collected. Generally, companies use one of two methods to estimate uncollectible accounts expense: (1) the percentage of sales method, or (2) the percentage of accounts receivable method.

The percentage of sales method uses a percentage based on the company's past experience or the industry average. This percentage is multiplied by the sales for the period to arrive at the estimate of uncollectible accounts expense. Theoretically, total credit sales should be used as the basis for the estimate; however, most companies use total sales because they do not separate cash and credit sales. For example, if sales for the period are $500,000 and, historically, the percentage of sales that has proven to be uncollectible is 2.5 percent, then the amount of uncollectible accounts expense is $12,500 ($500,000 × .025). This amount (1) appears as an expense on the income statement and (2) is added to the existing balance in the Allowance for Uncollectible Accounts account.

The percentage of accounts receivable method of estimating uncollectible accounts expense uses an aging schedule like the one shown in Exhibit 5–3. An aging schedule is prepared by the company and is used to identify each customer's account according to how many days each debt has been outstanding. The total for each category represents all outstanding receivables in that category. Each of the category totals is then multiplied by a historical percentage to determine the amount for each age category that will prove to be uncollectible. Higher percentages of uncollectibility are associated with older accounts. The sum of the amounts of estimated uncollectible accounts for each category represents the desired ending balance in the Allowance for Doubtful Accounts account. If Hypothetical Company (in Exhibit 5–3) had a current balance of $4,000 in the Allowance for Doubtful Accounts account, the amount of uncollectible accounts expense would be $12,520 ($16,520 − $4,000). This is the amount needed to bring the balance in that account to $16,520. The $12,520 figure is also the amount of uncollectible accounts expense appearing on the income statement.

Write-Off of Accounts Receivable

If a decision is made that an uncollected account is not collectible, the company removes the amount of the account by reducing both the Allowance for Uncollectible Accounts account and the Accounts Receivable account. This adjustment has no effect on uncollectible accounts expense or on the income statement because the expense was recognized in the year

EXHIBIT 5-3
Example of Aging Schedule

Hypothetical Company
Accounts Receivable Aging Schedule
December 31, 1996

Customer	Balance	Not Yet Due	Number of Days Past Due			
			1–30	31–60	61–90	Over 180
F. James	$ 20,000		$20,000			
B. Beck	66,000	$ 60,000	1,000	$ 5,000		
C. See	2,500				$ 2,500	
D. Green	15,000		6,000	5,000	3,000	$ 1,000
F. Green	8,000			2,000		8,000
R. Clame	44,000	33,000	2,000	4,000	1,500	3,500
S. Reed	28,000	28,000				
⋯	⋯	⋯	⋯	⋯	⋯	⋯
T. Send	42,300	42,300				
Totals	$293,000	$175,000	$54,000	$24,000	$17,500	$22,500
Estimated Uncollectible Percentage		1%	2.5%	8%	20%	40%
Amount Uncollectible	$ 16,520	$ 750	$ 1,350	$ 1,720	$ 3,500	$ 9,000

in which the sale took place and the receivable was recorded. This process is called "writing off" an account receivable. Remember, uncollectible accounts expense is estimated in the current period. Because a company does not know which accounts will prove to be uncollectible in future periods, it must increase the Allowance for Uncollectible Accounts account rather than reduce the Accounts Receivable account when recognizing the expense. After an uncollectible account has been identified, the amount can be removed (subtracted) from the Allowance for Uncollectible Accounts account and the Accounts Receivable account.

Accounts Receivable Disclosure in the Balance Sheet

If a company's balance in accounts receivable is $200,000 at year end and its allowance is $14,000, the current assets section of the balance sheet would show one of the following forms of presentation:

Accounts Receivable	$200,000
Less: Allowance for Uncollectible Accounts	(14,000)
	$186,000

or

Accounts Receivable (*less* Allowance for Uncollectible Accounts of $14,000)	$186,000

The $200,000 is called the gross amount of accounts receivable, and the $186,000—the amount the company expects to collect—is called the realizable value.

The presentation of accounts receivable 1994 annual report of Pfizer Inc., a global health care company, is reproduced in Exhibit 5–4.

Using Accounts Receivable to Generate Cash Prior to Maturity

A company may decide that the cost of waiting to collect its receivables is too high and elect to engage in accounts receivable financing. Typical

EXHIBIT 5-4
Pfizer Inc. and Subsidiary Companies, Excerpt from
Consolidated Balance Sheet

	December 31		
(millions of dollars)	1994	1993	1992
Assets			
Current assets:			
Cash and cash equivalents	$ 1,458.5	$ 729.4	$1,257.1
Short-term investments	560.1	447.1	446.6
Accounts receivable, less allowance for doubtful accounts:			
1994—$44.1; 1993—$40.6; 1992—$36.2	1,665.0	1,468.7	1,400.3
Short-term loans	361.3	456.9	620.3
Inventories			
Finished goods	528.0	413.3	413.5
Work in process	534.9	502.1	465.8
Raw materials and supplies	202.0	178.1	188.5
Total inventories	1,264.9	1,093.5	1,067.8
Prepaid expenses, taxes, and other current assets	478.6	537.6	592.7
Total current assets	5,788.4	4,733.2	5,384.8
Long-term loans and marketable securities	724.3	586.7	601.4
Property, plant, and equipment, less accumulated depreciation	3,073.2	2,632.5	2,305.1
Goodwill, less accumulated amortization	325.7	231.1	368.2
Other assets, deferred taxes, and deferred charges	1,186.9	1,147.4	930.6
Total assets	$11,098.5	$9,330.9	$9,590.1

examples of accounts receivable financing are pledging, assigning, or factoring accounts receivable.

Pledging   When a company pledges its accounts receivable, it uses its accounts receivable as collateral to obtain a loan. The borrowing company records the loan and related interest expense in the normal manner. The company agrees to collect its receivables and use the proceeds to repay the loan. Disclosure of the pledging of accounts receivable is made either parenthetically on the face of the balance sheet or in a note to the financial statements.

Assignment.   Assigning accounts receivable is a more formal type of pledging arrangement. Normally, the assignor (the borrower) signs both a financing agreement and a promissory note with the assignee (the lender). The lender advances cash based on specific assigned accounts. (The assignee usually lends less than the fair value of the accounts receivable (70 percent–90 percent) to insulate itself from credit losses.) The assignment normally specifies that the assignor must substitute new accounts for those that are past due or become uncollectible. The assignee charges interest on the loan as well as a financing charge for processing the assignment. The assignor collects the accounts receivable and remits the proceeds to the assignee to pay off the loan. Legally, the assignee has the same right to collect the receivables as the assignor had prior to signing the agreement. In some instances, therefore, payments may be made directly to the assignee.

Factoring.   In a factoring transaction, a company sells its accounts receivable to another company (a factor) in exchange for cash. In many cases, the factor is a bank or finance company. Generally, the factor takes control of the receivables and collects the accounts directly from the company's customers.

Receivables are sold (factored) on either a *without recourse* or a *with recourse* basis. When receivables are sold without recourse, the purchaser assumes the risk of collectibility; that is, title is transferred to the factor, who assumes the risk of the uncollectible accounts. In this situation, the transfer of accounts receivable is an outright sale. The receivables are removed from the selling company's books, and any gain or loss is recognized in the current period.

If the receivables are sold with recourse, the selling company guarantees payment to the purchaser should some or all of the receivables prove to be uncollectible. Because the selling company retains the same degree of risk after the transaction as it had prior to the transaction, the accounting profession requires that certain conditions must exist if the transaction is to be treated as an outright sale. Those conditions are:

1. The seller transfers control of the future economic benefits of the accounts receivable.

2. The seller's obligation under the recourse provisions can be reasonably estimated.

3. The purchaser cannot require the seller to repurchase the accounts receivable (except as specified in the recourse provisions).

When these conditions are met, control of the receivables has been effectively transferred to the purchaser and a sale has occurred. If these conditions are not met, the transaction is treated as a borrowing, the amount of the proceeds from the transfer is treated as a liability, and the accounts receivable are not removed from the borrowing company's books.

As an example of how a company might state its sale of accounts receivable, consider this note, which was among the footnotes for the 1994 annual report of Delta Woodside Industries, Inc.: The company operates principally in two segments: textiles and apparel. The company also manufactures and sells Nautilus fitness equipment primarily to the institutional market.

NOTE C—ACCOUNTS RECEIVABLE

The woven fabrics operation assigns a substantial portion of its trade accounts receivable to a bank under a factor agreement. The assignment of these receivables is primarily without recourse, provided that customer orders are approved by the bank prior to shipment of goods, up to a maximum for each individual account. At July 2, 1994, the Company had no significant concentrations of credit risk, since substantially all of the Company's accounts receivable are due from many companies that produce apparel, home furnishings and other products and from department stores and specialty apparel retailers located throughout the United States. The Company generally does not require collateral for its accounts receivable.

Short-Term Notes Receivable

Notes receivable are formal receivables that involve a legal negotiable instrument, such as a promissory note. (A negotiable instrument is unique in that it can be transferred to a third party.) Notes receivable differ from accounts receivable in several ways. Notes receivable generally are interest-bearing; accounts receivable are not. A note specifies the amount borrowed, the interest rate, and the due date; penalties for late payments or nonpayment; and, if the note is secured, a description of the security or collateral pledged by the borrower to secure the loan.

Notes receivable normally arise through transactions with customers, creditors, and suppliers. For example, if a manufacturing company lends money to one of its distributors to assist the distributor in building up its business, it might require the distributor to sign a note. A note receivable can also result when a customer seeks more time to pay for an overdue account receivable. In this case, one asset is exchanged for another: Notes Receivable replaces Accounts Receivable as a current asset.

If a borrower fails to pay the note at maturity, it is "in default." The company would reclassify the note to a separate account called Dishonored Notes Receivable. If material in amount, Dishonored Notes Receivable is an entry in the current asset section of the balance sheet, directly below Notes Receivable. This form of presentation separates the dishonored notes receivable from the notes receivable that are not in default.

Some companies will discount a note receivable at a bank. The company, in effect, sells the note to the bank to obtain cash before the note's maturity date. When a company discounts a note to a bank, it is normally done with recourse. The company is still contingently liable for the note; that is, if the note is not paid to the bank at maturity, the company that sold the note must pay to the bank the principal of the note plus interest and any late-payment penalty. If material, this contingent liability must be disclosed in the footnotes to the financial statements.

Disclosure of Notes Receivables in the Balance Sheet

Notes receivable are often combined with accounts receivable and presented as one amount in the balance sheet. AlliedSignal Inc. used this type of presentation in the current assets section of its 1994 annual report (see Exhibit 5–5). AlliedSignal Inc. is an advanced technology and manufacturing company serving customers worldwide with aerospace and automotive products, chemicals, fibers, plastics, and advanced materials.

Helene Curtis Industries, Inc. is a worldwide producer of brand-name personal care products. In its 1995 annual report, the company disclosed receivables as one amount.

EXHIBIT 5–5
AlliedSignal Inc., Excerpt from Consolidated Balance Sheet

(dollars in millions) December 31,	1994	1993
Assets		
Current assets:		
Cash and cash equivalents	$ 508	$ 892
Accounts and notes receivable	1,697	1,343
Inventories	1,743	1,745
Other current assets	637	587
Total current assets	4,585	4,567
Investments and long-term receivables	475	553
Property, plant, and equipment—net	4,260	4,094
Cost in excess of net assets of acquired companies—net	1,349	1,087
Other assets	652	528
Total assets	$11,321	$10,829

This breakdown of accounts and notes receivables appeared in the footnotes to the financial statements:

2. Receivables
Receivables, principally trade, consist of the following amounts at February 28:

	1995	1994
Less allowance for doubtful accounts	$111,111	$111,111
Accounts receivable	$210,755	$187,452
Notes receivable	66,282	60,161
	277,037	247,613
Less allowance for doubtful accounts	6,213	5,099
	$270,824	$242,514

Exhibit 5–6 is from Host Marriott Corporation's 1994 annual report. Notes receivable are disclosed separately in the balance sheet. Marriott is one of the largest owners of lodging properties in the world.

EXHIBIT 5–6
Host Marriott Corporation, Excerpt from
Consolidated Balance Sheet

December 30, 1994 and December 31, 1993 (in millions)	1994	1993
Assets		
Property and Equipment	$3,156	$3,026
Investments in Affiliates	203	220
Notes Receivables	50	111
Accounts Receivables	102	80
Inventories	40	52
Other Assets	176	256
Cash and Cash Equivalents	95	103
	$3,822	$3,848

Nontrade Receivables

Nontrade receivables—amounts due from noncustomers—arise from a wide variety of transactions. Because of their unusual character, they are sometimes classified separately, but may be combined with another current asset or assets. Exhibit 5–7, from the annual report of Kerr-McGee Corporation, shows that this company combines deposits with prepaid expenses in the current assets section of its balance sheet. Kerr-McGee is an energy and chemical company engaged in three businesses: oil and natural gas, coal, and inorganic industrial and speciality chemicals.

Examples of nontrade receivables include advances to officers, directors, stockholders, employees, and affiliated companies; claims for losses or damages; claims for tax refunds; interest or dividends to be received; or deposits with creditors and others, such as a utility or other agency.

EXHIBIT 5–7
Kerr-McGee Corporation, Excerpt from
Consolidated Balance Sheet

(In millions of dollars)	1994	1993
Assets		
Current assets:		
Cash	$ 82	$ 94
Notes and accounts receivable	422	373
Inventories	399	349
Deposits and prepaid expenses	60	50
Total current assets	963	866
Investments and other assets	95	101
Property, plant, and equipment—net	2,552	2,513
Deferred charges	88	67
	$3,698	$3,547

Prepaid Expenses

Companies normally make payments in advance for items such as insurance and rent. Often, these payments benefit more than one accounting period and are charged to future periods as expenses. On the balance sheet, items chargeable to the next accounting period are called prepaid expenses and are classified as current assets. As the benefits of the prepaid item are used up, the cost is transferred from the prepaid asset account to an expense account. The prepaid asset account decreases and the expense increases.

Assume that a company purchases a one-year insurance policy for $3,600 cash on August 1, and that the company's fiscal year ends on December 31. The company must recognize the expired portion of the Prepaid Insurance account. In this instance, a 5-month portion has expired. Because the policy is for 12 months, $300 expires each month ($3,600/12 months). Therefore, $1,500 (5 months × $300) should be charged to the insurance expense account in the current period. The balance in the Prepaid Insurance account is now $2,100 (7 months × $300, or $3,600 − $1,500), and this amount appears on the December 31 balance sheet as a current asset. The income statement will show $1,500 of Insurance Expense for the year ended December 31.

Prepaid expenses may also be classified as noncurrent assets. Continuing the example above, we might assume that the $3,600 insurance payment was for three years instead of one year. In this case, $100 of the insurance expires each month ($3,600/36 months). At the end of the current year, a 5-month portion has expired; thus, $500 is recognized in the Insurance Expense account. The current asset account, Prepaid Insurance, would have a balance of $1,200 ($100 × 12 months), representing the portion of insurance that expires in the next period. The noncurrent asset account, Prepaid Insurance, would have a balance of $1,900 ($100 × 19 months remaining after the next period).

Current period expense (5 months × $100)	$ 500
Balance of current asset Prepaid Expense	
(to be expensed next period) (12 months × $100)	1,200
Balance of noncurrent asset Prepaid Expense	
(to be expensed in periods following next period)	
(19 months × $100)	1,900
Total	$3,600

6

VALUING INVENTORIES

*W*hen a company purchases several million dollars' worth of inventories during the year (as many do), one of the major problems of preparing financial statements is determining the cost of inventory on hand and the cost of goods sold during the year. Accountants frequently do not know the cost of the specific units in inventory because shipments of identical units have been purchased at many different prices. But accountants must assign a cost to the units in inventory and the units sold, and how they do it affects both the income statement and the balance sheet.

Inventory Cost Flow Assumptions

Assume that the Donalds Company has a beginning inventory of 1 unit on June 1. The company purchases 2 additional units during the month, and sells 1 unit for $20 before month end. Ending inventory on June 30 is 2 units. If all the units are identical, what dollar amount should be given to Donalds' ending inventory on the balance sheet? How much should be charged to Donalds' cost of goods sold?

Assigning costs to inventory and cost of goods sold is no problem if all units are purchased for $10 each. Ending inventory is then $20 (2 × $10) and cost of goods sold is $10 (1 × $10). But if the units are purchased at three different prices, the problem is not so straightforward.

Assume Donalds' costs rise during the month as follows:

Beginning inventory on June 1	1 unit @ $5/unit	$ 5
Purchases:		
June 12	1 unit @ $10/unit	10
June 22	1 unit @ $15/unit	15
Totals	3 units	$30

Accounting principles allow accountants to use one of four main methods in accounting for inventories and cost of goods sold:

1. Specific identification.
2. First-in, first-out (FIFO).
3. Last-in, first-out (LIFO).
4. Weighted average.

A company can use any of these methods. Companies with several kinds of inventories may use several different methods.

Specific Identification

Many accountants do not like the specific identification inventory method because it lets managers manipulate income by choosing the unit to be sold. If Donalds sells one unit and uses specific identification, managers can select the unit to sell and create profit of $15, $10, or $5. Inventory shown on the balance sheet will then be $25 ($10 + $15), $20 ($5 + $15), or $15 ($5 + $10).

	Option 1	Option 2	Option 3
Income statement:			
Sales	$20	$20	$20
Cost of Goods Sold	5	10	15
Gross Profit	$15	$10	$ 5
Balance sheet:			
Inventory	$25	$20	$15

The specific identification method is most often used to account for unique, high-value items such as diamonds and computers because managers track each item and customers choose the item sold. The other three methods use different patterns of flowing costs that parallel the three options represented above.

First-In, First-Out (FIFO)

The first option is called first-in, first-out, or FIFO and charges the cost of the oldest unit to the cost of goods sold and assigns the costs of the most recent purchases to ending inventory. (In our example, the oldest unit is the $5 unit in beginning inventory.) This method flows costs through the records the way most merchants rotate stock and flow units of physical inventory on the shelves. People tend to understand and like FIFO because it follows the normal physical flow of goods in most companies.

Last-In, First-Out (LIFO)

Option 3, called last-in, first-out, or LIFO charges the cost of the most recently purchased units to cost of goods sold, and assigns to ending inventory the oldest costs of the first units purchased. Not many companies flow physical units in a LIFO pattern. One example is a coal pile: new coal is dumped on top of the pile, and the oldest coal is on the bottom. When coal is sold, workers load the last coal purchased (from the top of the pile) and keep the oldest.

Weighted Average

Option 2 uses the weighted average cost per unit for both cost of goods sold and ending inventory still on hand. The weighted average cost per unit is determined by dividing the total cost by the number of units available. Calculation of weighted average cost per unit for Donalds Company is as follows:

Total cost of units available for sale	$30
Divided by: Total units available for sale	÷ 3
Weighted average cost per unit	$10

How Inventory Methods Affect Financial Statements

Companies can use the specific identification, LIFO, FIFO, or weighted average method of valuing inventory to flow costs through the accounting system, *regardless of how individual physical units of inventory flow through the company.* Choosing to rotate stock in a FIFO pattern is a management decision. Deciding how to account for inventory is an accounting decision. The decisions are not related. A company can flow physical units in a FIFO pattern (as most do) and still use LIFO to prepare financial statements.

To understand the impact of each method on the financial statements, consider the effect on Donalds of selling one unit. Should gross profit be $15, $10, or $5? Should inventory in the balance sheet be $15, $20, or $25?

In judging which is the best method, accountants consider two questions:

1. How much better off is the company after the sale?

2. What is the "value" of the units in inventory?

How Much Better Off?

To decide how much better off Donalds is after selling one unit, we must realize that, to continue in business, Donalds must replace the unit it sold.

If replacement cost is increasing, as in the example, the next unit will cost $15 or more.

If a company sells a unit for $20 and must pay $15 or more to replace it, the company is only $5 or less better off. If it then pays taxes on the profit created, it is not even $5 better off. LIFO gives results that come closest to showing how much better off Donalds (or any company) is from selling one unit. Thus, LIFO provides the best measure of cost of goods sold and profit in the income statement.

When costs are rising, FIFO reports deceptively high profits. With FIFO, a company charges the cost of old, lower-cost inventory to cost of goods sold. When Donalds charges the old $5 inventory cost to cost of goods sold, the cost of goods sold expense is much less than the cash required to replace the inventory sold—again, probably $15 or more.

The weighted average method gives results that fall between LIFO and FIFO.

Value of Units in Inventory

As for the cost assigned to inventory on hand, LIFO weakens the balance sheet by charging the outdated costs of the oldest units to ending inventory. In contrast, FIFO charges the most recent costs to ending inventory and the oldest costs to cost of goods sold. FIFO maximizes the accuracy of the balance sheet by providing better information about the cost of units in ending inventory. Weighted average reports an inventory cost between LIFO and FIFO.

Which Method Do Accountants Prefer?

Most analysts believe the income statement is more important than the balance sheet. A weak balance sheet can be overlooked if a company has a strong earnings record, but a strong balance sheet will seldom outweigh poor earnings. Because of this, accountants attempt to use the best available information in the income statement, even if the balance sheet content is made less useful. As a result, accountants generally prefer LIFO inventory.

LIFO Reserve

When a company uses LIFO inventory, it often undervalues inventory on its balance sheet and creates a LIFO reserve. The amount of a LIFO reserve is the difference between LIFO cost of inventory and its replacement cost (usually, for simplicity, assumed to be the FIFO cost of the inventory). This difference occurs because LIFO shows inventories at older, usually lower costs than if a company uses FIFO or replacement cost. In our example, LIFO inventory is $15, and FIFO inventory is $25. The LIFO reserve is $10, the difference between the two.

FIFO inventory $25 (a surrogate for replacement cost)
LIFO inventory   15 (as shown on the balance sheet)

LIFO reserve $10 (the amount LIFO inventory is undervalued)

Companies that use LIFO may show the LIFO reserve either on the face of the balance sheet or in the notes. In the notes to its 1994 annual report, Sun Company's note on inventories gave the amount of the LIFO reserve:

8. Inventories

	December 31	
(Millions of Dollars)	*1994*	*1993*
Crude oil	$193	$140
Refined products	335	244
Materials, supplies and other	85	80
	$613	$464

The current replacement cost of all inventories valued at LIFO exceeded their carrying value by $459 and $390 million at December 31, 1994 and 1993, respectively.

The LIFO reserve allows readers to compare companies using LIFO with companies using FIFO. Companies often keep their books on a FIFO basis (the way their physical units flow) and convert to LIFO at year end.

Lower of Cost or Market

The accounting principle of conservatism requires that accountants show inventories in the balance sheet at the lower of their historical cost or their replacement cost (or market cost). Assume that Donalds uses FIFO and has ending inventory that originally cost $25 but can now be replaced for only $22. There is a strong argument that the market for those inventory items is falling and that Donalds' selling prices will also fall.

It follows that Donalds no longer has an asset of $25 and that the current "future benefit" of the asset is now only $22. Thus, ending inventory should be shown at $22 (the lower of cost or market), and the $3 loss should be shown in the income statement as an adjustment of cost of goods sold. In another excerpt from Sun Company's 1994 annual report, a note following the financial statements indicates that Sun values inventories at the lower of cost or market:

1. Summary of Significant Accounting Policies

• • •

Inventories
Inventories of crude oil and refined products are valued at the lower of cost or market. The cost of such inventories is determined principally using the last-in, first-out method ("LIFO"). Materials, supplies and other inventories are valued principally at the lower of average cost or market.

Inventory Estimating Methods

When a company sells many different items, all at different prices, a count of inventory is difficult and time-consuming. This is particularly true of retailers. But because many retailers mark up merchandise by the same percentage each period, cost of goods sold is often a predictable, continuing percentage of sales. Even retail companies that sell many types of products and mark each product up by a different percentage often have relatively constant gross margins and cost of goods sold percentages.

Retailers use the continuing relationship between cost and retail selling price to estimate the cost of inventories on hand from a count of inventories at retail. For example, if a clothing store counts its inventory and finds it has $100,000 of inventory at retail on hand, and knows the cost is 70 percent of retail, it can estimate ending inventory to be $70,000.

On quarterly financial statements, when inventory is not counted, the same clothing store may know that it had beginning inventory and purchases totaling $175,000 in inventory at cost available for sale. If the company also knows, from cash register tapes and other records, that total sales were $200,000 at retail, the company can estimate cost of goods sold to be $140,000 ($200,000 × .70) at cost, and ending inventory to be $35,000, calculated as follows:

Inventory at cost available for sale	$175,000
Cost of goods sold, calculated from retail sales	140,000
Ending inventory at cost	$ 35,000

A quarterly schedule of estimated ending inventory using the retail method is shown in Exhibit 6–1.

EXHIBIT 6–1
Quarterly Schedule of Estimated Ending Inventory
Using the Retail Method

	At cost	At retail
Beginning inventory	$ 70,000	$100,000
Plus purchases	105,000	150,000
Total available for sale	$175,000	$250,000
Cost/retail ratio ($175,000/$250,000)		.70
Sales at retail prices		$200,000
Cost/retail ratio		× .70
Estimated cost of sales ($200,000 × .7)	$140,000	
Estimated ending inventory	$ 35,000	

7

NONCURRENT
ASSETS: INVESTMENTS

Noncurrent investments, often simply called investments, generally consist of five types of assets.

1. Investments in securities, such as stocks or bonds, or warrants.

2. Investments in noncurrent receivables, such as notes.

3. Investments in tangible assets, such as real estate held for resale, that are not currently being used in operations.

4. Investments in special-purpose funds, such as a sinking fund to be used for the extinguishment of debt.

5. Investments in the cash surrender value of life insurance policies on key employees.

A company acquires these assets intending to hold them for the long term. Normally, they appear on the balance sheet just below current assets in a section titled Investments. However, it is not uncommon for a company to combine them with Other Assets or show them as a single item. Another form of presentation shows Investments as one amount, with detail presented in the footnotes to the financial statements.

Exhibit 7–1 is the asset portion of the balance sheet of Archer Daniels Midland Company's 1995 annual report. Archer Daniels Midland Company is in the business of procuring, transporting, storing, processing, and merchandising agricultural commodities and products.

Investments in Bonds or Stocks of Other Companies

Investments in securities are normally classified as either debt or equity, where debt represents bonds or notes and equity is in the form of shares of stock. The purchase of bonds is a lending transaction, while buying shares of stock results in ownership. All long-term investments are initially recorded at their acquisition cost, including additional costs such as brokerage fees.

Investment in Debt Securities

If a company invests in bonds or some other type of debt security as a long-term investment, the transaction is recorded at the fair value of the consideration given up—normally, cash. Whether a security is shown on the balance sheet at fair market value at the end of the accounting period is a function of whether it is classified as a trading security, a held-to-maturity security, or an available-for-sale security.

Trading debt securities—those bought and held primarily for resale in the short term—are always classified as short-term investments on the balance sheet. They are purchased primarily to generate profits on short-term price differences in the market. Trading securities are adjusted to fair value at each balance sheet date, and any resulting unrealized holding gains or losses appear as a component of income for that period. Thus, trading securities appear on the balance sheet at fair value. An unrealized holding gain or loss is the change in fair value of a security from one period to another.

EXHIBIT 7-1
Archer Daniels Midland Company, Excerpt from
Consolidated Balance Sheet

(In thousands)	June 30 1995	June 30 1994
Assets		
Current assets:		
Cash and cash equivalents	$ 454,593	$ 316,394
Marketable securities	664,690	1,019,059
Receivables	1,013,562	1,041,769
Inventories	1,473,896	1,422,147
Prepaid expenses	105,904	111,426
Total current assets	3,712,645	3,910,795
Investments and other assets:		
Investments in and advances to affiliates	502,698	297,147
Long-term marketable securities	1,604,219	891,073
Other assets	175,044	109,263
	2,281,961	1,297,483
Property, plant, and equipment:		
Land	113,098	101,854
Buildings	1,109,249	1,029,817
Machinery and equipment	5,443,561	5,073,631
Construction in progress	642,825	455,729
Less allowances for depreciation	(3,546,452)	(3,122,456)
	3,762,281	3,538,575
	$ 9,756,887	$ 8,746,853

For example, assume a company purchases a $1,000 face-value bond of Company A for $1,000 on January 1 of the current year. In preparing its financial statements for the year ending on December 31, the company determines that market forces have caused the fair value of Company A's bond to increase to $1,100. The company has experienced an unrealized holding gain of $100. The short-term investment in Company A's bond will be shown in the current assets section of the December 31 balance sheet at $1,100, and the $100 unrealized holding gain will appear in its income statement. (Trading debt securities as short-term investments is also discussed in Chapter 4.)

For a debt security to be classified as held-to-maturity, a company must demonstrate that it has the intent and ability to hold the security until maturity. Held-to-maturity securities are not adjusted to market value at each balance sheet date and are normally classified as noncurrent assets in the balance sheet. However, if the maturity date is within the next accounting period, the securities are classified as current assets.

Available-for-sale debt securities are securities not classified as either trading or held-to-maturity. This is to say that management's intent is not to immediately sell the securities nor is it to hold the securities until they mature. Available-for-sale debt securities should be classified as a current asset if they will mature within the next accounting period or if management intends to sell them. Otherwise, available-for-sale debt securities are classified as a noncurrent investment. Like trading securities, they are adjusted to fair value at the end of each period; however, unlike trading securities, the resulting unrealized holding gains or losses do not appear on the income statement but as a separate component of stockholders' equity. (Stockholders' equity is discussed in Chapter 16.)

Investments in Equity Securities

Equity securities are of two types: trading securities and available-for-sale securities. Because equity securities have no fixed maturity date, there is no held-to-maturity classification. Equity securities are classified as trading if they are purchased and held primarily to be sold in a short period of time; in other words, the purchaser company buys and sells frequently, hoping to generate profits from short-term price swings. These securities are always current assets and are reported at fair value, with unrealized holding gains and losses reported as a component of net income.

Equity securities not classified as trading are, by default, available-for-sale securities. Although available-for-sale securities are marketable, their classification as current or noncurrent depends on management's intent.

Available-for-sale equity securities are also reported at fair value; however, any unrealized holding gains or losses appear as a separate component of stockholders' equity rather than as a component of net income.

Exhibit 7–2 is an excerpt from the 1995 annual report of H&R Block, Inc. The company's policy contains footnote disclosure relating to its investment in marketable securities.

Summary of Significant Accounting Policies

• • •

Marketable securities: On May 1, 1994, the Company adopted Statement of Financial Accounting Standards No. 115, "Accounting for Certain Investments in Debt and Equity Securities." This Statement addresses the reporting for debt and equity securities by requiring such investments to be classified in held-to-maturity, available-for-sale or trading categories. All marketable debt and equity securities were classified as available-for-sale securities on the date of adoption, and are carried at market value, based on quoted prices, with unrealized gains and losses included in stockholders' equity. The adoption of the Statement resulted in an increase in stockholders' equity of $5,526, net of taxes. In accordance with the Statement, prior years' financial statements have not been restated.

For marketable securities held at April 30, 1994, municipal bonds and notes are stated at amortized cost, marketable equity securities are stated at the lower of aggregate cost or market value and other investments are stated at cost.

The cost of marketable securities sold is determined on the specific identification method and realized gains and losses are reflected in earnings.

Long-Term Investments in Stock

Many companies purchase equity securities of other companies with the intention that the investment will be long-term. Companies make this type of investment to secure the ability to influence or control the other companies' financial or operating policies, or to grow or diversify.

Noncurrent investments in stocks are initially recorded at cost. Subsequently, companies account for these investments by the cost method, the market value method, or the equity method. The choice of method is a

Understanding Balance Sheets

EXHIBIT 7–2
H&R Block, Inc., Excerpt from Notes to the Consolidated Balance Sheet

MARKETABLE SECURITIES

The amortized cost and market value of marketable securities at April 30, 1995 and 1994 are summarized below:

	1995			
	Amortized Cost	Gross Unrealized Gains	Gross Unrealized Losses	Market Value
Current:				
Municipal bonds and notes	$ 88,894	$ 310	$ 94	$ 89,110
U.S. Government obligations	52,091	48	—	52,139
Other equity investments	49,100	—	—	49,100
Other debt investments	72,830	61	1	72,890
	262,915	419	95	263,239
Noncurrent:				
Municipal bonds	82,702	1,676	1,325	83,053
Preferred stock	2,737	245	131	3,018
Common stock	1,511	396	115	1,625
Other equity investments	3,488	—	692	2,796
Other debt investments	999	3	—	1,002
	91,437	2,320	2,263	91,494
	$354,352	$2,739	$2,358	$354,733

All marketable securities at April 30, 1995 are classified as available-for-sale. Proceeds from the sales of available-for-sale securities were $299,702, $448,978 and $553,465 during 1995, 1994 and 1993, respectively. Gross realized gains on those sales during 1995, 1994 and 1993 were $7,014, $393 and $24, respectively; gross realized losses were $350, $86 and $147, respectively.

Contractual maturities of available-for-sale debt securities at April 30, 1995 are presented below. Since expected maturities differ from contractual maturities due to the issuers' rights to prepay certain obligations or the seller's rights to call certain obligations, the first call date, put date or auction date for municipal bonds and notes is considered the contractual maturity date.

	1994		
Amortized Cost	Gross Unrealized Gains	Gross Unrealized Losses	Market Value
$238,092	$ 266	$ 100	$238,258
—	—	—	—
118,263	5	—	118,268
116,688	4	—	116,692
473,043	275	100	473,218
92,154	3,176	1,316	94,014
1,511	415	131	1,795
7,479	7,287	—	14,766
4,561	—	649	3,912
—	—	—	—
105,705	10,878	2,096	114,487
$578,748	$11,153	$2,196	$587,705

	Amortized Cost	Market Value
Within one year	$213,815	$214,139
After one year through five years	36,184	37,444
After five years through ten years	47,517	46,611
	$297,516	$298,194

function of the level of influence that the investor company can exercise over the investee company. The investor company is the purchaser and owner of the stock and the investee company is the company whose stock is owned. Additionally, the availability of market prices must be considered.

If the investor owns less than 20 percent of the investee's outstanding common stock, the presumption is that the investor's position is passive. The investor does not possess enough of the investee's stock to influence its operating or financing policies. In this instance, either the cost method or the market value method is used.

On the other hand, when the investor company owns 20 percent or more of the investee's outstanding stock, the presumption is that the investor can significantly influence the investee and uses the equity method to account for its investment. (If the investor owns over 50 percent of the outstanding common stock of the investee, a parent–subsidiary relationship exists, and control is presumed. In this instance, consolidated financial statements are prepared, as shown in Chapter 3.)

The cost method is used when stock market prices are not available and the investor company cannot exercise significant influence. Under this method, the investment is initially recorded at cost. The recorded amount is not adjusted, and the investment is carried at cost until the stock is sold.

If the level of ownership does not allow the investor to exercise significant influence over the investee and market values are available, the investor uses the market value method. The stock is initially recorded at cost and subsequently adjusted to fair value at each balance sheet date. Because of management's intent to hold the stock for the long term, the stock is considered an available-for-sale security and any unrealized holding gains or losses appear as a component of stockholders' equity. They are not a component of net income, as are unrealized gains and losses on short-term investments. (Conversely, if management's intent changed and the company decided to sell the stock in the near future, it would be categorized as trading and classified as a short-term investment in the balance sheet. Any unrealized holding gains and losses resulting from the adjustment to fair value would then be included as a component of income.)

When significant influence over an investee's operating and financial policies can be exerted by the investor, the investor uses the equity method, which requires the investor to record the initial investment at cost and to make certain necessary periodic adjustments to the account balance. The adjustments made by the investor are:

1. Increase (or decrease) the investment for its proportionate share of the investee's net income (or net loss). For example, if the investee has net income of $200,000 and the investor has an ownership interest of 30 percent, then the investor recognizes $60,000 of investment income on its income statement and increases the balance in the investment account by the same amount.

2. Decrease the investment account for all dividends received by the investor company from the investee company. Because the investor has the ability to influence dividend policy, it would be inappropriate to record the dividends received as revenue on the investor's income statement.

These equity method adjustments give recognition to the fact that net income increases the net assets of the investee, while a net loss and dividend payments reduce the investee's net assets. Exhibit 7–3 displays the assets section of the balance sheet of Union Texas Petroleum. Regarding its equity investment, the company stated in a note:

Notes to Consolidated Financial Statements

• • •

Note 6   Equity Investment

At December 31, 1994 and 1993, an investment, accounted for using the equity method, consisted of the following:

	1994	*1993*
Unimar Company	$114,505	$103,111

The company has a 50% interest in Unimar Company ("Unimar"), a partnership through which the Company has an additional 11.56% working interest in the Indonesian joint venture, resulting in a total working interest of 37.81%. The Company's share of Unimar's nonrecourse debt of $18 million was redeemed on January 4, 1994.

EXHIBIT 7–3
Union Texas Petroleum Holdings, Inc., Excerpt from
Consolidated Balance Sheet

	December 31,	
(Dollars in thousands)	1994	1993
Assets		
Current assets:		
Cash and cash equivalents	$ 8,389	$ 18,143
Accounts and notes receivable,		
less allowance for doubtful accounts	54,773	49,599
Inventories	43,228	34,285
Prepaid expenses and other current assets	30,675	39,451
Total current assets	137,065	141,478
Equity investment	114,505	103,111
Property, plant, and equipment, at cost,		
less accumulated		
depreciation, depletion, and amortization*	1,286,278	1,088,884
Other assets	6,786	5,268
Total assets	$1,544,634	$1,338,741

* The Company follows the successful efforts method of accounting for oil and gas activities.

The ownership percentages and level of influence are only guidelines. Judgment must be used by management in determining the level of influence in each situation. For example, assume an investor company owns only 10 percent of an investee's outstanding common stock. Significant influence could still be present if the investor company's president is a member of the board of directors of the investee company.

Stock Warrants

Companies might also purchase stock warrants as long-term investments. Stock warrants entitle the holder to purchase new shares of stock at a set price—normally higher than the market price at the time of issuance—for a period of years or indefinitely into the future.

Long-Term Receivables

Investment in long-term notes receivable is an example of a debt instrument that is not a debt security. A note gives the holder that right to receive cash on demand or on fixed dates, along with periodic interest payments. Long-term notes receivable are initially recorded at the fair market value of the property, goods, or services given up, or the fair market value of the note, whichever is more reliable. Interest revenue is accounted for in the same manner as short-term notes receivable. (Short-term notes receivable are discussed in Chapter 5.)

Other types of long-term receivables include notes receivable and advances made to officers and key employees, and litigation claims to be paid to the company over an extended period of time.

Investments in Noncurrent Assets Not Currently Used in Operations

Investments in property, plant, and equipment held for future operations are also included in this section of the balance sheet. Examples include investments in mineral deposits, and real estate held for a future building site or for speculation. These assets are carried at original cost on the balance sheet, unless management determines that a permanent decline in value has occurred. In the latter case, the assets should be written down to fair value and a loss recognized.

EXHIBIT 7–4

Giant Food Inc., Excerpt from Consolidated Balance Sheet

February 25, 1995, February 26, 1994 and February 27, 1993
Dollar amounts in thousands

	1995	1994	1993
Property, plant, and equipment			
Land	$ 66,842	$ 58,820	$ 46,958
Buildings and improvements	295,245	268,640	231,947
Leasehold improvements	157,663	153,399	158,393
Fixtures and equipment	782,394	745,288	699,701
	1,302,144	1,226,147	1,136,999
Less accumulated depreciation	609,214	544,862	479,128
	692,930	681,285	657,871
Equipment deposits and construction in progress	27,255	32,506	30,400
	720,185	713,791	688,271
Property under capital leases, net of accumulated amortization (1995, $59,876; 1994, $54,679; 1993, $52,044)	105,502	107,580	110,439
Real estate held for future development	23,933	21,367	26,130
Other assets	10,751	9,537	10,132
	$1,416,710	$1,357,813	$1,296,600

Exhibit 7–4 is the noncurrent assets section of the balance sheet from the 1995 annual report of Giant Food Inc. On the balance sheet, the company lists an investment in real estate held for future development.

Investments in Special Funds

Companies establish funds for specific purposes. These purposes might include debt repayment (bond sinking fund), retiring preferred stock (stock redemption fund), pension commitments (pension fund), future plant expansion (plant expansion fund), or paying for some unforeseen future obligation (contingency fund). These funds do not relate to day-to-day operations in the way that petty cash and a payroll fund do. Some of these funds—a bond sinking fund, for example—originate because of contractual commitments made by the company. Others result from internal decisions made by management: a plant expansion fund may be created to construct an additional plant. These funds can be managed by the company's management or by an independent trustee, such as a bank or other financial institution.

The company sets aside cash and other assets (such as securities) in the fund. The fund balance is initially a contribution by the company. The fund is then increased by additional contributions and by interest and dividends, and it is reduced by the payment of expenses and the sales of the assets in the fund. Company management is responsible for monitoring the fund to determine whether the fund is accumulating assets at the forecasted level. If the fund has earnings that exceed those initially anticipated, future contributions might be reduced. If the assets of the fund are not generating earnings at the expected rate, future contributions might have to be increased to meet the company's objective for the fund. Although accounting for a long-term investment in a fund requires the use of several accounts, these accounts are aggregated and the fund balance is presented as a single amount on the balance sheet.

Cash Surrender Value of Life Insurance Policies

A company is heavily dependent on the expertise and skill of its officers and key executives. For this reason, many companies insure the lives of these individuals, naming the company as beneficiary of the life insurance policy in case of death. The rationale for this practice is to partly compensate the company for the loss of an officer's or executive's talents in the event of an unexpected death.

A company can purchase either a term or whole life insurance policy. A term insurance policy does not result in an investment. The company merely buys protection for the loss of the individual, and the payments are normally expensed as they are made. A whole life policy represents an investment because it has an accumulating cash surrender value (much like a savings plan), in addition to providing insurance coverage. The policy normally also has a loan value, which allows the company to borrow against the cash surrender value of the insurance policy. Also, if the company elects to discontinue the policy, the company can receive the cash surrender value in cash.

EXHIBIT 7–5
Winn-Dixie Stores, Inc., Excerpt from
Consolidated Balance Sheet

	1995	1994
	Amounts in thousands	
Assets		
Current assets:		
Cash and cash equivalents	$ 30,414	$ 31,451
Trade and other receivables, less allowance for doubtful items of $1,105,000 ($834,000 in 1994)	151,912	171,854
Associate stock loans	10,615	1,776
Merchandise inventories at lower of cost or market less LIFO reserve of $212,485,000 ($205,172,000 in 1994)	1,159,584	1,058,883
Prepaid expenses	103,135	97,220
Total current assets	1,455,660	1,361,184
Investments and other assets:		
Cash surrender value of life insurance, net	41,411	25,094
Other assets	58,873	12,493
Total investments and other assets	100,284	37,587
Deferred income taxes	29,025	41,024
Net property, plant, and equipment	897,823	706,779
	$2,482,792	$2,146,574

Each annual payment made on a whole life policy consists of two parts: (1) insurance expense and (2) an increase in the cash surrender value of the insurance policy. The portion of the annual premium that does not increase the cash surrender value is insurance expense. The portion of the annual premium that represents the increase in the investment in the policy is specified in the insurance policy. Generally, the adjustment for the annual increase in the investment is made at the end of the year. The investment is classified as a noncurrent asset on the company's balance sheet because it is doubtful that the company will terminate the policy in the near future.

Exhibit 7–5 presents the assets section of the balance sheet of Winn-Dixie Stores, Inc., a major food retailer. The company discloses its investment in the cash surrender value of life insurance for 1995 and 1994.

8

NONCURRENT ASSETS: LONG-LIVED PRODUCTIVE ASSETS

*F*or many companies, the largest dollar category of assets on the balance sheet is long-lived tangible productive assets, called plant, property, and equipment. For example, these assets comprised almost 81 percent of the total assets of Occidental Petroleum Corporation in 1994, as shown in Exhibit 8–1.

This class of assets is also referred to as plant assets or fixed assets. This chapter discusses how companies determine the cost of plant, property, and equipment and describes the methods used to depreciate those assets.

EXHIBIT 8-1
Occidental Petroleum Corporation, Excerpt from
Consolidated Balance Sheet

In millions, except share amounts Assets at December 31,	1994	1993
Current assets:		
Cash and cash equivalents	$ 129	$ 157
Receivables		
Trade, net of reserves of $17 in 1994 and $13 in 1993	831	539
Joint ventures, partnerships and other	134	128
Inventories	748	791
Prepaid expenses and other	416	319
Total current assets	2,258	1,934
Long-term receivables, net	131	93
Equity investments	692	482
Property, plant, and equipment, at cost:		
Oil and gas operations	8,180	7,335
Natural gas transmission operations	8,383	8,364
Chemical operations	6,621	6,530
Corporate and other	202	199
	23,386	22,428
Accumulated depreciation, depletion and amortization	(8,884)	(8,144)
	14,502	14,284
Other assets	406	330
	$17,989	$17,123

Cost of Plant Assets

The cost of a plant asset is the sum of all the costs of getting the asset in place and ready for its intended use. With minor exceptions, all of these costs have future benefit and are therefore part of the cost of the asset. These costs (with the exception of land) are expensed through the process of depreciation over the lives of the assets as the benefits are consumed. The reason for this treatment is derived from the matching principle, where, to measure periodic net income, revenue is matched against all expenses incurred in producing that revenue. For a company, the benefits of owning a plant asset are consumed over a period of time, perhaps eight years. The expenditures relating to the acquisition of the asset are included in its cost, so they will be matched against revenue obtained from the operation of the asset over the eight-year period.

Cost of Machinery or Equipment

What is the cost of machinery or equipment? The cost of a machine is the sum of its purchase price (including sales tax), transportation costs, insurance in transit, assembly, installation, painting, testing, and electrical connections. These costs are assets because the company (1) could not use the equipment if it were not delivered to the plant and (2) could not produce salable units if the machine were not installed, calibrated, and adjusted. In other words, all costs necessary to make the asset ready for its intended use are capitalized and become part of the machinery asset account.

Capitalized expenditures should include only those that are reasonable and necessary. For example, assume a company purchased equipment and it was damaged during installation by a negligent forklift operator. The repair costs are expensed, not capitalized, because these costs are not reasonable and essential.

Cost of Buildings

The cost of a building includes its purchase price, closing costs (such as attorney's fees and title insurance), real estate broker's commissions, and other costs necessary to prepare it for its intended use. There may also be expenditures for remodeling rooms and offices. Additionally, the cost of replacing or repairing roofs, floors, or plumbing, and any rewiring costs, are included in the cost of the building.

Companies often build their own assets because of lower initial costs, to satisfy the special nature of their needs, or for other reasons. Many companies routinely construct assets such as plants, garages, or loading docks. The cost of such self-constructed assets includes materials and labor plus other costs such as power, heat, light, and depreciation on assets (such as trucks) used in the construction of the asset.

Cost of Land

The cost of land includes the purchase price, attorney's fees, title search and other closing costs, real estate broker's commissions, and accrued property taxes and other liens assumed by the purchaser. When vacant land is purchased, clearing, drainage, filling, and grading might be necessary to make the land ready for some intended use. If a company purchases land that has an existing structure, such as a building that must be removed to make the land suitable for a new building, all demolition and other costs of removal (less any proceeds from sale of salvaged material) are costs of the land, not of the new building. Land is not depreciable because it does not deteriorate with usage and therefore has an unlimited life.

Improvements to Land

Although land lasts indefinitely, some land improvements have limited lives. For example, the cost of a new parking lot might include paving, fencing, and the installation of a lighting or security system. Because of their limited lives, these costs are included in a land improvement account and depreciated over their estimated useful lives.

Plant Assets Acquired by Capital Lease

Many companies lease capital assets rather than purchase them. A capital lease results when virtually all of the risks and rewards of ownership of the leased asset are passed from the lessor to the lessee. When a lease is deemed to be a capital lease, the lessee company records the asset on its books along with a corresponding liability for the lease payments. The impact of a capital lease is no different from purchasing the asset and signing a note payable. The company expenses the cost of the asset over the shorter of the asset's useful life or the lease term, and the leased asset appears under the plant asset category.

Acquisition of a Plant Asset by Noncash Exchange

Some companies acquire plant assets by issuing securities or paying with nonmonetary assets instead of cash. For example, a company could issue its own common stock to buy a plant or trade in an old plant asset for a new one. In the latter type of transaction, the recorded value of the acquired asset should be either the fair market value of (1) the securities or the asset given up, or (2) the asset received, whichever is more objectively determinable. The asset should be recorded at a value as close to its cash price as possible. For example, if a company decides to purchase land for a manufacturing plant by issuing 10,000 shares of its stock at a currently traded market value of $20 per share, the land would be valued on the balance sheet at $200,000. On the other hand, if the market value of the stock is not known (as in the case of a new start-up company whose stock is not widely traded), the appraised market value of the land should be used to record the acquisition. For example, if the land has been appraised at $190,000 and the value of the stock is in doubt, the appraisal would be used to value the asset on the company's books.

Donated Assets

Governmental units, such as cities and counties, sometimes donate land and buildings to companies to attract them to the area and provide jobs for residents. A company would record the plant asset received from such a donation at its appraisal or fair market value and would create an equity account called Donated Capital. Because the gift increases the equity of company stockholders, the Donated Capital account appears in the stockholders' equity section and the donated asset appears in the non-current asset section of the balance sheet.

Depreciating Plant Assets

Depreciation is the process of allocating the cost of a plant asset to expense over its useful service life in a rational and systematic manner. Depreciation is an estimate because it is impossible to know with a high degree of certainty an asset's actual service life and the pattern of its benefits. Depreciation is not the decline in economic value during the reporting period, but the expensing of a part of the asset's cost so as to match that cost with the revenues or services produced by that asset during each reporting period. This approach does not imply that the company is unconcerned with decline in the market values of its plant assets. The usefulness and market value of an asset fall because of physical wear and tear, obsolescence, and inadequacy, and these factors influence accounting estimates of the asset's useful life and its salvage value.

Inadequacy refers to the asset becoming incapable of meeting the increasing demands for its product or service because of a company's growth. Inadequacy generally occurs when a company grows more rapidly than expected.

Obsolescence occurs when technological advances create new assets that make older models out dated and relatively less efficient before they physically wear out. When this happens, an asset is reduced in value. Many types of assets, such as computers, have improved over time, thus rendering older models inadequate, if not obsolete.

Determining Depreciation Expense

After the cost of an asset is calculated, the amount of periodic expense is determined by estimating:

1. The periods of benefit, that is, the useful life of the asset.

2. The salvage value.

3. The pattern of consumption of the benefit, so that the appropriate depreciation method can be chosen.

The whole depreciation process is very exact mathematically, but very inexact from a practical standpoint because of the use of estimates. Annual depreciation expense is an estimate, as is the balance of plant and equipment in the balance sheet.

The asset's estimated economic life is an estimate of its productive life, which is not necessarily the same as its physical life. The life estimate may be expressed in terms of a time period, or units of activity (such as miles), or units of productive output. To estimate the economic life of an asset, management considers the effects of physical wear and tear, obsolescence, and inadequacy. Generally, an asset's useful life is shorter than its physical life.

The salvage or residual value of a plant asset is the amount expected to be received from disposing of the asset at the end of its useful life. This value might be zero or it might be quite high in relation to the original cost. The salvage value may be an estimate of the asset's trade-in value or of its value as scrap. The depreciable base—the cost of the asset less its residual value—is the total amount to be depreciated over the asset's useful life.

The pattern of depreciation expense over the useful life of the asset should reflect the pattern in which its benefits are consumed. In general, depreciation methods make the assumption that benefits are consumed in one of the following three patterns:

1. When benefits are consumed evenly over the useful life of the asset, use straight-line depreciation.

2. When benefits are consumed in the same pattern that utility is provided (for example, units produced, kilowatts generated, or miles traveled), the benefits are assumed to be directly linked to the activity. In this case, use units-of-activity depreciation.

3. When benefit consumption is greatest in the early years of the life of the asset and less in later years, use either of the following accelerated methods: sum-of-the-years'-digits depreciation or double-declining-balance depreciation. These methods are used when the company expects an asset to be more useful or productive in the early years of

its life. The assumption is that more benefit is received in the early years and therefore depreciation expense is greater in those years than in later years.

Straight-Line Method

Straight-line depreciation expenses an equal amount of the depreciable base in each period of an asset's useful life. The calculation is as follows:

$$\text{Annual Depreciation Expense} = \frac{\text{Cost of Asset} - \text{Salvage Value}}{\text{Useful Life}}$$

For example, if equipment cost \$55,000, with a five-year useful life and a salvage value of \$5,000, then annual depreciation expense is \$10,000 [(\$55,000 − \$,5000)/5].

At the end of the first year of the asset's life, the presentation relating to the equipment in the company's financial statements is:

Income Statement

Operating Expenses:

Depreciation Expense	\$10,000

Balance Sheet

Plant Assets:

Equipment	\$55,000
Less: Accumulated Depreciation	(10,000)
	\$45,000

Depreciation Expense appears on the income statement as an operating expense deducted in arriving at net income. The account Accumulated Depreciation appears in the balance sheet. An Accumulated Depreciation account is used to accumulate charges to depreciation expense over the life of the asset rather than directly reducing the asset account titled Equipment. Accumulated Depreciation is a contra asset to Equipment, just as the Allowance for Doubtful Accounts is a contra asset to Accounts Receivable. The difference between the historical cost of the equipment and its related accumulated depreciation is its book value.

Because salvage values and useful lives are estimates, the book value of a plant asset does not necessarily reflect its market value. The reason for showing the historical cost and accumulated depreciation of the equipment, rather than only its book value, is to permit the disclosure of the original cost of the asset and the total cost expensed to date. Also, this presentation allows the reader to gain some understanding of the condition of a company's plant assets. For example, a building costing $3,700,000 with $2,000,000 accumulated depreciation is probably quite different from one recently purchased for $1,700,000, even though both assets have the same book values.

Note that accumulated depreciation is not an amount of cash set aside to pay for replacing old assets. The amount is the cumulative cost of an asset charged to expense in prior periods.

In the footnotes to its financial statements, A. Schulman, Inc., an international supplier of high-performance plastic compounds and resins, indicated that the company depreciates the cost of property, plant, and equipment over the estimated useful lives of the assets, principally using the straight-line method:

Notes 1—Summary of Significant Accounting Policies

• • •

Depreciation

It is the Company's policy to depreciate the cost of property, plant, and equipment over the estimated useful lives of the assets generally using the straight-line method. The estimated useful lives used in the computation of depreciation are as follows:

Buildings and leasehold improvements	10 to 40 years
Machinery and equipment	5 to 12 years
Furniture and fixtures	10 years

The cost of property sold or otherwise disposed of is eliminated from the property accounts and the related reserve accounts, with recognition of gain or loss.

Maintenance and repair costs are charged against income. The cost of renewals and betterments are capitalized in the property accounts.

Units-of-Activity Method

The units-of-activity method is used when the benefit provided by the asset is linked to an activity (such as the number of units manufactured or services rendered), rather than to the mere passage of time. The annual depreciation expense is calculated by multiplying the depreciation rate per unit of activity by the number of activity units for the period. This method is particularly appropriate for assets whose benefits are easily measured.

To illustrate, assume the cost of equipment is $55,000, salvage value is $5,000, and management estimates the equipment will have a life of 100,000 machine hours. Depreciation per unit is then $0.50 ($50,000/100,000 machine hours). If production in 1996, 1997, 1998, 1999, and 2,000 is 25,000, 30,000, 20,000, 10,000, and 15,000 units, respectively, then depreciation expense is $12,500, $15,000, $10,000, $5,000, and $9,000 for those years.

Activity units might be miles driven, for trucks; machine hours, for machinery; or hours in use, for airplanes. Depreciating an asset based on activity units makes sense because it is in the use of the asset that the benefit is received. The method would not be appropriate for depreciating a building or office furniture because the expiration of the benefits of using these assets is more directly related to the passage of time.

The units-of-activity method of depreciating assets is used by Amerada Hess Corporation. In the notes to its 1994 annual report, the company indicated that it uses the units-of-production method to depreciate its refinery facilities:

1. Summary of Significant Accounting Policies

• • •

Depreciation, Depletion and Amortization: Depreciation, depletion and amortization of oil and gas production equipment, properties and wells are determined on the units-of-production method based on estimated recoverable oil and gas reserves. Depreciation of refinery facilities is determined on the units-of-production method based on estimated thruput volumes. Depreciation of all other plant and equipment is determined on the straight-line method based on estimated useful lives.

The estimated costs of dismantlement, restoration, and abandonment, less estimated salvage values, of offshore oil and gas production platforms and certain other facilities are taken into account in determining depreciation.

Accelerated Depreciation Methods

Accelerated methods are used when the benefits received from an asset are greater in the early years and less in the later years of the asset's life. This might occur because of technological innovations, early wear and tear, or increases in repairs and maintenance costs as the asset becomes older. Accelerated depreciation methods result in charges to depreciation expense that begin high (relative to straight-line depreciation) and decline over the useful life of the asset.

Sum-of-the-Years'-Digits Method.   The sum-of-the-years'-digits method depreciates a different fraction of the depreciable base each year. The numerator of the fraction is the number of years remaining in the asset's useful life at the beginning of the current year; the denominator is the sum of the years' digits. The sum of the years' digits for an asset with a 5-year useful life is calculated as:

$$\text{Sum of the years' digits} = 1 + 2 + 3 + 4 + 5 = 15$$

Depreciation in year 1 is $\frac{5}{15}$ times the depreciable base; in year 4, it is $\frac{2}{15}$ times the depreciable base. Recall that the machinery in our earlier example had a depreciable base of $50,000 and a useful life of 5 years. Summing the number of years' digits in the asset's life ($1 + 2 + 3 + 4 + 5$), the result is 15, which becomes the denominator. Next, the number of years remaining in the asset's life at the beginning of the period is used as the numerator. That fraction is multiplied by the depreciable base. A completed depreciation schedule for the equipment appears in Exhibit 8–2.

Imperial Holly Corporation uses both the straight-line and sum-of-the-years'-digits depreciation methods in depreciating its plant and equipment. The company gave this information in a note to its 1995 annual report:

1. ACCOUNTING POLICIES

• • •

Property and Depreciation—Property is stated at cost and includes expenditures for renewals and improvements and capitalized interest. Maintenance and repairs are charged to current operations. When property is retired or otherwise disposed of, the cost and related accumulated

EXHIBIT 8–2
Computation of Periodic Depreciation Expense Using
Sum-of-the-Years'-Digits Depreciation

Year		Depreciation Expense	Accumulated Depreciation	Book Value
				$55,000
1	5/15 × $50,000	$16,667	$16,667	38,333
2	4/15 × $50,000	13,333	30,000	25,000
3	3/15 × $50,000	10,000	40,000	15,000
4	2/15 × $50,000	6,667	46,667	8,333
5	1/15 × $50,000	3,333	50,000	5,000
		$50,000		

depreciation are removed from the respective accounts, and any gain or loss on disposition is included in income.

Depreciation is provided principally on the straight-line or sum-of-the-years' digits methods over the estimated service lives of the assets.

Double-Declining-Balance Method. The double-declining-balance method uses the straight-line rate (in our example, ⅕ or 20 percent). To use this method, we double the straight-line rate so that an asset with a 5-year life has a straight-line rate of 20 percent and a double-declining-balance rate of 40 percent. That rate is multiplied by the book value of the asset at the beginning of the year, not the depreciable base. Unlike other depreciation methods, salvage value is ignored when computing the amount to which the declining-balance rate is applied. However, the asset is still only depreciated down to salvage value. Exhibit 8–3 illustrates the calculations for the $55,000 piece of equipment in the earlier example.

In a note to its 1994 annual report, Alliant Techsystems Inc., a supplier of defense products and systems to the U.S. government and its allies, indicated that the company uses double-declining balance depreciation for new machinery and test equipment:

1. Basis of Presentation and Significant Accounting Policies

• • •

Property and Depreciation—Property, plant, and equipment is stated at cost and depreciated over estimated useful lives. New machinery and test equipment is depreciated using the double-declining-balance method. All other depreciable property is depreciated using the straight-line method.

Group and Composite Depreciation

Many large companies do not depreciate individual assets; instead, they combine assets into classes and depreciate them at an average rate. Group depreciation is used for collections of similar assets having approximately the same useful life (for example, a fleet of vehicles). Composite depreciation is used for a combination of dissimilar assets used as an integrated unit. For example, this method is appropriate for components of an integrated manufacturing assembly line.

The computation of depreciation expense is the same for both methods. Exhibit 8–4 illustrates group depreciation for a fleet of vehicles, using straight-line depreciation. The group rate is 16.2 percent, determined by dividing total depreciation expense per year by the total depreciable base

EXHIBIT 8–3
Computation of Periodic Depreciation Expense Using
Double-Declining-Balance Depreciation

Year		Depreciation Expense	Accumulated Depreciation	Book Value
				$55,000
1	(.40 × $55,000)	$22,000	$22,000	33,000
2	(.40 × $33,000)	13,200	35,200	19,800
3	(.40 × $19,800)	7,920	43,120	11,880
4	(.40 × $11,880)	4,752	47,872	7,128
5	(.40 × $ 7,128)	2,851*	50,723	4,277

* The amount would be $2,128 if the expected salvage value were still $5,000. This is the amount necessary to reduce the book value to $5,000.

EXHIBIT 8–4
Computation of Group Depreciation Assuming
Straight-Line Depreciation

Asset	Original Cost	Residual Value	Depreciable Base	Estimated Life (Years)	Depreciation Per Year
Vans	$ 40,000	$ 3,000	$ 37,000	5	$ 7,400
Trucks	60,000	6,000	54,000	8	6,750
Cars	160,000	22,000	138,000	6	23,000
	$260,000	$31,000	$229,000		$37,150

($37,150/$229,000). Annual depreciation expense is 16.2 percent of depreciable cost. The group life is 6.16 years ($229,000/$37,150). The composite and group methods save clerical time and cost because separate depreciation records are not maintained for each individual asset.

Texaco Inc. and Subsidiary Companies indicated, in a note to the 1994 annual report, that the company uses the group method for depreciating certain classes of plant assets:

NOTE 1. DESCRIPTION OF SIGNIFICANT ACCOUNTING POLICIES

• • •

PROPERTIES, PLANT AND EQUIPMENT AND DEPRECIATION, DEPLETION AND AMORTIZATION

• • •

Depreciation of properties, plant, and equipment related to facilities other than producing properties is provided generally on the group plan, using the straight-line method, with depreciation rates based upon estimated useful life applied to the cost of each class of property. Assets not on the group plan are depreciated based on estimated useful lives using the straight-line method.

In contrast, James River Corporation uses the composite method for depreciating selected plant assets. This information was contained in a note to the company's 1994 annual report:

Note 1. Summary of Significant Accounting Policies

• • •

Property, Plant, and Equipment

Property, plant, and equipment is stated at cost, less accumulated depreciation. Expenditures for improvements which increase asset values or extend useful lives are capitalized. Maintenance and repair costs are expensed as incurred. For financial reporting purposes, depreciation is computed using the straight-line method over the estimated useful lives of the respective assets, which range from 20 to 45 years for buildings and 5 to 20 years for machinery and equipment. For income tax purposes, depreciation is calculated using accelerated methods. Certain assets are depreciated using composite depreciation methods; accordingly, no gain or loss is recognized on partial sales or retirements of these assets.

Depreciation and Income Taxes

Tax regulations do not require companies to use the same depreciation method for both income tax and financial reporting. Therefore, it is not unusual for many companies to use the straight-line method for financial reporting purposes and a special accelerated method for income tax purposes. The use of an accelerated method for tax purposes results in the company paying less income tax in the early years of an asset's life and more in the later years. Thus, the income taxes are postponed, and the company has these postponed payments available for other uses; the funds become much like an interest-free loan.

The Modified Accelerated Cost Recovery System (MACRS) was enacted by Congress in the Tax Reform Act of 1986. MACRS establishes classes of property (for example, automobiles, computers, and so on) with established lives, which are subject to a certain depreciation method. There are eight classes, as shown in Exhibit 8–5. When one of the accelerated methods is used to depreciate an asset for tax purposes, a switch to the

EXHIBIT 8-5
MACRS Depreciation Schedule

Classes	Applicable Assets	Depreciation Method
3 year	Small tools, tractors, horses, and specialized manufacturing devices	200% declining balance
5 year	Computers, automobiles and light trucks, small aircraft, construction equipment, and research and development property	200% declining balance
7 year	Office furniture, fixtures, and equipment; commercial aircraft, and most machinery	200% declining balance
10 year	Specialized heavy manufacturing machinery and equipment, and mobile homes	200% declining balance
15 year	Billboards, service station buildings, and telephone equipment	150% declining balance
20 year	Sewer pipes, most utility property, and land improvements	150% declining balance
27½ year	Residential real estate property	Straight-line
39* year	Office and other nonresidential real estate property	Straight-line

* The recovery period for nonresidential real property placed in service after May 12, 1993, is 39 years. However, for property placed in service prior to 1994, the recovery period is 31½ years provided that before May 13, 1993, a written binding contract was entered into to buy or build the property or, prior to that date, construction on such property had begun.

straight-line method is made in the first year when straight-line depreciation equals or exceeds the accelerated depreciation. For tax purposes, the salvage value is assumed to be zero, sometimes causing depreciation for tax purposes to differ from the depreciation expensed on the income statement. Companies can elect to use the straight-line method, instead of MACRS, in computing depreciation for tax purposes, but, in general, MACRS permits a faster recovery of an asset's cost (MACRS life is generally shorter than the asset's useful life) and larger tax benefits (because 100 percent of the asset's cost is depreciated) during the early years of an asset's life. The intent of Congress in enacting the legislation creating MACRS was to encourage and stimulate capital investment.

Revising Depreciation Expense

Because estimation is an inherent part of the accounting process, it is sometimes necessary to revise computations of depreciation when new information or developments arise. This may occur if a company determines that, because of wear or tear, inadequacy, or obsolescence, annual depreciation charges are inadequate or excessive. When this happens, the company must change its estimate of the asset's useful life.

The procedure for changing a depreciation calculation is to spread the book value remaining at the date of revision over the asset's remaining useful life. The rationale for not adjusting previously recorded depreciation is that the company's original estimates for salvage value and useful life were not wrong but were based on the best information available at that time. When new information becomes available, the initial estimate is revised from that point forward.

To illustrate, assume that a company purchases a machine costing $100,000, with a salvage value of $10,000 and a useful life of 10 years. Annual depreciation expense is $9,000 per year. At the beginning of the fourth year, the book value of the machine is $73,000 [$100,000 − ($9,000 × 3 years)]. If, because of improved maintenance procedures, the machine has a remaining useful life of 10 years and the salvage value remains the same, the annual charge to depreciation expense for the current year and each of the next 9 years is $6,300. Delta Air Lines, Inc. increased the useful lives of its flight equipment from 15 to 20 years in 1993, which decreased the amount of annual depreciation. This information was contained in this note to Delta's 1995 annual report which covered the years 1993, 1994, and 1995:

1. Summary of Significant Accounting Policies

• • •

Depreciation and Amortization—Prior to April 1, 1993, the Company depreciated substantially all of its flight equipment on a straight-line basis to residual values (10% of cost) over a 15-year period from the dates placed in service. As a result of a fleet plan review, effective April 1, 1993, the Company increased the estimated useful lives of substantially all of its flight equipment. Flight equipment that was not already fully depreciated is being depreciated on a straight-line basis to residual values (5% of cost) over a 20-year period from the dates placed in service. The effect of this change was a $34 million decrease in depreciation expense and a $22 million ($0.44 per common share) decrease in net loss for fiscal 1993.

Ground property and equipment are depreciated on a straight-line basis over their estimated service lives, which range from 3 to 30 years. Flight equipment under capital leases are amortized on a straight-line basis over the lives of their respective leases, which range from 8 to 15 years.

Because companies continually make expenditures to maintain the operating efficiency of plant assets, it is necessary to distinguish between revenue and capital expenditures. Expenditures for routine maintenance (such as machine lubrication) or repairs (replacing a worn-out part) are expensed as incurred because they do not extend the asset's life or increase its operating efficiency or productive output. On the other hand, capital expenditures:

1. Increase the service quality or operating efficiency of the asset.

2. Extend the asset's useful life.

3. Increase the asset's productive capacity.

These costs are capitalized as plant assets and may cause a change in the calculation of annual depreciation expense.

For example, assume a piece of equipment has an initial cost of $80,000, no salvage value, and an estimated useful life of 5 years. Annual depreciation expense is $16,000 ($80,000/5 years). Now assume that, at the beginning of year 3, when the book value of the equipment is $48,000 [$80,000 − ($16,000 × 2)], the company makes a $6,000 expenditure that increases the equipment's productive capacity but does not extend its useful life. Annual depreciation is now $18,000 [($48,000 + $6,000)/3 years remaining in useful life].

The proper classification of revenue and capital expenditures is important. Incorrect classification of these expenditures leads to inaccurate balance sheet and income statement amounts.

Disclosures Relating to Plant Assets

The following disclosures relating to depreciable assets and depreciation should be made in the financial statements or the related notes:

1. Depreciation expense for the period.
2. Balances of major classes of depreciable assets by nature or function.
3. Accumulated depreciation by classes or in total.
4. The methods used, by major classes of assets, in computing depreciation.

Kimball International, Inc., which manufactures and markets a broad range of diversified consumer durable products, disclosed its accounting policies relating to plant assets in these two notes to its 1994 annual report:

NOTE 1 SUMMARY OF SIGNIFICANT ACCOUNTING POLICIES

• • •

Property, Equipment and Depreciation: Property and equipment are stated at cost. Depreciation is provided over the estimated useful life of the assets using the straight-line method for financial reporting purposes and accelerated methods for income tax purposes. Maintenance, repairs and minor renewals and betterments are expensed; major improvements are capitalized.

• • •

NOTE 4 PROPERTY AND EQUIPMENT

Major classes of property and equipment consist of the following:

(Amounts in Thousands)	*1994*	*1993*
Land	$ 5,501	$ 4,150
Buildings and improvements	119,544	117,877
Machinery and equipment	224,792	211,550
Construction-in-progress	26,433	3,242
Totals	376,270	336,819
Less: Accumulated depreciation	205,027	184,458
Net property and equipment	$171,243	$152,361

Construction-in-progress at June 30, 1994, includes $24 million of expenditures on a new plant facility which was substantially complete at June 30, 1994.

The useful lives, based on the Company's estimate of the service life of the classes of property, used in computing depreciation are as follows:

	Years
Buildings and improvements	5 to 40
Machinery and equipment	3 to 15
Automotive equipment	3 to 5
Office equipment	3 to 10
Leasehold improvements	Life of Lease

Depreciation and amortization of property and equipment totaled, in millions, $26.9 for 1994, $26.2 for 1993 and $24.9 for 1992. Imputed interest costs, related to the financing of certain construction projects, of $345,000, $112,000 and $84,000 were capitalized during 1994, 1993 and 1992, respectively.

9

NONCURRENT ASSETS: NATURAL RESOURCES

*M*any companies own assets such as stands of timber, oil fields, and mineral deposits (coal, copper, gold, and silver, for example). These assets are called natural resources or wasting assets. The term wasting assets indicates that they are physically exhausted during the production process; in other words, the asset can be replaced only by a process of nature. Exhibit 9–1 reproduces the asset section of the balance sheet from the 1994 annual report of Champion International Corporation, a manufacturer of paper and wood products. Note that timber and timberlands represent a substantial portion (almost 21 percent) of the company's total assets.

The basis for recording these assets is the same as with other long-lived assets—that is, cost. Cost is defined as outlays for acquiring the property and placing it in service; they include expenditures for exploration, development, and production. These capitalized costs comprise the depletion

99

EXHIBIT 9–1
Champion International Corporation and Subsidiaries,
Excerpt from Consolidated Balance Sheet

	December 31,	
(In Thousands of Dollars)	1994	1993
Assets		
Current assets:		
Cash and cash equivalents	$ 90,948	$ 55,653
Short-term investments	—	7,197
Receivables	562,085	494,426
Inventories (Note 2)	441,430	469,269
Prepaid expenses	23,286	22,818
Deferred income taxes (Note 12)	61,032	65,064
Total current assets	1,178,781	1,114,427
Timber and timberlands, at cost—less cost of timber harvested	1,846,823	1,838,550
Property, plant, and equipment, at cost (Notes 3, 6 and 7)	8,579,254	8,467,756
Less—Accumulated depreciation	2,976,640	2,665,720
	5,602,614	5,802,036
Other assets and deferred charges	335,410	387,756
	$8,963,628	$9,142,769

base and constitute the total amount that will be expensed over the period of removal and production of the natural resource. The process of allocating the costs of natural resources to the periods of benefit is called depletion. Accounting for these costs is similar to the process of depreciating plant and equipment. Depletion is an appropriate term because natural resources are physically depleted during the extraction phase.

Computing Depletion

Depletion is computed in the same manner as units-of-activity depreciation (discussed in Chapter 8). The computation requires estimates of the residual value of the property and of the total resource obtainable (such as tons of coal, barrels of oil, or board feet of timber). The result is the depletion rate, an estimate of the cost per unit of the natural resource. For example, assume that a company acquired the rights to a mineral deposit for $10,000,000. Exploration and development costs are $2,000,000, resulting in a total cost of $12,000,000. The company estimates that, after the deposit is exhausted and the land reclaimed, it can sell the property for $1,500,000. The $1,500,000 is the estimated residual value and reduces the depletion base. The company estimates that the deposit contains 3,000,000 tons of mineral, which it expects to extract and sell over the life of the natural resource. This results in a depletion rate per ton of $3.50 [($12,000,000 − $1,500,000)/3,000,000]. Assume that 300,000 tons are extracted in 1996 and 200,000 tons are sold. The amount of depletion for the year is $1,050,000 ($3.50 per ton × 300,000 tons). Two-thirds (200,000/300,000) of the mineral extracted were sold. One-third remains on hand and is included on the balance sheet as inventory. Therefore, one-third of the amount of depletion, or $350,000 ($1,050,000 × ⅓), is treated as inventory, and two-thirds, or $700,000 ($1,050,000 × ⅔), is charged to the income statement as a cost of production. Notice that there is no depletion expense per se because the amount of depletion is allocated between the inventory and the cost of product sold (an expense) when the minerals are sold. Also, note that the depletion that is expensed in each period is always a function of the number of units *sold,* not *produced.* The cost of product sold appears in the income statement and is matched against the revenues from the sale of the natural resource.

   The inventory of minerals account appears in the current asset section of the balance sheet. The presentation of the natural resource appears in the noncurrent asset section of the balance sheet in the following manner:

           Mineral deposits, net $10,950,000

The $10,950,000 represents the depletion base of $12,000,000 less the amount of depletion for the period ($1,050,000). The amount of depletion directly reduces the natural resource, and this is the form of balance sheet presentation most commonly used. In a note to its 1994 annual report, Champion International stated that it "credits" or reduces its natural resource account for depletion:

Note 1. Summary of Significant Accounting Policies

• • •

E. Fixed Assets

Property, Plant and Equipment, which includes capitalized leases, is stated at cost. Timber and Timberlands, which includes original costs, road construction costs, and reforestation costs, such as site preparation and planting costs, is stated at unamortized cost. Property taxes, surveying, fire control and other forest management expenses are charged to expense as incurred. When fixed assets are sold or retired, cost and accumulated depreciation are eliminated from the accounts and gains or losses are recorded in income.

For financial reporting purposes, plant and equipment are depreciated using the straight-line method over the estimated service lives of the individual assets. Machinery and equipment lives range from 3 to 35 years, buildings from 10 to 40 years and land improvements from 5 to 24 years. Leasehold improvements are amortized over the shorter of the lives of the leases or estimated service lives. Cost of timber harvested is based on the estimated quantity of timber available during the growth cycle and is credited directly to the asset accounts (Notes 3, 6 and 7).

It is acceptable for a company to use the contra asset account, Accumulated Depletion, which would result in the following form of presentation on the balance sheet:

Mineral deposits	$12,000,000
Less: Accumulated depletion	1,050,000
Net Mineral deposits	$10,950,000

Similar to the presentation of plant assets in the balance sheet, use of the historical cost of the asset along with a contra asset account may assist readers in determining the percentage of the cost of the resource that has been extracted. However, this form of presentation does not assist in ascertaining the value of the natural resource, which may be greatly in excess of its recorded value.

Normally, assets such as equipment and buildings are constructed or purchased in connection with the removal of natural resources. The cost of these assets should be depreciated over the shorter of (1) the physical life of the asset or (2) the life of the natural resource. The amount of depreciation is treated as an expense by including it as a part of the cost of product sold for the period.

Estimates of recoverable resources and residual value are subject to reevaluation and are changed if necessary. The depletion rate is revised by dividing the remaining undepleted balance, less any residual value, by the estimate of the remaining recoverable units. The procedure parallels the one used for plant assets when new information suggests that the initial estimates of depreciable lives have changed.

Information about natural resources is permitted to be presented in numerous ways in published financial statements. Exhibit 9–2 presents the disclosure relating to natural resources from the 1994 annual report of Exxon Corporation, whose primary business is energy. Note that Exxon presents property, plant, and equipment as one amount in its balance sheet.

Details relating to natural resources and depletion are given in the following two notes to Exxon's financial statements:

1. Summary of Accounting Policies

• • •

Property, Plant, and Equipment. Depreciation, depletion, and amortization, based on cost less estimated salvage value of the asset, are primarily determined under either the unit of production method or the straight-line method. Unit of production rates are based on oil, gas and other mineral reserves estimated to be recoverable from existing facilities. The straight-line method of depreciation is based on estimated asset service life taking obsolescence into consideration.

Maintenance and repairs are expensed as incurred. Major renewals and improvements are capitalized, and the assets replaced are retired.

EXHIBIT 9–2
Exxon Corporation, Excerpt from
Consolidated Balance Sheet

	December 31,	
(Millions of Dollars)	1994	1993
Assets		
Current assets:		
Cash and cash equivalents	$ 1,157	$ 983
Other marketable securities	618	669
Notes and accounts receivable, less		
estimated doubtful amounts	8,073	6,860
Inventories		
Crude oil, products and merchandise	4,717	4,616
Materials and supplies	824	856
Prepaid taxes and expenses	1,071	875
Total current assets	16,460	14,859
Investments and advances	5,394	4,790
Property, plant, and equipment, at cost, less		
accumulated depreciation and depletion	63,425	61,962
Other assets, including intangibles, net	2,583	2,534
Total assets	$87,862	$84,145

The corporation's exploration and production activities are accounted for under the "successful efforts" method. Under this method, costs of productive wells and development dry holes, both tangible and intangible, as well as productive acreage are capitalized and amortized on the unit of production method. Costs of that portion of undeveloped acreage likely to be unproductive, based largely on historical experience, are amortized over the period of exploration. Other exploratory expenditures, including geophysical costs, other dry hole costs and annual lease rentals, are expensed as incurred.

8. Investment in Property, Plant, and Equipment

	Dec. 31, 1994		Dec. 31, 1993	
	Cost	Net	Cost	Net
	(millions of dollars)			
Petroleum and natural gas				
Exploration and production	$ 64,483	$32,177	$ 62,131	$32,263
Refining and marketing	30,389	17,422	28,103	16,185
Total petroleum and natural gas	94,872	49,599	90,234	48,448
Chemicals	9,124	4,892	9,155	5,006
Other	12,330	8,934	11,746	8,508
Total	$116,326	$63,425	$111,135	$61,962

Accumulated depreciation and depletion totaled $52,901 million at the end of 1994 and $49,173 million at the end of 1993. Interest capitalized in 1994, 1993 and 1992 was $405 million, $374 million and $364 million, respectively.

National Gypsum Company, a manufacturer and supplier of gypsum wallboard and related products, presents the cost of mineral deposits on the face of its balance sheet. Exhibit 9–3 displays the asset section of the company's balance sheet.

In a note to its 1994 annual report, the company made this disclosure:

2. Significant Accounting Policies
• • •

Property, plant, and equipment are stated on the historical cost basis.

Depreciation of fixed assets is provided on the straight-line method over estimated useful lives. Depletion of mineral deposits is provided at rates per ton extracted, based on the cost of individual deposits divided by estimated recoverable proven tonnage.

Exhibit 9–4 is from the 1994 annual report of CMS NOMECO Oil & Gas Co., an oil and gas exploration and production company. In its balance

EXHIBIT 9-3
National Gypsum Company and Subsidiaries,
Excerpt from Consolidated Balance Sheet

(Thousands)	December 31,	
	1994	1993
Assets		
Current assets:		
Cash and cash equivalents	$ 85,033	$120,476
Trade and sundry receivables, less		
allowances (1994—$9,340; 1993—$12,401)	63,855	58,115
Inventories:		
Finished goods	11,551	11,451
Products in process	1,442	917
Materials and supplies	29,057	22,395
	42,050	34,763
Other current assets	9,049	13,753
Total current assets	199,987	227,107
Property, plant, and equipment:		
Mineral deposits	11,181	11,095
Plant and office sites	22,005	22,005
Buildings	78,480	77,681
Machinery and equipment	294,960	259,403
	406,626	370,184
Less allowances for depreciation, depletion,		
and amortization	54,428	17,936
	352,198	352,248
Other noncurrent assets	45,149	33,823
Total assets	$597,334	$613,178

EXHIBIT 9–4
CMS NOMECO Oil & Gas Co., Excerpt from
Consolidated Balance Sheet

	December 31,	
(Dollars in thousands)	1994	1993
Assets		
Current assets:		
Cash	$ 1,117	$ 932
Temporary cash investments	4,969	—
Accounts receivable:		
Revenues and other	10,973	9,680
Income tax benefits	3,527	5,442
Affiliates	83	2,170
Other	1,435	1,059
	22,104	19,283
Investments and other assets	12,539	7,088
Oil and gas properties (full cost method)	934,460	841,524
Less accumulated depletion and amortization	496,403	465,534
	438,057	375,990
Total assets	$472,700	$402,361

sheet, the company shows the historical cost of its oil and gas properties and uses a contra asset account, Accumulated Depletion and Amortization.

In a note to the financial statements, CMS NOMECO clarifies its policy as follows:

1. SIGNIFICANT ACCOUNTING POLICIES

• • •

A. OIL AND GAS PROPERTIES

The Company follows the full cost method of accounting and capitalizes all costs related to its exploration and development program, including the cost of nonproductive drilling and surrendered acreage, in cost centers on a country-by-country basis. The capitalized costs in each cost center are amortized on an overall unit-of-production method based on total estimated proven oil and gas reserves. Additionally, certain costs associated with major development projects and all costs of unevaluated leases are excluded from the depletion base until reserves associated with the projects are proven or until impairment occurs.

Costs associated with exploration and development activities in nonproducing cost centers are not amortized until proven reserves are discovered and produced or a determination is made that the value of the property is less than the costs incurred. Accordingly, the Company has written off $4.9 million ($3.2 million after taxes) in 1994, $7.7 million ($5.0 million after taxes) in 1993 and $1.9 million ($1.2 million after taxes) in 1992 for prediscovery international expenditures. Also, the Company wrote down the value of Papua New Guinea ($.7 million in 1994) and Colombia ($1.9 million in 1993 and $3.1 million in 1992) oil properties in excess of the cost center ceiling. These charges are included in international write-offs on the Consolidated Statements of Income.

Taxes and Depletion

Our discussion of cost depletion in this chapter relates to financial reporting. The Internal Revenue Code permits companies to deduct the greater of cost depletion or percentage depletion for oil, gas, or minerals. Percentage depletion, or statutory depletion as it is sometimes called, is computed by multiplying a stated percentage by the gross income derived from the sale of the natural resource during the period. The rates change over time, based on changes in the tax law, and they vary depending on the type of natural resource. Currently, the rates range from 5 percent to 22 percent. If the income from the property is a significant amount, the deductions for percentage depletion can exceed the historical cost of the natural resource. Recent changes in the tax law have significantly diminished the effects of percentage depletion; that is, percentage depletion is not available for all natural resources, such as timber and large oil and gas reserves.

10

NONCURRENT ASSETS: INTANGIBLES

*I*ntangibles are long-lived noncurrent assets that are characterized by a lack of physical existence. There is also a high degree of uncertainty regarding the future benefits to be provided by these assets. Intangibles derive their value from the rights and privileges granted to the company that owns them. Examples include copyrights, franchises, goodwill, leasehold improvements, organization costs, patents, trademarks, and tradenames.

Intangible assets are recorded at original cost. The process of allocating the cost of intangible assets to the periods of benefit is called amortization. Current generally accepted accounting principles (GAAP) require that these assets be amortized over the shorter of (1) their legal lives, (2) their economic (useful) lives, or (3) 40 years. Other than for leaseholds and leasehold improvements, GAAP require that a company use straight-line amortization to expense an intangible asset. Another method can be used if the company can demonstrate that the method is more appropriate in the circumstances. As a result of the process of amortization, an Amortization Expense account appears in the income statement, and the specific intangible asset account is reduced. This method is similar to the process of depreciating a fixed asset; however, it differs in that an accumulated amortization account is generally not shown on the balance sheet.

Exhibit 10–1 is the income statement and balance sheet from the 1994 annual report of Whitman Corporation and Subsidiaries. Note the Amortization Expense account on the income statement and the description of intangible assets (net of accumulated amortization) on the balance sheet. Whitman Corporation is engaged in three distinct businesses: Pepsi-Cola and other nonalcoholic beverage products, Midas automotive services, and Hussman refrigeration systems and equipment.

Copyrights

A copyright indicates exclusive control of a literary or artistic work by giving the copyright owner the sole right to reproduce and sell that work. A copyright is not renewable and is granted for the life of the author plus 50 years; however, the useful life of a copyright is normally less than its legal life, and the cost of a copyright should be allocated over its estimated economic life, not to exceed 40 years.[1] Because it is very difficult to estimate the economic life of copyrighted properties, companies normally amortize these costs over a relatively short period. In fact, the cost of many musical and literary copyrights are amortized to expense over the estimated life of the first printing. This is a reasonable procedure because of the difficulty of predicting how successful these works might be. Copyrights can be sold or assigned to other parties. *Tom Sawyer* (1876) and *Huckleberry Finn* (1884), by Samuel L. Clemens (alias Mark Twain), are examples of books off copyright since Clemens died in 1910. On the other hand, books currently under copyright include *Jurassic Park* by Michael Crichton (1990), *The Client* by John Grisham (1994), and *Apollo 13* by Jim Lovell and Jeffrey Kluger (1994).

---

[1] Prior to 1978, copyrights were granted for 28 years with the right to renew for an additional 28 years. Since 1978 they are issued for the length of the author's life plus 50 years.

EXHIBIT 10–1
Whitman Corporation and Subsidiaries, Consolidated
Income Statement and Balance Sheet

(in millions)	For the years ended December 31		
	1994	1993	1992
Sales and revenues	$2,658.8	$2,529.7	$2,388.0
Cost of goods sold	1,704.7	1,625.0	1,545.6
Gross profit	954.1	904.7	842.4
Selling, general and administrative expenses	609.8	582.3	550.7
Amortization expense	17.5	17.1	17.3
Operating income	326.8	305.3	274.4
Interest expense	(71.1)	(96.2)	(97.7)
Interest income	6.4	12.8	9.0
Other expense, net	(25.2)	(9.7)	(15.1)
Unrealized investment loss	(24.2)	—	—
Income before income taxes	212.7	212.2	170.6
Income tax provision	88.1	90.7	68.5
Income from continuing operations before minority interest	124.6	121.5	102.1
Minority interest	18.2	15.1	10.0
Income from continuing operations	106.4	106.4	92.1
Loss from discontinued operations after taxes (Note 2)	(3.2)	—	—
Loss from dispositions of discontinued operations after taxes (Note 2)	—	—	(32.3)
Extraordinary loss on early debt retirement after taxes (Note 4)	—	(4.2)	—
Cumulative effect of change in accounting principle after taxes (Note 6)	—	(24.0)	—
Net income	$ 103.2	$ 78.2	$ 59.8
Average number of common shares outstanding	106.2	107.5	107.2
Income (Loss) Per Common Share (In Dollars):			
Continuing operations	$ 1.00	$ 0.99	$ 0.86
Discontinued operations	(0.03)	—	(0.30)
Extraordinary loss on early debt retirement	—	(0.04)	—
Cumulative effect of change in accounting principle	—	(0.22)	—
Net income	$ 0.97	$ 0.73	$ 0.56
Cash dividends per common share	$ 0.330	$ 0.290	$ 0.255

(Continued)

EXHIBIT 10-1 *(Continued)*

(in millions)	As of December 31 1994	As of December 31 1993
Assets:		
Current assets:		
Cash and cash equivalents	$ 71.3	$ 93.0
Receivables—net of allowance for doubtful accounts of $7.9 million in 1994 and $7.8 million in 1993	362.5	324.1
Inventories:		
Raw materials and supplies	73.8	67.6
Work in process	41.2	39.5
Finished goods	118.6	115.6
Total inventories	233.6	222.7
Other current assets	40.3	51.4
Total current assets	707.7	691.2
Investments	222.6	238.5
Property (at cost):		
Land	63.5	59.9
Buildings and improvements	308.4	298.1
Machinery and equipment	833.3	748.9
Total property	1,205.2	1,106.9
Accumulated depreciation and amortization	(591.4)	(534.1)
Net property	613.8	572.8
Intangible assets, net of accumulated amortization of $123.6 million in 1994 and $106.7 million in 1993	524.3	525.9
Other assets	67.0	74.8
Total assets	$2,135.4	$2,103.2

EXHIBIT 10–1 *(Continued)*

(in millions)	As of December 31	
	1994	1993
Liabilities and Shareholders' Equity:		
Current liabilities:		
Short-term debt, including current maturities of long-term debt	$ 90.0	$ 90.0
Accounts and dividends payable	238.7	232.9
Income taxes payable	10.6	10.7
Accrued expenses:		
Salaries and wages	40.2	39.0
Interest	26.6	22.8
Other expenses	77.0	77.3
Total current liabilities	483.1	472.7
Long-term debt	723.0	749.3
Deferred income taxes	15.6	66.6
Other liabilities	154.9	124.7
Minority interest	206.2	172.9
Shareholders' equity:		
Common stock (no par, 250.0 million shares authorized; 105.0 million outstanding at December 31, 1994 and 107.1 million outstanding at December 31, 1993)	413.2	404.4
Retained income	239.9	172.4
Cumulative translation adjustment	(51.8)	(52.3)
Unrealized investment gain	1.3	—
Treasury stock	(50.0)	(7.5)
Total shareholders' equity	552.6	517.0
Total liabilities and shareholders' equity	$2,135.4	$2,103.2

Franchises and Licenses

Franchises are rights granted by a franchisor to an individual or company (the franchisee) to sell a product or service under a tradename. Examples include Kentucky Fried Chicken and McDonald's restaurants; Midas Muffler, in the automotive parts market; and the San Francisco Forty-Niners, a professional sports team. To secure the franchise rights, the franchisee normally pays the franchisor a substantial initial fee and also agrees to pay an annual fee. The initial fee should be amortized over the life of the franchise, not to exceed 40 years. Exhibit 10–2 shows the balance sheet from the 1993 annual report of PepsiCo, Inc.

EXHIBIT 10–2
PepsiCo, Inc., Consolidated Balance Sheet

	December	
(in millions except per share amount)	1993	1992
Assets		
Current assets:		
Cash and cash equivalents	$ 226.9	$ 169.9
Short-term investments, at cost which approximates market	1,629.3	1,888.5
	1,856.2	2,058.4
Accounts and notes receivable, less allowance: $128.3 in 1993 and $112.0 in 1992	1,883.4	1,588.5
Inventories	924.7	768.8
Prepaid expenses, taxes and other current assets	499.8	426.6
Total current assets	5,164.1	4,842.3
Investments in affiliates and other assets	1,756.6	1,707.9
Property, plant, and equipment, net	8,855.6	7,442.0
Intangible assets, net	7,929.5	6,959.0
Total assets	$23,705.8	$20,951.2

In an accompanying note relating to intangibles, the company created an intangible titled Reacquired Franchise Rights. This explanation was given:

Note 7—Intangible Assets

Identifiable intangible assets arose from the allocation of purchase prices of businesses acquired, and consist principally of reacquired franchise rights and trademarks. Reacquired franchise rights relate to acquisitions of franchised bottling and restaurant operations, and the trademarks principally relate to acquisitions of international snack food operations and KFC. Values assigned to such identifiable intangibles were based on independent appraisals or internal estimates. Goodwill represents any residual purchase price after allocation to all identifiable net assets.

	1993	*1992*
Other identifiable intangibles	$1,111.1	$1,111.1
Reacquired franchise rights	3,959.7	3,476.9
Trademarks	898.5	734.2
Other identifiable intangibles	154.7	159.6
Goodwill	2,916.6	2,588.3
	$7,929.5	$6,959.0

Intangible assets are amortized on a straight-line basis over appropriate periods generally ranging from 20 to 40 years. Accumulated amortization was $1.3 billion and $1.0 billion at year-end 1993 and 1992, respectively.

The recoverability of carrying values of intangible assets is evaluated on a recurring basis. The primary indicators of recoverability are current or forecasted profitability of the related acquired business, measured as profit before interest, but after amortization of the intangible assets. Consideration is also given to the estimated disposal values of certain identifiable intangible assets compared to their carrying values. For the three-year period ended December 25, 1993, there were no adjustments to the carrying values of intangible assets resulting from these evaluations.

A license agreement is similar to a franchise and is normally entered into by a governmental unit and a company that uses public properties. Examples include the use of the rights associated with radio airwaves and phone lines for cable television, and the right to provide mass transit (bus)

EXHIBIT 10–3
AT&T Corporation and Subsidiaries, Consolidated Balance Sheet

(Dollars in millions except per share amount)	1994	1993
Assets		
Cash and temporary cash investments	$ 1,208	$ 671
Receivables, less allowances of $1,251 and $1,040		
Accounts receivable	13,671	12,294
Finance receivables	14,952	11,370
Inventories	3,633	3,222
Deferred income taxes	3,030	2,079
Other current assets	1,117	732
Total current assets	37,611	30,368
Property, plant, and equipment—net	22,035	21,015
Licensing costs—net	4,251	3,995
Investments	2,708	3,060
Finance receivables	4,513	3,815
Prepaid pension costs	4,151	3,575
Other assets	3,993	3,565
Total assets	$79,262	$69,393

services. The initial license fee should be amortized to expense over the life of the agreement, not to exceed 40 years.

Licensing costs are disclosed separately on the face of the balance sheet for AT&T Corporation and Subsidiaries, shown in Exhibit 10–3.

Other details relating to these licensing costs were presented in the following notes to the AT&T financial statements:

1. Summary of Significant Accounting Policies

• • •

Licensing Costs

Licensing costs represent costs incurred to develop or acquire cellular and messaging licenses. Generally, amortization begins with the commencement of service to customers and is computed using the straight-line method over a period of 40 years.

5. Supplementary Financial Information

Supplementary Income Statement Information

Dollars in millions	1994	1993	1992
Included in costs			
Amortization of software production costs	$ 370	$ 359	$ 315
Amortization of licensing costs	115	108	105

In Exhibit 10–4, the 1994 balance sheet of Witco Corporation and Subsidiary Companies, worldwide manufacturer of specialty chemical and petroleum products, includes licenses as part of the intangible assets.

The following note to the company's 1994 annual report delineated the intangible assets:

Note 5—Intangible Assets

Intangible assets consist of the following:

(Thousands of dollars)	1993
Goodwill	$160,091
Patents and licenses	37,341
Other	58,212
	255,644
Less accumulated amortization	38,612
	$217,032

Amortization expense amounted to $16,916,000 (1994), $18,686,000 (1993), and $9,111,000 (1992).

Goodwill

Goodwill is the least understood and most complex of a company's intangible assets. Unlike other assets that can be exchanged or sold, goodwill can be understood only in the context of the company as a whole. Conceptually,

EXHIBIT 10–4
Witco Corporation and Subsidiary Companies,
Consolidated Balance Sheet

(in thousands except per share data)	December 31, 1993
Assets	
Current assets:	
Cash and cash equivalents	$ 183,050
Accounts and notes receivable, less allowances of $8,863 and $6,821	340,850
Inventories	227,469
Prepaid and other current assets	41,204
Total current assets	792,573
Property, plant, and equipment, less accumulated depreciation of $696,043 and $621,684	696,462
Intangible assets, less accumulated amortization of $43,760 and $38,612	217,032
Deferred costs and other assets	132,931
Total assets	$1,838,998
Liabilities and Shareholders' Equity	
Current liabilities:	
Notes and loans payable	$ 4,194
Accounts payable and other current liabilities	337,144
Total current liabilities	341,338
Long-term Debt	496,266
Deferred Federal and Foreign Income Taxes	74,612
Deferred credits and other liabilities	213,367
Shareholders' Equity	
$2.65 Cumulative Convertible Preferred Stock, par value $1 per share	
Authorized—14 shares	
Issued and outstanding—7 shares and 9 shares	9
Common stock, par value $5 per share	
Authorized—100,000 shares	
Issued—56,312 shares and 50,818 shares	254,089
Capital in excess of par value	6,123
Equity adjustments:	
Foreign currency translation	(23,723)
Pensions	(6,548)
Retained earnings	488,241
Treasury stock, at cost—165 and 318 shares	(4,776)
Total shareholders' equity	713,415
Total liabilities and shareholders' equity	$ 1,838,998

the factors contributing to a company's goodwill include the reputation of its products or services, superior management or personnel, strategic location, a secret formula or process, favorable government regulation, or monopoly status. The presence of goodwill generally results in above-average earnings for the company, leading to a higher-than-average return on funds invested in the company.

Measuring the dollar effects of the aforementioned factors is difficult, if not impossible, and because goodwill cannot be bought or sold separately, companies report goodwill in their financial statements only in relation to a purchase. This occurs when one company purchases another for a price greater than the fair market value of the identifiable net assets (both tangible and intangible) of the acquired company.

To illustrate, assume that Catlett Company purchases Olson International, Inc., for $50,000,000 and also assumes an $8,000,000 note payable. Additionally, the fair market values of Olson's assets are as shown in Exhibit 10–5.

The $1,800,000 excess of the amount paid ($50,000,000) over the identifiable net assets ($48,200,000) is goodwill. Goodwill is a residual amount—that is, the excess of the price paid over the fair value of the net assets acquired.

EXHIBIT 10–5
Computation of Goodwill

Amount paid		$50,000,000
Less fair market value of identifiable		
net assets:		
Accounts receivable	$ 900,000	
Inventory	2,800,000	
Machinery	18,000,000	
Land	23,000,000	
Building	10,000,000	
Patents	1,500,000	
Note payable	(8,000,000)	48,200,000
Goodwill		$ 1,800,000

Like other intangible assets, goodwill is amortized to expanse over a period not to exceed 40 years.[2] Exhibit 10–6 reproduces the asset section of the balance sheet from the 1995 annual report of Medtronic, Inc., a therapeutic medical technology company. The company's Goodwill account is net of accumulated amortization. The disclosure relating to goodwill appeared in the notes to Medtronic's financial statements:

Note 1—Summary of Significant Accounting Policies

• • •

Goodwill and Other Intangible Assets

Goodwill represents the excess of cost over net assets of businesses acquired, while other intangible assets consist primarily of purchased technology and patents. These assets are being amortized using the straight-line method over their estimated useful lives, of which periods up to 25 years remain.

Prosperous companies constantly make expenditures to develop and maintain goodwill, but because of the complexity of identifying and measuring the effects of these expenditures, they are treated as period expenses. Therefore, internally generated goodwill is not capitalized and does not appear on the balance sheet. This causes an inconsistency in the treatment of internally generated goodwill and purchased goodwill.

Because of the interpretational problems associated with goodwill on the balance sheet, some companies use a more descriptive title, such as Excess of Cost Over Net Assets of Acquired Companies, where cost is the price paid. Exhibit 10–7 presents the asset section of Great Lakes Chemical Corporation and Subsidiaries' 1994 annual report, which uses this type of reporting for goodwill. The company is a well-diversified specialty chemicals company.

---

[2] Prior to August 10, 1993 goodwill could not be deducted for tax purposes. Goodwill purchased after August 10, 1993 in a business combination is tax deductible.

EXHIBIT 10-6
Medtronic, Inc., Excerpt from Consolidated Balance Sheet

| | April 30, | |
	1995	1994
Assets		
Current assets:		
Cash and cash equivalents	$ 98,292	$ 108,720
Short-term investments	225,357	72,694
Accounts receivable, less allowance for doubtful accounts of $22,416 and $20,123	413,942	340,927
Inventories:		
Finished goods	97,048	102,163
Work in process	59,311	50,751
Raw materials	65,573	60,384
Total inventories	221,932	213,298
Prepaid income taxes	92,563	79,809
Prepaid expenses and other current assets	51,823	30,409
Total current assets	1,103,909	845,857
Property, plant, and equipment:		
Land and land improvements	17,920	16,624
Buildings and leasehold improvements	174,592	165,822
Equipment	501,134	409,050
Construction in progress	21,830	18,449
	715,476	609,945
Accumulated depreciation	(384,415)	(308,160)
Net property, plant, and equipment	331,061	301,785
Goodwill, net of accumulated amortization of $39,990 and $27,842	278,724	279,514
Other intangible assets, net of accumulated amortization of $31,482 and $21,042	84,622	87,724
Other assets	148,416	108,372
Total assets	$1,946,732	$1,623,252

EXHIBIT 10–7
Great Lakes Chemical Corporation and Subsidiaries,
Excerpt from Consolidated Balance Sheet

	December 31,	
(in thousands of dollars)	1994	1993
Assets		
Current assets:		
Cash and cash equivalents	$ 144,666	$ 179,734
Accounts and notes receivable, less allowance		
of $7,758 and $7,088, respectively	493,614	383,129
Inventories	316,623	275,062
Prepaid expenses	24,774	18,994
Total current assets	979,677	856,919
Plant and equipment	605,924	468,010
Excess of investment over net assets of		
subsidiaries acquired	411,028	341,079
Investments in and advances to unconsolidated		
affiliates	66,479	185,789
Other assets	48,357	49,067
	$2,111,465	$1,900,864

Leaseholds

A leasehold is a contractual agreement between the owner of a property (the lessor) and the renter of the property (the lessee) that gives to the lessee the right to use the property for a specified period of time in exchange for periodic payments. Examples of leased assets include machinery, buildings, land, and vehicles.

The presentation of a lease in the financial statements depends on whether the lease is a capital lease or an operating lease. The rules for classifying leases as operating or capital are complex. Capital leases are for extended periods of time. In many instances, they cover the entire useful life of the asset. A company that leases an asset for essentially all of its useful life is, in essence, buying the asset. Capital leases are, in substance, installment purchases whereby the lessee is essentially acquiring the asset and the risks and rewards of ownership are transferred from the lessor to the lessee. Operating leases, in contrast, do not transfer the risks and rewards of ownership from the lessor to the lessee.

Regardless of whether a lease is an operating or a capital lease, the lessee may be required to prepay lease payments. The prepayment is treated as an intangible asset and appears on the balance sheet. The cost of the prepayment is amortized to the periods benefited.

Leasehold Improvements

Leasehold improvements are expenditures made by a lessee to modify or improve the quality of service of leased property. Examples include constructing interior walls in a retail store, painting, installing carpeting, or adding parking space or shrubbery to leased land. These improvements become the property of the lessor at the termination of the lease, unless the parties contractually agree otherwise. If the estimated economic life of the leasehold improvements is longer than one year, they are capitalized and appear on the balance sheet as intangible assets in the account Leasehold Improvements. The improvements are amortized over the shorter of (1) the useful life of the improvement or (2) the lease term. Though they are intangible assets, leasehold improvements are sometimes presented in the tangible plant asset section of the balance sheet. Reebok International Ltd. presents leasehold improvements under property and equipment. Exhibit 10–8 shows the asset section of the balance sheet from Reebok's 1994 annual report.

Classification of leasehold improvements as a component of the Property and Equipment account appeared in this note to the financial statements:

EXHIBIT 10–8
Reebok International Ltd., Excerpt from
Consolidated Balance Sheet

	December 31,	
(Amounts in thousands, except share data)	1994	1993
Assets		
Current assets:		
Cash and cash equivalents	$ 83,936	$ 79,347
Accounts receivable, net of allowance for doubtful accounts (1994, $44,862; 1993, $46,455)	532,475	457,399
Inventory	624,625	514,027
Deferred income taxes	66,456	54,784
Prepaid expenses	29,952	21,558
Total current assets	1,337,444	1,127,115
Property and equipment, net	164,848	130,607
Non-current assets:		
Intangibles, net of amortization	96,196	94,262
Deferred income taxes	2,910	1,250
Other	48,063	38,477
	147,169	133,989
	$1,649,461	$1,391,711

3. Property and Equipment

Property and equipment consist of the following:

December 31	1994	1993
Land	$ 32,243	$ 27,994
Buildings	60,440	41,709
Machinery and equipment	156,046	124,568
Leasehold improvements	34,506	25,355
	283,235	219,626
Less accumulated depreciation and amortization	118,387	89,019
	$164,848	$130,607

Organization Costs

Organization costs are the initial costs incurred in forming a company. They include legal and accounting fees, state incorporation fees, compensation to promoters, initial stock and bond issuance costs, and other miscellaneous organization costs. These costs are carried on the balance sheet as an asset. In most instances, companies choose an arbitrary amortization period ranging from 5 to 10 years.

Patents

A patent is an exclusive right, issued by the U.S. Patent Office, that grants the holder the right to use, produce, and sell a particular product or process. The legal life of a patent is 17 years, although its economic life (and period of benefit) may be shorter because of changing technology, such as in the computer industry. A patent that is purchased from an individual or another company is valued at cost. Other costs, such as legal fees incurred in securing the patent, are capitalized as part of the cost of the asset.

Companies also spend significant amounts developing processes and products to be patented. For example, Exhibit 10–9, a portion of the Upjohn Company's income statement for 1994, 1993, and 1992, shows that the company had significant research and development expenditures.

A note to the financial statements gave this report breakdown of research and development expenditures for the three years as a percentage of sales:

Costs and Expenses

Consolidated operating expenses, stated as a percent of sales, were as follows:

	1994	*1993*	*1992*
Cost of products sold	25.7%	23.5%	23.2%
Research and development	18.5	18.3	17.0
Marketing and administrative	39.5	39.4	39.7
Restructuring		6.3	0.7
Operating income	18.3	13.8	20.4

EXHIBIT 10–9
Upjohn Company and Subsidiaries, Excerpt from
Consolidated Statements of Earnings

(Dollar amounts in thousands, except per-share data)	December 31,		
	1994	1993	1992
Operating revenue:			
Net sales	$3,274,996	$3,339,957	$3,256,188
Other revenue	69,542	40,579	28,560
Total	3,344,538	3,380,536	3,284,748
Operating costs and expenses:			
Cost of products sold	843,152	783,590	754,483
Research and development	607,187	612,490	553,297
Marketing and administrative	1,294,752	1,316,138	1,292,204
Restructuring		208,789	22,055
Total	2,745,091	2,921,007	2,622,039
Operating income	599,447	459,529	662,709
Interest income	59,624	50,789	50,054
Interest expense	(24,600)	(31,496)	(31,253)
Foreign exchange losses	(1,087)	(4,556)	(3,397)
All other, net	9,912	5,771	(6,210)
Earnings from continuing operations before income taxes and minority equity	643,296	480,037	671,903
Provision for income taxes	154,400	84,201	145,900
Minority equity in losses	(192)	(535)	(987)
Earnings from continuing operations	$ 489,088	$ 396,371	$ 526,990

In contrast to the costs associated with purchased patents, the costs of internally developed patents are much more difficult to determine because of the need to allocate the costs of ongoing research to individual patents. Therefore, the accounting profession has decided that all research and development costs should be expensed as incurred. As a result, virtually all costs associated with internally developed patents are expensed rather than capitalized. Only legal and registration fees, other costs such as models and drawings needed for registration, and legal fees paid to defend the patent are capitalized as assets. A potential problem is that this treatment can result in removing from the balance sheet significant and valuable assets. This is certainly true in the biotechnology industry, where significant research and development expenditures are required for product development.

Additionally, when the dollar amount of an internally developed patent appears on the balance sheet, it will be understated by the amount of research and development costs expended in developing that asset.

Patents may be disclosed on the face of the balance sheet or in the notes to the financial statements. Exhibit 10–10 is the asset section of the balance sheet of Carter-Wallace, Inc. and Subsidiaries, from its 1995 annual report. Patents are presented under the caption Intangible Assets. Carter-Wallace is involved in the processing and sale of consumer and health products.

Warner-Lambert Company discloses patents in a note to its financial statements. Exhibit 10–11 is the asset section of Warner-Lambert's balance sheet from its 1994 annual report, which shows an Intangible Assets account. Warner-Lambert is a worldwide marketer of distinguished brands; its three core lines of business are consumer health care products, confectionery products, and pharmaceuticals.

The note disclosing patents was as follows:

NOTE 8—INTANGIBLE ASSETS

December 31,	*1994*	*1993*
Purchased patents, trademarks and other intangibles	$236.7	$179.9
Goodwill	205.3	181.5
	442.0	361.4
Less accumulated amortization	(62.3)	(47.3)
	$379.7	$314.1

Trademarks and Tradenames

Trademarks and tradenames entitle their owners to exclusive use of certain names, phrases, designs, labels, and symbols that companies use to encourage product identification in hopes of improving product marketability. Trademarks are normally unique symbols or designs, such as McDonald's golden arches, Philip Morris Corporation's Marlboro cowboy, the unique patch on Guess jeans, and the Rolls Royce emblem. Examples of

EXHIBIT 10–10
Carter-Wallace, Inc., and Subsidiaries, Excerpt from
Consolidated Balance Sheet

	March 31,	
	1995	1994
Assets		
Current assets:		
Cash and cash equivalents	$ 40,098,000	$ 23,311,000
Short-term investments, principally government securities and certificates of deposit	18,188,000	32,883,000
Accounts receivable-trade, less allowances of $6,344,000 in 1995 and $5,955,000 in 1994	119,077,000	112,367,000
Other receivables	4,728,000	4,703,000
Inventories		
Finished goods	55,499,000	60,515,000
Work in process	12,359,000	22,121,000
Raw materials and supplies	21,359,000	39,553,000
	89,217,000	122,189,000
Deferred taxes	24,832,000	10,051,000
Prepaid expenses and other current assets	7,177,000	9,922,000
Total current assets	303,317,000	315,426,000
Property, plant, and equipment, at cost		
Land	2,519,000	3,544,000
Buildings and improvements	99,128,000	108,033,000
Machinery, equipment, and fixtures	126,887,000	142,354,000
Leasehold improvements	23,692,000	25,109,000
	252,226,000	279,040,000
Accumulated depreciation and amortization	114,618,000	121,981,000
	137,608,000	157,059,000
Intangible assets		
Excess of purchase price of businesses acquired over the net assets at date of acquisition, less amortization	90,352,000	68,292,000
Patents, trademarks, contracts and formulae, less amortization	39,500,000	41,921,000
	129,852,000	110,213,000
Deferred taxes	57,752,000	26,594,000
Other assets	51,695,000	19,270,000
	$680,224,000	$628,562,000

EXHIBIT 10–11
Warner-Lambert Company and Subsidiaries, Excerpt from
Consolidated Balance Sheet

(Millions of dollars)	December 31, 1994	1993
Assets:		
Cash and cash equivalents	$ 217.9	$ 440.5
Short-term investments	247.2	61.2
Receivables, less allowances of $21.8 in 1994 and $20.5 in 1993	1,096.0	890.8
Inventories	636.2	476.5
Prepaid expenses and other current assets	318.0	349.7
Total current assets	2,515.3	2,218.7
Investments and other assets	557.6	487.4
Equity investments in affiliated companies	234.2	208.6
Property, plant, and equipment	1,846.0	1,599.3
Intangible assets	379.7	314.1
	$5,532.8	$4,828.1

tradenames include Pepsi-Cola, Ford, Wheaties, Microsoft, and the Chicago Bears.

The cost of an acquired tradename or trademark is its purchase price. The cost of an internally developed tradename or trademark includes registration fees, legal fees, design costs, successful legal defense costs, and other costs directly related to the acquisition of the tradename or trademark. Research and development expenditures are excluded from this cost.

The right to use these names, designs, phrases, labels, and symbols is granted by the U.S. Patent Office and can be renewed for consecutive 20-year periods, yielding a legal life that is indefinite. However, for accounting purposes, the cost associated with trademarks and tradenames must be amortized over the periods benefited, not to exceed 40 years.

ConAgra, Inc., a diversified international food company, reports brands (tradenames), trademarks, and goodwill as one amount on the face of its

EXHIBIT 10–12
ConAgra, Inc., and Subsidiaries, Excerpt from
Consolidated Balance Sheet

	May	
(Dollars in millions except per share amount)	1995	1994
Assets		
Current assets:		
Cash and cash equivalents	$ 60.0	$ 166.4
Receivables, less allowance for doubtful accounts		
of $63.9 and $55.9 (Note 2)	1,540.0	1,589.6
Margin deposits and segregated funds	—	286.0
Inventories (Note 3)		
Hedged commodities	925.4	723.4
Other	2,241.9	2,161.0
Total inventories	3,167.3	2,884.4
Prepaid expenses	372.9	216.9
Total current assets	5,140.2	5,143.3
Property, plant, and equipment:		
Land	141.2	140.7
Buildings, machinery, and equipment	3,953.7	3,633.7
Other fixed assets	227.2	219.9
Construction in progress	215.7	156.1
	4,537.8	4,150.4
Less accumulated depreciation	(1,741.8)	(1,564.1)
Property, plant, and equipment, net	2,796.0	2,586.3
Brands, trademarks, and goodwill, at cost less		
accumulated amortization of $420.9 and $363.1	2,420.1	2,626.4
Other assets	444.7	365.8
	$10,801.0	$10,721.8

1995 balance sheet. The asset section from that balance sheet appears as Exhibit 10–12.

In the notes to the financial statement, ConAgra offered this statement of its accounting policy:

1. Summary of Significant Accounting Policies

. . .

Brands, Trademarks, and Goodwill

Brands and goodwill arising from the excess of cost of investment over equity in net assets at date of acquisition and trademarks are being amortized using the straight-line method, principally over a period of 40 years. The carrying value of such brands, trademarks and goodwill is periodically evaluated on the basis of management's estimates of future undiscounted operating income associated with the acquired businesses.

Exhibit 10–13 on page 132 is a portion of the 1994 annual report of Harcourt General, Inc., which operates businesses in publishing, specialty retailing, and human resource consulting services. The company reports intangibles as one amount in the asset section of its balance sheet.

EXHIBIT 10–13

Harcourt General, Inc., and Subsidiaries, Excerpt from Consolidated Balance Sheet

	October 31,	
(in thousands)	1994	1993
Assets		
Current assets:		
Cash and equivalents	$ 819,659	$ 466,925
Accounts receivable—trade, net	578,575	493,384
Inventories	466,177	470,525
Deferred income taxes	90,501	20,016
Other current assets	66,096	53,095
Total current assets	2,021,008	1,503,945
Property and equipment:		
Land, buildings, and improvements	445,968	494,438
Fixtures and equipment	378,691	301,941
	824,659	796,379
Less accumulated depreciation and amortization	302,989	279,838
Total property and equipment, net	521,670	516,541
Other assets		
Prepublication costs, net	164,160	137,959
Intangible assets	422,566	400,028
Other	112,960	108,807
Total other assets	699,686	646,794
Net assets of discontinued operations	—	464,127
Total assets	$3,242,364	$3,131,407

11

OTHER
NONCURRENT ASSETS

*T*he items classified as other assets vary widely in practice. These non-current assets may be listed under the general heading Other Assets or (if material in amount) may be shown individually under a specific descriptive heading or title. Additionally, because the heading Other Assets tends to be vague, companies often clarify the items included in this category in the notes to the financial statements. This section consists of all assets not included under alternative asset classifications. Some common examples include:

1. Debt issuance costs.

2. Software development costs.

3. Advances to subsidiaries.*

4. Noncurrent deferred tax assets.

5. Long-term rental, insurance, or license prepayments.

---

* Sometimes classified as investments.

6. Long-term receivables, notes, or advances from officers, employees, customers, or others.*

7. Long-term prepaid pension cost.

8. Assets of a discontinued business segment.

9. Deposits made with taxing agencies or utility companies.

10. Plant relocation or rearrangement costs.

11. Restricted funds.

12. Deferred start-up costs.

13. Other deferred charges (discussed below).

14. Long-lived assets held for resale.*

15. Other idle fixed assets.*

Exhibit 11–1 reproduces the asset section of the balance sheet from the
1994 financial statements of United States Surgical Corporation and Subsidiaries. The company's Other Assets account was detailed in this note to
the financial statements:

Note E—Other Assets
   At December 31, 1994 and 1993, Other Assets (net of accumulated
amortization of $57 million and $61 million in 1994 and 1993, respectively) were comprised of the following items:

	1994	*1993*
	In thousands	
Patents	$ 57,200	$ 59,200
Computer software costs	8,300	12,500
Deferred start-up costs	4,200	8,300
Goodwill	5,200	5,600
Prepaid rent	19,700	10,400
Other	29,400	17,500
	$124,000	$113,500

During 1994 the Company removed from its Balance Sheet fully amortized Other Assets with a cost of $23 million.

EXHIBIT 11–1
United States Surgical Corporation and Subsidiaries,
Excerpt from Consolidated Balance Sheet

	December 31,	
(In thousands except share data)	1994	1993
Assets		
Current assets:		
Cash and cash equivalents	$ 11,300	$ 900
Receivables, less allowance of $7,300 (1994);		
$5,000 (1993)	211,500	197,900
Inventories:		
Finished goods	95,500	113,000
Work in process	27,100	36,900
Raw materials	44,600	62,300
	167,200	212,200
Other current assets	49,500	53,800
Total current assets	439,500	464,800
Property, plant, and equipment (net)	540,000	592,200
Other assets (net)	124,000	113,500
Total assets	$1,103,500	$1,170,500

The asset section of the balance sheet for Lincoln Electric Company and Subsidiaries is presented in Exhibit 11–2. The Other Asset category includes long-term notes receivable from employees. Ideally, the Other Asset section should be restricted to assets that are distinct from those included in other categories. However, as indicated in Exhibits 11–1 and 11–2, some companies include intangibles in this section of the balance sheet. Items chosen for classification within this category should be carefully scrutinized by company management because many items listed under Other Assets might be more accurately classified in one of the other categories.

EXHIBIT 11–2
**Lincoln Electric Company and Subsidiaries, Excerpt from
Consolidated Balance Sheet**

	December 31,	
(Dollars in thousands)	1994	1993
Assets		
Current assets:		
Cash and cash equivalents	$ 10,424	$ 20,381
Accounts receivable (less allowances of $4,251 in 1994; $6,258 in 1993)	126,007	110,504
Inventories		
Raw materials and in-process	72,302	66,987
Finished goods	82,974	76,698
	155,276	143,685
Deferred income taxes—Note E	11,601	42,960
Prepaid expenses	2,899	3,241
Other current assets	7,220	4,937
Total current assets	313,427	325,708
Other assets:		
Notes receivable from employees	3,151	4,747
Goodwill—Note C	39,213	39,732
Other	16,855	19,665
	59,219	64,144
Property, plant, and equipment		
Land	12,655	12,802
Buildings	118,903	113,927
Machinery, tools and equipment	312,957	279,933
	444,515	406,662
Less allowances for depreciation and amortization	260,304	236,971
	184,211	169,691
Total assets	$556,857	$559,543

Deferred Charges

Sometimes this section of the balance sheet is inappropriately referred to as deferred charges. A deferred charge is defined as a long-term prepayment of an expense. The problem with using this terminology is that many items classified as other assets do not fit the definition of a deferred charge. True deferred charges must be amortized over the periods of benefit, not to exceed 40 years. Rearrangement and relocation costs, long-term prepayments of expenses, bond issue and financing costs, and noncurrent prepaid pension costs are all examples of deferred charges. Many companies avoid this classification because of the problems in interpreting its meaning. If the classification is used in the balance sheet, companies normally make adequate disclosure of the nature of the charges in the footnotes to the financial statements.

Exhibit 11–3 is from the 1995 annual report of Alliant Techsystems, a company primarily engaged in the defense industry. The following note to the financial statements amplified the last three asset accounts on the balance sheet:

5. Goodwill, Deferred Charges, and Other Long-Term Assets

Goodwill, deferred charges, and other long-term assets consist of the following:

	Years Ended	
	Mar. 31, 1995	Mar. 31, 1994
Goodwill, net of accumulated amortization 1995—$4,211, 1994—$3,518	$18,215	$18,908
Debt issuance costs, net of accumulated amortization 1995—$0, 1994—$3,405	$12,997	$ 820
Other	5,367	453
	$18,364	$ 1,273
Prepaid and intangible pension asset	$32,839	$ 9,866
Other	717	1,349
	$33,556	$11,215

No goodwill resulted from the Aerospace acquisition transactions.

EXHIBIT 11–3
Alliant Techsystems Inc. and Subsidiaries,
Excerpt from Consolidated Balance Sheet

(Dollars in thousands)	March 31, 1995	1994
Assets		
Current assets:		
Cash and cash equivalents	$ 26,138	$ 45,584
Marketable securities	348	5,325
Receivables	284,911	113,853
Net inventory	103,886	89,049
Income tax refund receivable	—	1,491
Deferred income tax asset	44,032	29,908
Other current assets	4,996	2,103
Total current assets	464,311	287,313
Net property, plant, and equipment	517,373	119,482
Goodwill	18,215	18,908
Deferred charges	18,364	1,273
Other assets	33,556	11,215
Total assets	$1,051,819	$438,191

Exhibit 11–4 is a portion of the balance sheet from the 1995 annual report of American Greetings, one of the world's premier greeting card companies. The heading Other Assets was explained in this note to the company's financial statements:

NOTE C—OTHER ASSETS

The other assets classification consists of various long-term assets such as deferred costs relating to agreements with certain customers, corporate-owned life insurance, goodwill and equity investments. The largest component of other assets is deferred costs, which are $311,503 and $174,524 at February 28, 1995 and 1994, respectively. Deferred costs are charged to

EXHIBIT 11–4
American Greetings Corporation, Excerpt from
Consolidated Statement of Financial Position

(Thousands of dollars)	February 28, 1995	February 28, 1994
Assets		
Current assets:		
Cash and cash equivalents	$ 87,151	$ 101,066
Trade accounts receivable, less allowances for sales returns of $102,004 ($97,903 in 1994) and for doubtful accounts of $14,968 ($13,084 in 1994)	324,329	322,675
Inventories:		
Raw material	54,196	48,845
Work in process	40,608	38,956
Finished products	225,959	202,620
	320,763	290,421
Less LIFO reserve	86,169	84,970
	234,594	205,451
Display material and factory supplies	44,676	37,906
Total inventories	279,270	243,357
Deferred income taxes	66,409	62,075
Prepaid expenses and other	136,290	121,022
Total current assets	893,449	850,195
Other assets	419,477	286,117
Property, plant, and equipment:		
Land	5,533	5,975
Buildings	266,375	265,220
Equipment and fixtures	590,071	522,770
	861,979	793,965
Less accumulated depreciation	413,154	365,043
Property, plant, and equipment—net	448,825	428,922
	$1,761,751	$1,565,234

operations on a straight-line basis over the effective period of the agreement, generally three to six years. At February 28, 1995, these costs include amounts which, during 1995, were committed for future payment. Deferred costs estimated to be charged to operations during the next year are classified with prepaid expenses and other.

12

CURRENT LIABILITIES AND SPONTANEOUS FINANCING

Generally, current liabilities are obligations that a company expects to pay from current assets within one year of the balance sheet date. Because current liabilities must be paid from current assets, the amount of a company's current liabilities directly affects its short-term liquidity.

All equities are listed on the balance sheet in the general order of preference upon liquidation. Current liabilities are listed first and within the current liabilities group, debts to workers and vendors are listed first, accrued liabilities last.

The order of preference upon liquidation is not an absolute, but does describe the general sequence in which accountants arrange groups of equities and the individual equities within each group. Debts to creditors are listed before the equity of owners because creditors have preference upon liquidation. Preferred stock is listed before common stock for the same reason.

The current liabilities section of the balance sheet follow this general order:

Current Liabilities:

Accounts payable

Short-term notes payable

Unearned revenues

Short-term contingencies

Accrued payables

Current portion of long-term debt

Other short-term liabilities

A collection of the types of current liabilities typically shown on the balance sheet are discussed in the following listing:

- Accounts Payable. Amounts owed to vendors for merchandise or services purchased. Examples include amounts payable for inventory or delivery costs.

- Short-Term Notes. Formal, interest-bearing debt instruments. The principal amount of a short-term note is shown on the balance sheet; any interest that has accrued is shown as interest payable.

- Vacation Wages Payable. Vacation pay earned by employees but not yet paid. This debt is satisfied when employees take vacations.

- Current Portion of Long-Term Debt. Any long-term debt principal that will be paid within the next year. This occurs when a mortgage or other debt is repaid in installments. (Interest on long-term debt is Interest Payable.)

- Unearned Revenues. Customer payments accepted before a product or service is provided. The company is liable for delivering the product or service, or for returning the payment.

- Income Taxes Payable. The portion of income taxes the business has not yet paid. These are taxes due on the company's earnings (not withholdings for employees).

- Withholdings. Withholdings from employees. Federal and state laws require companies to withhold (and pay quarterly) income taxes and social security taxes (FICA taxes) from employees' paychecks. (The company's portion of FICA taxes, and unemployment taxes accrued but not paid are also current liabilities.)

- Deferred Taxes Currently Payable. Taxes associated with income reported to stockholders but not yet due to be paid because of the timing difference between accounting net income and taxable net income. Chapter 8 explains how taxable income is often different from income reported to stockholders in the financial statements, creating a deferred tax liability.

- Interest Payable. Unpaid interest on debt (short- or long-term) for the period from the last interest payment to the balance sheet date.

- Current Warranty Costs. Estimated costs to repair and service inventory sold under warranty.

The current liabilities portion of the balance sheets of RJR Nabisco and SCANA Corporation are shown in Exhibits 12–1 and 12–2, respectively. The current liability titled Current Portion of Preferred Stock, in the SCANA balance sheet, results from a commitment to retire the stock, according to the notes to the financial statements.

EXHIBIT 12–1
RJR Nabisco, Excerpt from Consolidated Balance Sheet

($ in millions)	December 31, 1994		December 31, 1993	
	Holdings	RJRN	Holdings	RJRN
Current liabilities:				
Notes payable (Note 8)	$ 296	$ 296	$ 301	$ 301
Accounts payable	548	548	515	515
Accrued liabilities (Note 9)	2,532	2,488	2,751	2,705
Current maturities of long-term debt (Notes 10 and 17)	1,970	1,970	142	142
Income taxes accrued (Note 3)	248	248	234	234
Total current liabilities	$5,594	$5,550	$3,943	$3,897

EXHIBIT 12–2
SCANA Corporation, Excerpt from
Consolidated Balance Sheet

	December 31,	
(Thousands of Dollars)	1994	1993
Current liabilities:		
Short-term borrowings (Notes 8 and 9)	$183,027	$ 43,019
Current portion of long-term debt (Note 3)	38,055	34,322
Current portion of preferred stock (Note 6)	2,418	2,504
Accounts payable	117,959	129,495
Estimated rate refunds and related interest		
(Note 2)	—	2,509
Customer deposits	13,768	13,498
Taxes accrued	46,670	50,063
Interest accrued	25,226	21,784
Dividends declared	35,530	33,637
Other	17,220	12,649
Total current liabilities	$479,873	$343,480

Spontaneous Financing from Current Liabilities

When companies grow, managers must plan ahead to secure capital to finance the growth. Companies may issue additional debt or stock, or they may restrict dividends or cut operating budgets when plants must be built, advertising campaigns mounted, or other strategies implemented. But some financing occurs automatically, without management's help. Let's consider the Baba Company, which has the following characteristics:

Annual Sales	$1,800,000
Cost of Goods Sold	
(annual)	$1,200,000 (⅔ of sales)
Accounts Receivable	$ 150,000 (one month's sales)

Cost of Goods Sold
   (one month) $ 100,000 (⅔ of each month's sales)
Accounts Payable $ 100,000 (one month's purchases)
Inventory $ 25,000 (¼ of a month's requirement)
Salaries Payable $ 40,000 (½ of this amount is linked to sales
                                  activity)

Now assume Baba has a 10 percent increase in sales. Immediately, Baba must increase its inventory on hand and the amount of money tied up in receivables (discussed in detail in the following paragraphs). Baba's managers must finance this increase in assets. But from where?

When companies increase sales of merchandise, several things happen. Increased sales result in a higher average accounts receivable balance. If Baba Company has a 10 percent increase in sales—say, from $1,800,000 to $1,980,000 ($1,800,000 × 110 percent)—receivables can be expected to increase by the same percentage. If average receivables before the increase are one month's sales, or $150,000, Baba's accounts receivable average will increase to $165,000 ($150,000 × 110 percent).

Because Baba's cost of inventory sold is 66.7 percent of sales, we know that, with sales of $1,800,000, the cost of inventory sold (and hence purchased) is $1,200,000 ($1,800,000 × 66.7 percent) per year, or $100,000 per month. If suppliers are paid in 30 days, the balance in accounts payable will average one month's purchases, or $100,000. After the 10 percent increase in sales, the accounts payable balance averages $110,000.

Increased sales also cause Baba to need more inventory on hand, which must be acquired by purchase or by production from raw materials (which must be purchased). With a 10 percent increase in sales, inventory on hand may be increased by a like percentage, to support the increased sales. If Baba's average inventory is 25 percent of one month's purchases, average inventory on hand before the increase is $25,000 ($100,000 × 25 percent); after the increase, it is $27,500 (110,000 × 25 percent).

(Because inventory levels are a marketing decision, the relationship of inventories on hand to purchases or to sales is not as certain as the relationship of sales to receivables, which is affected directly by the activity of the company.)

Some portion of salaries may increase because of increased sales activity. Quite arbitrarily, we let half of the salaries be directly linked to the

EXHIBIT 12–3
Baba Company, Spontaneous Sources of Financing

At sales of $1,800,000:

Current Assets		Current Liabilities	
Cash	$ 30,000	**Salaries payable**	**$ 40,000**
Accounts receivable	**150,000***	**Accounts payable**	**100,000**
Inventory	**25,000**	Notes payable	50,000
Prepaids	10,000		
Total	$215,000	Total	$190,000

At a 10 percent increase, or sales if $1,980,000:

Current Assets		Current Liabilities	
Cash	$ 30,000	**Salaries payable**	**$ 42,000**
Accounts receivable	**165,000**	**Accounts payable**	**110,000**
Inventory	**27,500**	Notes payable	50,000
Prepaids	10,000		
Total	$232,500	Total	$202,000

Increase in current assets and liabilities due to increase in sales	$17,500		$12,000

* Relationship of balances to sales, and changes in account balances when sales increase are explained in the text.

level of sales: half of the salaries payable are increased by 10 percent ($40,000 × .5 × 110 percent).

Current assets and liabilities, before and after the 10 percent increase in sales, are shown in Exhibit 12–3. The accounts directly impacted are shown in bold type; other account balances are not changed. Notice that investment in current assets increases $17,500 when sales increase, but financing of $12,000 "spontaneously" occurs because of the increase in current liabilities caused by the increased activity.

13

THE TIME
VALUE OF MONEY

*M*any state lotteries that make million-dollar payoffs normally pay these amounts over 10-, 20-, or 30-year payout periods. Publishers' Clearinghouse and The Reader's Digest mail sweepstakes are other examples of situations where substantial amounts of prize money can be paid to winners over some future period of time. In some instances, though, winners have the option of accepting a lump-sum payment immediately, rather than receiving payments over a stipulated period. Would you prefer $2.4 million today or $120,000 per year for 20 years (a total of $2.4 million)? All things equal, and ignoring income tax considerations, you would opt for the $2.4 million today because a dollar received today is worth more than a dollar to be received at some future time. This is because today's dollars can be invested and will yield a greater amount in the future. If we were to change the amounts to, say, $2.4 million to be received today versus $130,000 per year for 20 years (a total of $2.6 million), the analysis becomes more complicated; however, the basic premise is still the same—the *time value of money* is important for any receipt or payment of cash at some future point or points in time.

Business Applications of the Time Value of Money

Like individuals, companies are interested in the time value of money because they invest and borrow substantial amounts. In both instances, interest is involved. Interest is defined as the cost of using money over time, or, simply, the time value of money. Company managers are keenly aware of the importance of this concept. They monitor its effect on their cash inflows and outflows because it affects the measurement and valuation of assets and liabilities. In measuring assets and liabilities, company managers must understand the concepts of compound interest, present value, and annuities. Specifically, annuities and present value concepts are used by companies in the measurement of the following:

1. Noncurrent notes receivable and notes payable.

2. Bonds.

3. Leases.

4. Pensions and postretirement benefits.

5. Noncurrent asset valuation.

Companies make internal investment decisions and must choose among alternative projects. The alternative projects must be made comparable in terms of the time value of money. This chapter discusses the concepts necessary to assist in the measurement of assets and liabilities and the impact of the time value of money.

The Concept of Present Value

The time value of money is a very important consideration in measuring certain accounting transactions because decisions need to be made about cash inflows and/or outflows over an extended period of time. Absolute dollar amounts cannot be used in measuring these inflows or outflows because money has a time value. As we previously stated, the right to receive $100 today is worth more than the right to receive $100 in, say, 2 years, because that $100 can be invested to earn interest over that 2-year period. Earning interest on interest as well as on principal is referred to as *compounding,* whereby an amount invested today grows to a larger sum in the future. Discounting, or calculating present values, is used to adjust future cash inflows or outflows to the present.

Discounted cash flow refers to the present value, at a point in time, of a single amount—or a stream of receipts or payments—to be received or paid in the future. The receipts or payments are normally referred to as rents. If (1) the stream of rents is the same each period, (2) the time between rents is the same, and (3) interest is compounded once each period, the pattern is referred to as an annuity.

Future Value of a Single Sum

The concept of present value is related to the application of compound interest. For example, assume that we invest $1,000 in a savings account at a rate of 10 percent compounded annually. The balance in the account after 5 years would be $1,611, computed as follows:

Year	Principal at Beginning of Year (a)	Interest at 10% (b)	Principal at End of Year (a + b)
1	$1,000	$1,000 × 10% = $100	$1,100
2	$1,100	$1,100 × 10% = $110	$1,210
3	$1,210	$1,210 × 10% = $121	$1,331
4	$1,331	$1,331 × 10% = $133	$1,464
5	$1,464	$1,464 × 10% = $147	$1,611

The future value of a $1,000 deposit made today would grow to $1,611 at the end of 5 years. We can depict this sequence of deposits in the form of a time line, as shown in Exhibit 13–1.

EXHIBIT 13–1
Example of a Timeline

Today	Year 1	Year 2	Year 3	Year 4	Year 5

$1,000 ——➤ invested at an annual rate of 10 percent grows to ——➤ $1,611

There are formulas for calculating future and present values. Let us assume that:

F_n = the future value of an amount at the end of the stipulated time period,
i = the annual rate of interest,
n = number of periods,
P = the principal amount.

The formula for the future value of an investment is

$$F_n = P(1 + i)^n.$$

In our example, $F_n = \$1,000(1 + .10)^5 = 1.611$. We can express

$$F_n = P(1 + i)^n \text{ as } P \times [\text{Table } (i, n)],$$

where Table (i, n) is the future value interest factor for $1, found in a table derived from this formula. The future value of $1 invested today at vari-

Table 13–1
Future Value of $ Due in N Periods

No. of Periods	*Interest Rate*							
	1%	*4%*	*5%*	*6%*	*8%*	*10%*	*12%*	*15%*
1	1.010	1.040	1.050	1.060	1.080	1.100	1.120	1.150
2	1.020	1.082	1.103	1.124	1.166	1.210	1.254	1.323
3	1.030	1.125	1.158	1.191	1.260	1.331	1.405	1.521
4	1.041	1.170	1.216	1.263	1.361	1.464	1.574	1.749
5	1.051	1.217	1.276	1.338	1.469	1.611	1.762	2.011

ous interest rates and for equal time periods appears here as Table 13–1. Note that the value for 5 periods at a 10 percent interest rate is 1.611. And, $1,000 multiplied by the table value of 1.611 equals $1,611.

Present Value of a Single Sum

The present value of an amount views the compound interest concept in reverse; for example, the present value of $1,611 to be received over 5 equal periods is $1,000, as depicted in Exhibit 13–2.

Present value factors are computed in the same manner, using a present value formula (not presented here). Table 13–2 in an example of a present value table for 5 periods at various interest rates. Many calculators and computer programs include future and present value functions.

From Table 13–2, we can see that the present value factor for $1 for 5 periods at 10 percent is .621. Multiplying $1,611 by this factor results in a present value of $1,000 (rounded).

EXHIBIT 13–2
Example of Present Value

Today	Year 1	Year 2	Year 3	Year 4	Year 5

$1,000 ⟶ invested at an annual rate of 10 percent grows to ⟶ $1,611

Table 13–2
Present Value of $1 Due in N Periods

No. of Periods	Interest Rate							
	1%	4%	5%	6%	8%	10%	12%	15%
1	.990	.962	.952	.943	.926	.909	.893	.870
2	.980	.925	.907	.890	.857	.826	.797	.756
3	.971	.890	.864	.840	.794	.751	.712	.658
4	.961	.855	.823	.792	.735	.683	.636	.572
5	.951	.822	.784	.747	.681	.621	.567	.497

Present Value of an Ordinary Annuity

The present value of an annuity is simply the combined present values of the individual payments or receipts discounted back to today. An ordinary annuity assumes that rents occur at the end of the period. Suppose we wish to know whether we should accept a lump-sum payment of $3,500 today, or 5 receipts of $1,000 each, to be received at the end of each of the periods. Exhibit 13–3 is a diagram of the annuity.

The interest rate is 8 percent. Using the present value factors from Table 13–2, we can calculate the present value of this annuity:

			Payments		
Present Value	*1*	*2*	*3*	*4*	*5*
$ 926 =	$1,000 × .926				
857 =		$1,000 × .857			
794 =			$1,000 × .794		
735 =				$1,000 × .735	
681 =					$1,000 × .681
$3,993					

Because the present value of the receipts is greater than the lump sum, we would opt to receive the annuity rather than the lump sum (all things considered equal, and ignoring income taxes).

There is also a formula (not presented here) for calculating the present value of an ordinary annuity. The formula can be used to derive factors for an annuity table. Table 13–3 is an example of an annuity table.

EXHIBIT 13–3
Present Value of an Annuity

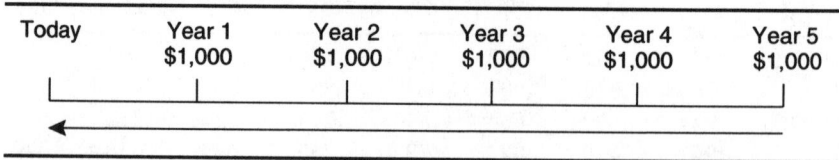

Today	Year 1	Year 2	Year 3	Year 4	Year 5
	$1,000	$1,000	$1,000	$1,000	$1,000

Table 13–3
Present Value of an Ordinary Annuity for N Periods

No. of Periods	Interest Rate							
	1%	*4%*	*5%*	*6%*	*8%*	*10%*	*12%*	*15%*
1	.990	.962	.952	.943	.926	.909	.893	.870
2	1.970	1.886	1.859	1.833	1.783	1.736	1.690	1.626
3	2.941	2.775	2.723	2.673	2.577	2.487	2.402	2.283
4	3.902	3.630	3.546	3.465	3.312	3.170	3.037	2.855
5	4.853	4.452	4.329	4.212	3.993	3.791	3.605	3.352

Remember our earlier statement: The present value of an ordinary annuity is the combined present values of the individual payments or receipts discounted back to today. If, using the present values in Table 13–2, we sum the individual present value factors for 5 periods at 8 percent, we obtain 3.993 (.926 + .857 + .794 + .735 + .681). This is the present value factor from the annuity table (Table 13–3) for five periods at 8 percent.

Present Value of an Annuity Due

A number of accounting transactions involve deposits or payments at the beginning of the period, rather than the end. An annuity that involves equal periodic rents at the beginning of the period is known as an annuity due. The difference between the present value of an annuity due and the present value of an ordinary annuity of the same number of rents is that the rents, in the case of an annuity due, are each one period closer in time even though the same number of rents is involved. If we use the information from our previous example (receipt of $1,000 a period for 5 periods, compounded at 8 percent per period) and assume receipt is at the beginning of the period, we can present the annuity as shown in Exhibit 13–4.

In the same way that we calculated the present value of an ordinary annuity, we can calculate the present value of an annuity due. We simply sum the present value of each of the periodic rents using the present value

EXHIBIT 13–4
Example of Present Value of an Annuity Due

Today $1,000	Year 2 $1,000	Year 3 $1,000	Year 4 $1,000	Year 5 $1,000

factors from Table 13–2. Note that the present value of $1 to be received today is $1, which results in a present value of $1,000 for the first rent.

		Payments				
Present Value	*Today*	*1*	*2*	*3*	*4*	*5*
$1,000 =	$1,000 × 1.0					
926 =		$1,000 × .926				
857 =			$1,000 × .857			
794 =				$1,000 × .794		
735 =					$1,000 × .735	
$4,312						

We could also use a formula to construct an annuity due present value table such as the one in Table 13–4.

From Table 13–4, we see that the factor for $1 for 5 periods at 8 percent is 4.312. If we multiply this factor by $1,000, the result is $4,312.

Table 13–4
Present Value of an Annuity Date for N Periods

No. of Periods	Interest Rate							
	1%	*4%*	*5%*	*6%*	*8%*	*10%*	*12%*	*15%*
1	1.000	1.000	1.000	1.000	1.000	1.000	1.000	1.000
2	1.990	1.962	1.952	1.943	1.923	1.909	1.893	1.870
3	2.970	2.886	2.860	2.833	2.783	2.736	2.690	2.626
4	3.941	3.775	3.723	3.673	3.577	3.487	3.402	3.283
5	4.902	4.630	4.546	4.465	4.312	4.170	4.037	3.855

The present value of an ordinary annuity of $1 for 5 periods at 8 percent is $3,993; the present value of an annuity due of $1 for 5 periods at 8 percent is $4,312. The present value of an annuity due for N periods will always be larger than the present value of an ordinary annuity for the same N periods because the cash flows occur at the beginning of the period instead of at the end. Thus, one additional interest period exists with an annuity due. We can prove this by checking the difference in the amounts of the annuity due and the ordinary annuity in our example ($4,312 − $3,993 = $319). The amount accumulated with the ordinary annuity after the fifth rent is $3,993. If we multiply that amount by 8 percent for one more period, we obtain $319.

Future Value of an Ordinary Annuity and an Annuity Due

There are formulas and tables that can be used to compute the future amount of an ordinary annuity and an annuity due. A calculator or computer program can also be used to generate the accumulated amounts resulting from these annuities. Because substantially all business transactions affecting the measurement of balance sheet accounts relate to the application of present value techniques, we will not discuss the future value of an ordinary annuity or an annuity due.

Examples

Future Value of a Single Sum

The company controller wishes to know the amount that will be on deposit in 4 years if $4,300 is invested at 12 percent today. The amount is:

Present Value × Table 13–1 Value = Future Value

$4,300 × 1.574 = $6,768

If $4,300 is invested today at 12 percent annual interest, it will be worth $6,768 in 4 years.

Present Value of a Single Sum

Your son will be attending college in 4 years. You want to have the total amount of his tuition on hand when he begins his studies. You anticipate that the cost of tuition in 4 years will be $25,000. If the interest rate is 8 percent, what amount would you need to deposit today in order to have the $25,000 on hand in 4 years? The present value of $25,000 due in 4 years at 8 percent is:

Future Value × Table 13–2 Value = Present Value

$25,000   ×   .735   = $18,375

That is, $18,375 invested today at 8 percent would grow to $25,000 in 4 years.

Present Value of an Ordinary Annuity

A friend has won a lottery. She has been given the option of taking a $4,000 lump-sum payment today or receiving a $1,000 payment for each of the next 5 years, payable at the end of the year. The interest rate is 12 percent. The present value of an annuity of $1,000 for 5 periods at 12 percent is:

Periodic Payment × Table 13–3 Value = Present Value

$1,000   ×   3.605   = $3,605

All things being equal, your friend should take the lump-sum payment.

Present Value of an Annuity Due

You are examining whether your company should buy (obtain a mortgage) or lease a warehouse. The lessor has quoted you an annual lease payment of $120,000 for each of the next 5 years. The warehouse has a fair value of

$400,000 today, the annual interest rate is 10 percent, and the mortgage note would be paid off in 5 equal installments over the next 5 years. The payments are to be made at the beginning of the year. You need to determine the mortgage payment for 5 years at 10 percent and compare it to the annual lease payments.

$$\text{Periodic Payment} \times \text{Table 4 Value} = \text{Present Value}$$

$$\text{Periodic Payment} \times \quad 4.170 \quad = \quad \$400,000$$

$$\text{Periodic Payment} = \frac{\$400,000}{4.170} = \quad \$95,923$$

Again, all things equal, your company should buy rather than lease the warehouse.

14

NONCURRENT
NOTES AND
MORTGAGE LIABILITIES

*B*anks sometimes classify loans as short-term, intermediate, and long-term, with long-term being three years or more. Accounting rules governing financial statement presentation, however, classify as long-term or noncurrent liabilities all debts a company will not pay for at least one year or one operating cycle, whichever is longer. These debts include borrowings by the company in the form of long-term notes, mortgages, or bonds, and debts that arise from the company's pensions, leases, and deferred taxes.

Some noncurrent liabilities require the company to make periodic payments of principal and interest, usually monthly or annually. Any portion of a debt that will be paid within the next year (or operating cycle) is classified as a current liability. Exhibit 14–1 reproduces the balance sheet of Eaton Corporation and shows a current portion of long-term debt included in the current liabilities section and three types of long-term debt.

EXHIBIT 14–1
Eaton Corporation, Consolidated Balance Sheet

(Millions)	December 31, 1994	December 31, 1993
Assets		
Current assets:		
Cash	$ 18	$ 32
Short-term investments	23	268
Accounts receivable	889	550
Inventories	698	434
Deferred income taxes	151	127
Other current assets	67	55
	1,846	1,466
Property, plant, and equipment:		
Land	50	41
Buildings	539	486
Machinery and equipment	2,321	1,959
	2,910	2,486
Accumulated depreciation	(1,441)	(1,298)
	1,469	1,188
Excess of cost over net assets of business acquired	850	265
Deferred income taxes	158	112
Other assets	359	237
	$ 4,682	$ 3,268
Liabilities and Shareholders' Equity		
Current liabilities:		
Short-term debt	$ 14	$ 14
Current portion of long-term debt	22	110
Accounts payable	449	266
Accrued compensation	163	106
Accrued income and other taxes	60	23
Other current liabilities	394	268
	1,102	787
Long-term debt	1,053	649
Postretirement benefits other than pensions	573	509
Other long-term liabilities	274	218
Shareholders equity:		
Common Shares (78.0 in 1994 and 71.3 in 1993)	39	36
Capital in excess of par value	806	535
Retained earnings	988	708
Foreign currency translation adjustments	(71)	(78)
Unallocated Employee Stock Ownership Plan shares	(82)	(96)
	1,680	1,105
	$ 4,682	$ 3,268

This chapter discusses long-term notes and mortgages. Chapter 15 discusses bonds.

Long-Term Notes Payable

The amount of a liability that will actually be paid at some future date is called its *future value*. Current liabilities are shown in balance sheets at their future values. Noncurrent liabilities, because they are not due for over one year, are shown in balance sheets at their *present values*. As discussed in Chapter 13, the present value of a debt is the amount required to pay the debt off on the date of the balance sheet. To illustrate, assume that on December 31, Year 1, Frommer Company borrows $10,000 on a two-year note payable at 10 percent annual interest. The future value of the note is calculated as follows:

Present value of the note at balance sheet date, Year 1	$10,000
Times one plus the interest rate	× 1.10
Due in one year (principal and interest)	11,000
Times one plus the interest rate	× 1.10
Future value due in two years (principal and interest)	$12,100

Frommer's note payable is shown in the balance sheet for Year 1 (dated December 31, Year 1, the date of the note) at the $10,000 owed on that date. At the end of Year 2, the note is again shown at the amount owed on the balance sheet date. When Frommer pays the note in two years, the $12,100 payment is composed of $2,100 in interest and $10,000 in principal. The note is paid on December 31, Year 3, and does not appear in the balance sheet as of that date. Examples of how Frommer's long-term note payable might be shown are contained in Exhibit 14–2.

Some notes are made payable for the total amount, which must be paid (principal plus interest) when the note becomes due. (This amount is the future value of the note.) If Frommer's accountant had initially recorded the note payable at $12,100 (its future value) instead of $10,000 (its present value), the note would still be shown in the balance sheets of Years 1

EXHIBIT 14–2
Balance Sheet Disclosure of a Long-Term Note Payable
Recorded at Its Present Value

December 31, Year 1
Noncurrent liabilities:
Note payable (due in two years) $10,000

December 31, Year 2
Current liabilities:
Note payable (due in one year) $10,000
Interest payable (on note due in one year)   1,000 $11,000

and 2 at the same amounts: $10,000 for Year 1, and $11,000 for Year 2. The calculation is:

Future value, end of Year 1, of note due in two years	$12,100
Less interest not yet earned on December 31, Year 1	2,100
Present value of the note at balance sheet date, Year 1	$10,000
Future value, end of Year 2, of note due in one year	$12,100
Less interest not yet earned on December 31, Year 2	1,100
Present value of the note at balance sheet date, Year 2	$11,000

Exhibit 14–3 shows how Frommer's accountant might use a valuation account titled Discount on Note Payable to show the notes correctly in the Year 1 and Year 2 balance sheets.

Mortgages

A mortgage loan is a debt agreement that gives the lender (the mortgagee) a claim against the borrower's (the mortgagor's) property in case the loan is not repaid. Commercial mortgages frequently require 20 percent or 25 percent of the appraised value of a property as a down payment, and payments

EXHIBIT 14–3
Balance Sheet Disclosure of a Long-Term Note Payable
Recorded at Its Future Value

December 31, Year 1		
Noncurrent liabilities:		
Note payable (due in two years)	$12,100	
Less discount on note payable	2,100	$10,000

December 31, Year 2		
Current liabilities:		
Note payable (due in one year)	$12,100	
Less discount on note payable	1,100	$11,000

over 10 to 20 years. For example, a company might purchase an office building by paying 25 percent down and financing the rest with a mortgage that gives the bank the right to take the building if the loan is not repaid.

A mortgage is essentially a long-term installment note secured by property. Like long-term notes, mortgage liabilities are shown on balance sheets at their present values. On any date, the present value of a mortgage liability is the discounted amount of unpaid principal plus the accrued interest required to pay off the mortgage debt.

Mortgage terms generally require the borrower to make payments monthly, but can require quarterly, semiannual, or annual payments. Each payment reduces the loan principal and pays the interest for the period. If we know only the payment arrangement and the mortgage interest rate, we can determine the present value of a mortgage, using the formula in Chapter 11 to find the present value of an annuity.

$$\text{Periodic Payment} \times \text{Annuity Factor} = \text{Present Value}$$

If the interest rate is 10 percent and the mortgage payment is $1,000 per year for 5 years, the annuity value from Table 13–3 is 3.791, and the present value of the stream of mortgage payments is $3,791.

Periodic Payment × Annuity Factor = Present Value

$1,000   ×   3.791   = $3,791

Calculating a Mortgage Payment

The relationship in the present value formula is used to calculate the amount of a mortgage payment. For example, if a mortgage is for $100,000 payable annually for 5 years at 10 percent, the present value in the equation is the amount borrowed ($100,000), and the factor is the annuity factor (from Table 13–3) for a 5-period annuity at 10 percent (3.791). If we insert these amounts in the equation, we find that the periodic payment is $26,378.26.

Periodic Payment × Annuity Factor = Present Value

Periodic Payment ×   3.791   = $100,000

$$\text{Periodic Payment} = \frac{\$100,000}{3.791} = \$26,378.26$$

A *mortgage loan amortization schedule* shows how each payment is split between principal and interest. A loan amortization schedule for our $100,000 5-year mortgage at 10 percent interest is shown in Exhibit 14–4. The schedule contains six vertical columns with a horizontal row for each payment. The first column identifies the year for which calculations are shown. The third column states the periodic interest rate of each payment, and the fifth column lists the amount of the periodic payment.

The fourth column shows the interest due each period, calculated as Interest = Principal × Periodic Interest Rate. The annual interest rate in our example is 10 percent. Because the mortgage requires annual payments, the periodic rate is also 10 percent. (If the mortgage instead required monthly payments, the periodic rate would be 10 percent divided by 12 months.)

Subtracting from the payment the amount of interest due in a period gives the amount of the payment applied to principal (as in the sixth column). The second column shows the decreasing amount of principal remaining at the start of each period.

EXHIBIT 14-4
Mortgage Loan Amortization Schedule

A mortgage for $100,000 at 10 percent interest with 5 annual payments.

Period (Year)	Principal Amount (p)	Periodic Rate (r)	Interest Expense (i = pr)	Periodic Payment (a)	Applied to Principal (a − i)
1	$100,000.00	.10	$10,000.00	$26,378.26	$16,378.26
2	83,621.74	.10	8,362.17	26,378.26	18,016.09
3	65,605.65	.10	6,560.56	26,378.26	19,817.70
4	45,787.95	.10	4,578.79	26,378.26	21,799.47
5	23,988.48	.10	2,398.84	26,378.26	23,979.42*

* Difference due to rounding.

If the mortgage in Exhibit 14–4 is dated January 1, Year 1, the present value of the mortgage loan in the December 31, Year 1, balance sheet is $100,000 (the principal amount) plus $10,000 in Year 1 interest. A $26,378.26 payment is made on January 1, Year 2, and the value of the loan on December 31, Year 2, is $83,621.74 (principal) plus $8,362.17 in Year 2 interest. An amortization table makes it easy to determine the amount of the debt at any point in time.

Exhibit 14–5 on page 166 reproduces the financial statement note related to long-term debt, as it appeared in the 1994 Fluor Corporation annual report. Fluor has both long-term notes and mortgages, including a "first mortgage note" which the company intends to prepay within one year (causing this debt to be reclassified as current). A first mortgage note is simply a note secured by property.

EXHIBIT 14–5

Fluor Corporation, Financial Statement Note Related to Long-Term Debt, in the 1994 Annual Report

Long-Term Debt

Long-term debt comprises:

$ in thousands/At October 31,	1994	1993
Deutsche mark financing, with a currency exchange agreement fixing the repayments in U.S. dollars at an effective interest rate of 9.5%, due in 1996	$23,644	$23,644
13.50% first mortgage note, due in 2000, prepayable at par in 1995	34,701	35,000
Other notes and mortgages	4,022	2,680
	62,367	61,324
Less: Current portion	38,001	1,687
Long-term debt due after one year	$24,366	$59,637

Long-term debt maturities are as follows: 1996, $24.1 million; 1997, $60 thousand; 1998, no maturities; 1999, no maturities; and $.2 million thereafter. All long-term debt (including current portion) outstanding at October 31, 1994, bears interest at fixed rates. In 1995, the company intends to prepay the 13.50 percent first mortgage note of $34.7 million, and accordingly, this amount has been classified as current at October 31, 1994.

The company has unsecured committed revolving long-term lines of credit with banks from which it may borrow for general corporate purposes up to a maximum of $250 million. Commitment and facility fees are paid on these lines. In addition, the company has $784 million in short-term uncommitted lines of credit. Borrowings under lines of credit and revolving credit agreements bear interest at prime or rates based on the London Interbank Offered Rate (LIBOR), domestic certificates of deposit or other rates which are mutually acceptable to the banks and the company. At October 31, 1994, no amounts were outstanding under the committed lines of credit. As of that date, $193 million of the short-term uncommitted lines of credit were used to support undrawn letters of credit issued in the ordinary course of business.

The company had unsecured commercial paper outstanding in the amount of $20 million and $30 million at October 31, 1994 and 1993, respectively. The commercial paper was issued at a discount with an effective interest rate of 5.0 percent and 3.2 percent in 1994 and 1993, respectively. Maturities range from 9 to 90 days in 1994 and 18 to 90 days in 1993. The weighted average maturity at both October 31, 1994 and 1993 was 16 days. The maximum and average balances outstanding for the years ended October 31, 1994 and 1993 were $52.9 million and $24.1 million, respectively, and $92 million and $44.9 million, respectively, with weighted average interest rates of 3.6 percent and 3.2 percent, respectively.

15

BOND LIABILITIES

Each individual bond is a debt agreement, typically in the amount of $1,000, to be repaid in 10 to 20 years. A $10,000,000 bond issue might consist of 10,000 individual $1,000 bonds. Instead of searching for a lender who will agree to a $10,000,000 loan, the company can place the bond issue with up to 10,000 separate lenders. A lender who provides $10,000 receives 10 bond contracts at $1,000 each. Each bond contract (called an indenture) sets out the coupon interest rate (also called the nominal or contract rate), the interest payment schedule (annually or semiannually), and the maturity date when the face amount of the bonds will be repaid in a single amount.

Generally, all bonds in an issue are due for repayment on the same date, but they may mature over several years. Bonds that mature in such increments are called serial bonds. To illustrate, an issue of $20,000,000 in serial bonds might be scheduled to mature in the 10th, 11th, 12th, and 13th years, with the company repaying $5,000,000 each year. This spreads out the burden of repayment and may prevent the company from needing to refinance part of the debt. Because the market demands different interest

167

EXHIBIT 15–1
Schedule of Long-Term Debt from Eaton Corporation
Financial Statement Notes

Debt and Other Financial Instruments

The Company's subsidiaries outside the United States have lines of credit, primarily short-term, aggregating $115 million from various banks worldwide. Most of these arrangements are reviewed periodically for renewal. At December 31, 1994, the Company had $19 million outstanding under these lines of credit with banks. The weighted average interest rate on short-term debt, excluding immaterial amounts for highly inflationary countries, at December 31, 1994 and 1993 was 6.8% and 8.1%, respectively.

Long-term debt at December 31, excluding the current portion, follows (in millions):

	1994	1993
Notes of Employee Stock Ownership Plan due through 1999	$ 66	$ 82
6⅜% notes due 1999	100	
9% notes due 2001	100	100
8% debentures due 2006 (due 1996 at option of debenture holders)	86	86
8.9% debentures due 2006	100	100
7% debentures due 2011, net of unamortized discount of $93 million in 1994 and $95 million in 1993 (effective interest rate 14.6%)	107	105
8⅞% debentures due 2019 (due 2004 at option of debenture holders)	38	38
8.1% debentures due 2022	100	100
7⅝% debentures due 2024	100	
Unsecured notes (6% to 6.4%)	210	
Other	46	38
	$1,053	$649

rates for debts of different terms, serial bonds sometimes have interest rates that vary among maturities.

A mortgage bond is secured by a pledge of property; a debenture bond is not. The complete balance sheet of Eaton Corporation is reproduced in Exhibit 14–1. The schedule of long-term debt from the notes to Eaton's financial statements is shown here as Exhibit 15–1. The interest rate and repayment date are given for each debt. A number of Eaton's debenture issues will mature between 2006 and 2024.

Issuing Bonds

When a company issues a bond, it is making two promises:

1. To pay the lender the face amount of the bond at maturity.
2. To pay interest on the bond each period.

Suppose ABC Company issues $1,000,000 in 10-year, 12 percent bonds, with interest payable semiannually. Assume the market rate of interest (also called the effective interest rate) for bonds of the same characteristics (maturity, risk, etc.) as the bond issue is also 12 percent. ABC can expect to issue its bond at face value, receiving $1,000 for each bond. ABC will thus receive the $1,000,000 face amount of the bonds (less any issue costs) and will begin to pay $60,000 ($1,000,000 × .12 × ½ year) in interest at the end of each six-month period. The payment schedule is:

The face amount at the maturity of the bonds (10 years)	$1,000,000
Interest in 20 equal semiannual payments ($60,000 × 20)	1,200,000
Total amount paid	$2,200,000
Less amount received from lender at issue	1,000,000
Excess paid over amount received (interest expense)	$1,200,000

When ABC keeps its promises as spelled out in the bond contract, it will pay the $1,000,000 face amount when the bonds mature, plus $1,200,000 in semiannual interest payments during the 10 years.

Bonds Issued at a Discount

Now assume instead that, before the ABC bonds are issued, the market interest rate rises above the 12 percent nominal rate. Under these conditions, a lender will no longer purchase a $1,000 bond (that is, lend $1,000) to receive 12 percent interest, but will demand the higher market rate of return. But the bond contracts are printed, and the issue is ready to go. What can ABC do?

The problem is resolved by issuing the bonds at less than face, allowing lenders to invest less than the $1,000,000 face amount of the issue to receive the payments (principal and interest) promised in the bond contract. Because interest rates change continuously, it is unlikely that the bond contract rate will match the market rates on the date of issue.

Suppose that, at the higher market rate of interest, the lender agrees to lend only $800,000 for the bonds. In this case, to keep the two promises cited previously, ABC will pay:

The face amount at the maturity of the bonds (10 years)	$1,000,000
Interest in 20 equal semiannual payments ($60,000 × 20)	1,200,000
Total amount paid	$2,200,000
Less amount received from lender at issue	800,000
Excess paid over amount received (interest expense)	$1,400,000

Again, ABC pays the $1,000,000 face when the bonds mature, plus $1,200,000 in semiannual interest payments. Again, the interest expense is the excess paid over the amount received. ABC pays $120,000 in interest per year, but the average annual cost of the funds borrowed is $140,000 ($140,000/10 years).

At the time of issue, the bonds might appear in ABC's balance sheet as follows. The debt is shown at its present value—conceptually, the amount ABC would be required to pay if it retired its bonds immediately after they were issued. (ABC would need to pay the same market price paid by the lenders.)

Bonds Payable	$1,000,000	
Discount on Bonds Payable	200,000	$800,000

Each year, ABC pays cash of $120,000 and amortizes (or reduces) the amount of the discount by an average of $20,000. Thus, each year, the carrying value of the bond liability increases by $20,000; in 10 years, the discount is reduced to zero (10 × $20,000 = $200,000) and the carrying value of the bond liability is increased to the face amount of the bonds, which is the amount owed to lenders ($1,000,000).

Balance sheet presentation at the end of year 1 and in years 2 through 5 might be as shown below. Note the decrease in the amount of the discount and the increase in the carrying amount of the bond liability.

End of Year 1

Bonds Payable	$1,000,000	
Discount on Bonds Payable	180,000	$820,000

End of Year 2

Bonds Payable	$1,000,000	
Discount on Bonds Payable	160,000	$840,000

End of Year 3

Bonds Payable	$1,000,000	
Discount on Bonds Payable	140,000	$860,000

End of Year 4

Bonds Payable	$1,000,000	
Discount on Bonds Payable	120,000	$880,000

End of Year 5

Bonds Payable	$1,000,000	
Discount on Bonds Payable	100,000	$900,000

Bonds Issued at a Premium

If, instead of rising, the interest rate falls before the ABC bonds are issued, lenders will be willing to pay more than the face amount of the issue to receive the $60,000 semiannual interest payments. Assume, after market interest rates have fallen, lenders agree to lend $1,100,000 in exchange for the two promises made in the bond contract.

In this case, ABC will pay:

The face amount at the maturity of the bonds (10 years)	$1,000,000
Interest in 20 equal semiannual payments ($60,000 × 20)	1,200,000
Total amount paid	$2,200,000
Less amount received from lender at issue	1,100,000
Excess paid over amount received (interest expense)	$1,100,000

At the time of issue, the bonds might appear in ABC's balance sheet as shown below. The debt is shown at its present value—conceptually, the amount ABC would pay if it retired its bonds immediately after issue.

Bonds Payable	$1,000,000	
Premium on Bonds Payable	100,000	$1,100,000

Again, the excess paid over the amount received is the true interest cost of the funds, and the average interest expense over the 10-year life of the bonds is $110,000 ($1,100,000/10 years). Each year, ABC pays cash of $120,000 and amortizes (or reduces) the amount of the premium by an average of $10,000. Thus, each year, the carrying value of the bond liability decreases by $10,000; in 10 years, the premium is reduced to zero (10 × $10,000 = $100,000) and the carrying value of the bond liability is decreased to the amount owed to lenders ($1,000,000).

Balance sheet presentation at the end of year 1 and in years 2 through 5 might be as shown below. Note the decrease in the amount of the discount and the increase in the carrying amount of the bond liability.

End of Year 1

Bonds Payable	$1,000,000	
Premium on Bonds Payable	90,000	$1,090,00

End of Year 2

Bonds Payable	$1,000,000	
Premium on Bonds Payable	80,000	$1,080,000

End of Year 3

| Bonds Payable | $1,000,000 | |
| Premium on Bonds Payable | 70,000 | $1,070,000 |

End of Year 4

| Bonds Payable | $1,000,000 | |
| Premium on Bonds Payable | 60,000 | $1,060,000 |

End of Year 5

| Bonds Payable | $1,000,000 | |
| Premium on Bonds Payable | 50,000 | $1,050,000 |

Effective Interest Rate Amortization

In the preceding examples, we have used the *straight-line method* to amortize the discount or premium. This method is simple, but when the discount or premium is material, the *effective interest rate method*, a more complex method, must be used. The straight-line method, which gives the same interest expense in each period, is thought to be misleading because this method causes the effective interest rate in each period to change.

To illustrate, we return to our example and calculate average annual interest expense ($110,000) as a percentage of the bonds' value at issue and at the end of years 1 through 5. Because the value of the bond liability in the balance sheet changes each period as the premium is amortized, and the straight-line method uses the same interest expense each period, the *apparent* interest rate increases over the life of the bonds. (When bonds are issued at a discount, the straight-line rate causes the apparent interest rate to decrease each period.)

$$\textit{Date issued} \quad \frac{\$110,000}{\$1,100,000} = 10.00 \text{ percent}$$

$$\textit{Year 1} \quad \frac{\$110,000}{\$1,090,000} = 10.09 \text{ percent}$$

$$\text{Year 2} \quad \frac{\$110,000}{\$1,080,000} = 10.18 \text{ percent}$$

$$\text{Year 3} \quad \frac{\$110,000}{\$1,070,000} = 10.28 \text{ percent}$$

$$\text{Year 4} \quad \frac{\$110,000}{\$1,060,000} = 10.38 \text{ percent}$$

$$\text{Year 5} \quad \frac{\$110,000}{\$1,050,000} = 10.48 \text{ percent}$$

Total interest expense (here, $1,100,000) is the same, regardless of the method used to amortize the bond premium. When the effective interest rate is used, total annual interest payments are still $120,000, but the interest expense changes each period, much as it did in the amortization schedule for a mortgage in Chapter 14.

Market Interest Rate and the Amount Received

The market interest rate determines the amount received when a bond is issued. ABC Company issued $1,000,000 face value, 10-year bonds. The bonds have a contract rate of 12 percent, but we do not know the market rate at the time of issue. We know only that it is lower than the contract rate because the price of the bonds was bid up and we received more than their face amount. However, we can use factors from present value tables to determine the relationship among the present value of the two promises contained in the bond contract (the market interest rate, and the amount received when the bonds are issued). In the calculation below, we try a 10 percent market rate, which is a bit low. The present value (PV) of $1 at 10 percent for 10 periods is $0.386, and the PV of a $1 annuity at 5 percent (10% × .5) for 20 6-month periods is $12.462. (Present value concepts are explained in Chapter 13.)

(Promise)   × (10% PV Factor) = (Present Value)

To pay, in 10 years, $1,000,000 × .   .386   = $ 386,000

To pay 12 percent interest on
the face amount of the bonds
each year, for 20 6-month
periods:

$1,000,000× .12 = $120,000

$120,000   × %12 = $ 60,000   ×   12.462   =   747,720

     Present value of the two bond contract promises $1,133,720

     Actual amount received   1,100,000

     Error $ 133,720

Because 10 percent is low, we try 11 percent and find we are slightly high. Extrapolating between the two, we find the effective market rate to be 10.64 percent:

(Promise)   × (11% PV factor) = (Present Value)

To pay, in 10 years, $1,000,000 ×   .354   = $ 354,000

To pay 12 percent interest on
the face amount of the bonds
each year, for 20 6-month
periods:

$1,000,000× .12 = $120,000

$120,000   × %12 = $ 60,000   ×   12.000   =   720,000

     Present value of the two bond contract promises $1,074,000

     Actual amount received   1,100,000

     Error $ −74,720

We can extrapolate to arrive at an approximate rate, or calculate one using an electronic spreadsheet. Exhibit 15–2 is an amortization table for ABC Company's 12 percent bonds issued at a premium, using the effective

EXHIBIT 15-2
Bond Amortization Table Using the Effective Interest Rate Method;
12 Percent Bonds Issued at a Premium,
Effective Market Interest Rate of 10.64 Percent

Period	Bond Face Amount f	Premium p	Total Debt (p + f)
1	$1,000,000.00	$100,000.00	$1,100,000.00
2	1,000,000.00	97,033.90	1,097,033.90
3	1,000,000.00	93,914.01	1,093,914.01
4	1,000,000.00	90,632.36	1,090,632.36
5	1,000,000.00	87,180.56	1,087,180.56
6	1,000,000.00	83,549.78	1,083,549.78
7	1,000,000.00	79,730.75	1,079,730.75
8	1,000,000.00	75,713.71	1,075,713.71
9	1,000,000.00	71,488.39	1,071,488.39
10	1,000,000.00	67,043.99	1,067,043.99
11	1,000,000.00	62,369.16	1,062,369.16
12	1,000,000.00	57,451.94	1,057,451.94
13	1,000,000.00	52,279.76	1,052,279.76
14	1,000,000.00	46,839.42	1,046,839.42
15	1,000,000.00	41,116.99	1,041,116.99
16	1,000,000.00	35,097.87	1,035,097.87
17	1,000,000.00	28,766.66	1,028,766.66
18	1,000,000.00	22,107.18	1,022,107.18
19	1,000,000.00	15,102.41	1,015,102.41
20	1,000,000.00	7,734.46	1,007,734.46

Effective Rate e	Interest Expense E = e (p + f)	Contract Rate r	Interest Payment P = rf	Applied to Premium P − E
5.1849%	$57,033.90	6%	$60,000.00	$2,966.10
5.1849	56,880.11	6	60,000.00	3,119.89
5.1849	56,718.35	6	60,000.00	3,281.65
5.1849	56,548.20	6	60,000.00	3,451.80
5.1849	56,369.22	6	60,000.00	3,630.78
5.1849	56,180.97	6	60,000.00	3,819.03
5.1849	55,982.96	6	60,000.00	4,017.04
5.1849	55,774.68	6	60,000.00	4,225.32
5.1849	55,555.60	6	60,000.00	4,444.40
5.1849	55,325.16	6	60,000.00	4,674.84
5.1849	55,082.78	6	60,000.00	4,917.22
5.1849	54,827.83	6	60,000.00	5,172.17
5.1849	54,559.65	6	60,000.00	5,440.35
5.1849	54,277.58	6	60,000.00	5,722.42
5.1849	53,980.87	6	60,000.00	6,019.13
5.1849	53,668.79	6	60,000.00	6,331.21
5.1849	53,340.52	6	60,000.00	6,659.48
5.1849	52,995.24	6	60,000.00	7,004.76
5.1849	52,632.05	6	60,000.00	7,367.95
5.1849	52,250.02	6	60,000.00	7,749.98

interest rate method and an effective annual market interest rate of 10.3698 percent (or 5.1849 percent per 6-month interest period). When the effective interest rate method is used, interest expense is the same percentage of the total debt (face amount plus or minus premium or discount) each period. This certainly makes better sense to balance sheet readers.

A bond amortization table lets us see how each payment is applied to interest and principal. For example, Exhibit 15–2 shows that, in period 5, the total debt is on the balance sheet as $1,087,180.56.

Bonds payable at face	$1,000,000.00	
Plus premium on bonds payable	87,180.56	$1,087,180.56

The interest payment to bondholders is $60,000 in each period. Interest expense for the fifth 6-month period is shown to be $56,369.22, leaving $3,630.78 to be applied to reduction of the premium.

Bond Disclosure in the Notes to the Annual Report

A company that has bond debt must show, in the notes to its financial statements, the details of the bond security agreement, the maturity date, and the interest rate of each bond issue. The noncurrent portion of bond debt is shown in the long-term liabilities section of the balance sheet at its face amount, minus or plus the discount or premium.

Convertible Bonds

Some bond contracts include a provision that gives bondholders the right to exchange their bonds for common stock. Bonds containing this provision are called convertible bonds. Companies issue convertible bonds because:

1. Creditors may accept a lower interest rate, knowing that they have the option of converting to common stock if the stock increases in value.

2. The debt may be essentially self-retiring, in that the liability to bondholders is satisfied when they exchange their debt securities for equity (ownership) securities.

Convertible bonds work like this. Assume Wilson Company issues $2,000,000 in 15-year, $1,000 face value bonds paying 10 percent interest in each 6-month period. Each bond is convertible into 20 shares of Wilson's stock. When the bonds are issued, the stock is selling for $40 per share. At date of issue, when the market value of 20 shares at $40 per share ($800) is less than the value of the bond, bondholders prefer bonds over common stock. But as the market price of the stock rises, bondholders will, at some point, exercise their option to convert and exchange their $2,000,000 in debt for shares of common stock.

When (and if) this happens, Wilson's debt is satisfied.

Zero Coupon and Junk Bonds

Some bonds do not pay periodic interest. On these bonds, the company makes only one of the two promises discussed earlier: to pay the face amount of the bond at maturity. This type of bond is called a *zero coupon bond* or a *zero*. Because zeros pay no interest, the lender is compensated only by the bond's increase in value; hence, zeros are issued at a large discount.

Bonds with a credit rating of BB or lower are speculative and are often called junk bonds. Paid-in-kind junk bonds (called PIKs) are essentially zeros because the bondholders receive additional bonds instead of interest during the bonds' life. As with zeros, the company pays no cash until the bonds mature.

16

STOCKHOLDERS' EQUITY

*T*he stockholders' equity section of the balance sheet shows the investment of owners in the assets of a company and their equity interest in those assets. Stockholders have a residual claim to the assets; it is honored only after creditors' interests have been satisfied.

There are two basic components of stockholders' equity: (1) invested or paid-in capital and (2) retained earnings. Paid-in capital is the amount invested by the stockholders of the company; retained earnings is the amount of profits that have been retained by the company since its inception, after dividend distributions to stockholders. Exhibit 16–1 presents the balance sheet for Southwest Airlines Co., from its 1994 annual report. The stockholders' (also called shareholders' or shareowners') equity section is the final section of the balance sheet.

EXHIBIT 16–1
Southwest Airlines Co., Consolidated Balance Sheet

	December 31,	
	1994	1993
Assets		
Current assets:		
Cash and cash equivalents	$ 174,538	$ 295,571
Accounts receivable	75,692	70,484
Inventories of parts and supplies, at cost	37,565	31,707
Deferred income taxes (Note 11)	9,822	10,475
Prepaid expenses and other current assets	17,281	23,787
Total current assets	314,898	432,024
Property and equipment, at cost (Notes 3, 4, and 7):		
Flight equipment	2,564,551	2,257,809
Ground property and equipment	384,501	329,605
Deposits on flight equipment purchase contracts	393,749	242,230
	3,342,801	2,829,644
Less allowance for depreciation	837,838	688,280
	2,504,963	2,141,364
Other assets	3,210	2,649
	$2,823,071	$2,576,037
Liabilities and Stockholders' Equity		
Current liabilities:		
Accounts payable	$ 117,599	$ 94,040
Accrued liabilities (Note 5)	288,979	265,333
Air traffic liability	106,139	96,146
Income taxes payable	—	7,025
Current maturities of long-term debt	9,553	16,068
Total current liabilities	522,270	478,612
Long-term debt less current maturities (Note 6)	583,071	639,136
Deferred income taxes (Note 11)	232,850	183,616
Deferred gains from sale and leaseback of aircraft	217,677	199,362
Other deferred liabilities	28,497	21,292
Commitments and contingencies (Notes 4, 7, and 11)		
Stockholders' equity (Notes 8 and 9):		
Common stock, $1.00 par value: 500,000,000 shares authorized; 143,255,795 shares issued and outstanding in 1994 and 142,756,308 shares in 1993	143,256	142,756
Capital in excess of par value	151,746	141,168
Retained earnings	943,704	770,095
Total stockholders' equity	1,238,706	1,054,019
	$2,823,071	$2,576,037

Sources of Paid-in Capital

The primary source of paid-in capital is the issuance of shares of common stock and preferred stock. A corporation's charter indicates the number of shares of stock authorized for issue in each class of stock. The number of shares issued is the total number sold by the company since its inception. The number of shares outstanding is the number of shares currently held by stockholders. In Exhibit 16–1, Southwest Airlines Co. had 500,000,000 shares authorized and 143,255,795 shares issued and outstanding on December 31, 1994.

Common Stock

Common stock, the basic ownership equity of a corporation, is evidenced by a stock certificate issued by the company. Common stockholders all have the same rights and privileges:

1. The right to elect the members of the board of directors of the company.

2. The right to share in earnings.

3. The right to purchase additional shares of new issues of stock in the same proportion as they presently hold (called the preemptive right).

4. The right to a proportionate share in assets upon liquidation of the company.

Companies sometimes issue more than one class of common stock. The classes are distinguished by differences in dividend preferences and/or voting rights. Exhibit 16–2, from the 1995 annual report of Helene Curtis Industries, Inc., indicates that the company has issued two classes of common stock.

This note to the financial statement details how the two classes differ in voting rights and the amount of dividends per share:

6. Common Stock and Stock Plans

At February 28, 1995, 5,000,000 shares of $.50 par value Preferred Stock were authorized and unissued, and 15,000,000 shares each of $.50 par

EXHIBIT 16–2
Helene Curtis Industries, Inc., and Subsidiaries,
Excerpt from Consolidated Balance Sheet

	As of February 28,	
	1995	1994
• • •		
Stockholders' equity:		
Common Stock, issued 7,933,611 shares (1995)		
and 7,921,471 shares (1994)	$ 3,967	$ 3,96
Class B Common Stock, issued 3,060,529 shares		
(1995) and 3,072,669 shares (1994)	1,530	1,53
Capital in excess of par value	42,027	40,54
Retained earnings	177,997	161,04
Currency translation adjustment	5,539	1,23
Treasury Stock (Common), 1,123,990 shares (1995)		
and 1,114,031 shares (1994), at cost	(10,642)	(8,86)
Total stockholders' equity	$220,418	$199,44

value Common Stock and $.50 par value Class B Common Stock were authorized. In April 1995, the Board of Directors recommended, subject to stockholders' approval at the 1995 Annual Meeting, an amendment to the Company's Certificate of Incorporation to increase the number of authorized shares of Common Stock to 30,000,000.

The Class B Common Stock is identical to the Common Stock, except that it has ten-times greater voting power but lesser dividend rights per share than the Common Stock. While transfer of the Class B Common Stock is restricted, the Class B Common Stock is convertible at no cost into Common Stock on a share-for-share basis; under certain conditions, all outstanding shares of the Class B Common Stock must be converted.

Most major corporations report the proceeds of the issuance of common stock in two accounts: (1) the par value account and (2) the paid-in capital account. Par value (sometimes called "legal capital") is the minimum contribution required by law from stockholders. It establishes the maximum responsibility of a stockholder should the company become insolvent. Exhibit 16–1 reveals that the par value of Southwest Airlines common stock is $1.00 per share. Note that any excess of the proceeds over the par value is presented in an account titled Capital in Excess of Par. Sometimes this account is called Additional Paid-in Capital or Paid-in Capital in Excess of Par.

It is possible for a stockholder to pay less than par value for his or her shares of stock. In accounting terminology, the stock was then sold at a discount. If a company becomes insolvent, the creditors can force the original stockholders to pay to the company the amount of the discount on their shares of stock. Thus, the purchasers of stock issued at a discount are contingently liable to creditors of the company. To avoid this situation, many companies use a low par value, such as $1, when initially selling their stock. In addition, many states allow companies to issue stock with no par value, avoiding the sale of stock at a discount. No-par-value stock is reported in the balance sheet at its total issue price, without any separate Paid-in Capital in Excess of Par account. Exhibit 16–3, from the 1994 annual report of Wm. Wrigley Jr. Company, makers of chewing gum, shows that the company has two classes of no-par-value stock.

Many states that allow the issuance of no-par stock still adhere to the concept of "legal capital" in that they require or permit the company to designate part of the proceeds from the sale of stock as stated or legal capital. Assignment of a stated value makes no-par stock identical to par-value stock for accounting purposes.

Other Issuances of Common Stock Affecting Stockholders' Equity

A corporation might issue stock in exchange for assets such as buildings, machinery, or land. In such instances, the assets received are recorded on the company's books at their fair market value. A corresponding increase in stockholders' equity results from the issuance of the stock.

In other instances, stock can be issued to employees under an employee stock ownership plan (ESOP). ESOPs vary from company to company; however, in many plans, a trustee borrows money from a bank or other

EXHIBIT 16–3
Wm. Wrigley Jr. Company and Associated Companies,
Excerpt from Consolidated Balance Sheet

	As of December 31,	
	1994	1993
• • •		
Stockholders' equity:		
Preferred stock—no par value		
Authorized: 20,000 shares		
Issued: None		
Common stock—no par value		
Common stock		
Authorized: 400,000 shares		
Issued: 1994—91,326 shares; 1993—90,589		
shares	$ 12,177	12,078
Class B common stock—convertible		
Authorized: 80,000 shares		
Issued and outstanding: 1994—25,075 shares;		
1993—25,812 shares	3,343	3,442
Additional paid-in capital	1,781	1,467
Retained earnings	685,850	564,640
Foreign currency translation adjustment	(13,502)	(24,757)
Unrealized holding gains on marketable equity		
securities	7,855	18,312
Common Stock in treasury, at cost		
(1994—192 shares; 1993—0 shares)	(9,034)	—
Total stockholders' equity	$688,470	575,182

financial institution and uses the proceeds to purchase shares of stock for the employees.

Stock might also be issued to key employees participating in a stock award (option) plan. A stock option plan is a form of compensation that gives these employees, over an extended period of time, the right to exercise stock options and purchase common stock at a stipulated price.

Preferred Stock

Preferred stockholders are normally not entitled to vote; instead, they receive other rights or privileges not given to common stockholders. The rights or privileges attached to preferred stock vary. They include preference as to dividends and preference as to assets upon liquidation. Based on market conditions, preferred stock might also have some of the following features: cumulative dividends; participation in additional dividends; callable under certain conditions; conversion to other securities; or, redeemable. Each of these features is discussed below.

Preference as to Dividends. The dividend on preferred stock is expressed as a percentage of par or stated value. For example, a 9 percent $100 par value preferred stock pays a dividend of $9 per share. (No-par-value stock has a dividend of a set dollar amount.) The dividend preference entitles the preferred stockholder to a dividend payment before any dividends can be paid to the common stockholders. This right ensures that, should a dividend be declared, the preferred stockholders will be paid first.

Preference as to Assets upon Liquidation. If a company is liquidated, preferred stockholders normally have a preference over common stockholders as to the distribution of assets. For this reason, preferred stock has a *liquidation value*—an amount payable to the preferred stockholders, upon liquidation of the company, before any payment is made to the common stockholders but after payments are made to creditors. The preference is usually stated as a dollar amount or as a percentage of par or stated value.

Cumulative Dividends. If preferred stock is cumulative with respect to dividends, the accumulated amount of any undeclared dividends from prior years must be paid before any dividends can be declared and paid to common stockholders. Undeclared cumulative dividends from prior periods are also referred to as dividends in arrears or simply arrearages. These arrearages are not liabilities until they are formally declared by the board of directors. Normally, they are disclosed in the notes to the financial statements.

Participative Feature. In some cases, preferred stockholders receive dividends above the preferential rate. Specifically, after both the common and preferred stockholders have received their respective dividends, any remaining share of the total dividends is distributed between common and preferred shareholders in a specified manner, as described in the stock contract. Participating preferred stock is rare.

Callable Under Certain Conditions. Some issuances of preferred stock are callable—the company can redeem them at a stipulated price at its option. The call price and specified conditions for calling the stock are stated in the stock contract. The call price is usually somewhat higher than the issuance price. This has the effect of establishing an upper limit on the market price of the company's stock.

Convertible to Other Securities. Convertible preferred stock can be exchanged for common stock at a predetermined price (or ratio) at the option of the stockholder. Convertible preferred stock allows a preferred stockholder to become a common stockholder and participate without limitation in the profits and dividends of the company.

Exhibit 16–4 is from the 1995 annual report of Quaker Oats Company. The company has issued shares of preferred stock with a liquidating preference of $78 per share. The stock is also cumulative and convertible.

Redeemable. Redeemable preferred stock requires (1) mandatory redemption of the stock by the company on a specified date at a specific price, or (2) at the option of the holder (as opposed to being callable at the option of the issuer), the right to redeem the shares at a specified date and price. Exhibit 16–5, excerpted from the 1994 annual report of Valero Energy Corporation, indicates that the company has issued redeemable preferred stock.

In a note to the financial statement, the company made this disclosure:

7. REDEEMABLE PREFERRED STOCK

Energy is required to redeem and, commencing in 1986, has redeemed in December of each year its Cumulative Preferred Stock, $8.50 Series A ("Series A Preferred Stock"), at $100 per share at the rate of 11,500 shares annually ($1,150,000 per year). The redemption requirement for the Series A Preferred Stock for each of the five years following December 31, 1994 is also $1,150,000 per year. Energy also has the option to redeem

EXHIBIT 16–4
Quaker Oats Company and Subsidiaries, Excerpt from
Consolidated Balance Sheet

Dollars in Millions	June 30,		
	1995	1994	1993
Liabilities and Shareholders' Equity			
Current liabilities:			
Short-term debt	$ 510.1	$ 211.3	$ 128.0
Current portion of long-term debt	38.8	45.4	48.9
Trade accounts payable	423.8	406.3	391.6
Accrued payroll, pension and bonus	123.8	158.9	161.3
Accrued advertising and merchandising	165.0	149.6	130.6
Income taxes payable	180.1	40.6	33.7
Other accrued liabilities	371.3	247.0	211.0
Total current liabilities	1,812.9	1,259.1	1,105.1
Long-term debt	1,103.1	759.5	632.6
Other liabilities	530.0	481.4	426.2
Deferred income taxes	233.3	82.2	89.5
Preferred stock, series B, no par value, authorized 1,750,000 shares; issued 1,282,051 of $5.46 cumulative convertible shares (liquidating preference of $78 per share)	100.0	100.0	100.0
Deferred compensation	(74.9)	(80.8)	(85.9)
Treasury preferred stock, at cost, 81,194 shares, 47,817 shares and 34,447 shares, respectively	(6.3)	(3.9)	(2.7)
Common shareholders' equity:			
Common stock, $5 par value, authorized 400 million, 200 million and 200 million shares, respectively	840.0	420.0	420.0
Reinvested earnings	1,499.3	1,273.6	1,190.1
Cumulative translation adjustment	(61.4)	(75.4)	(65.4)
Deferred compensation	(132.2)	(143.5)	(154.0)
Treasury common stock, at cost	(1,016.9)	(1,028.9)	(839.6)
Total common shareholders' equity	1,128.8	445.8	551.1
Total liabilities and shareholders' equity	$ 4,826.9	$ 3,043.3	$2,815.9

EXHIBIT 16–5
Valero Energy Corporation and Subsidiaries, Excerpt from
Consolidated Balance Sheet

	December 31,	
	1994	1993
Liabilities and Stockholders' Equity		
Current liabilities:		
Current maturities of long-term debt	$ 62,230	$ 28,737
Accounts payable	341,694	90,994
Accrued interest	19,693	5,063
Other accrued expenses	37,150	28,233
	460,767	153,027
Long-Term Debt, less current maturities	1,021,820	485,621
Deferred Income Taxes	264,236	232,564
Deferred Credits and Other Liabilities	59,405	37,128
Redeemable Preferred Stock, Series A, issued 1,150,000 shares, outstanding 126,500 (1994) and 138,000 (1993) shares	12,650	13,800
Common stock and other stockholders' equity:		
Preferred stock, $1 par value—20,000,000 shares authorized including redeemable preferred shares:		
$3.125 Convertible Preferred Stock, issued and outstanding 3,450,000 (1994) and -0- (1993) shares ($172,500 aggregate involuntary liquidation value)	3,450	—
Common stock, $1 par value—$75,000,000 shares authorized; issued 43,463,869 (1994) and 43,391,685 (1993) shares	43,464	43,392
Additional paid-in capital	536,613	371,303
Unearned Valero Employees' Stock Ownership Plan Compensation	(13,706)	(15,958)
Retained earnings	442,659	446,931
Treasury stock, -0- (1994) and 145,119 (1993) common shares, at cost	—	(3,371)
	1,012,480	842,297
	$2,831,358	$1,764,437

shares of the Series A Preferred Stock at any time at $105 per share until November 30, 1995, with such amount being reduced by $.50 per share each year thereafter to $100 per share.

In the event of an involuntary liquidation, the holders of the outstanding Series A Preferred Stock would be entitled, after the payment of all debts, to $100 per share, plus any accrued and unpaid dividends. In the event of a voluntary liquidation, the holders of the outstanding Series A Preferred Stock would be entitled to $100 per share, any applicable premium Energy would have had to pay if it had elected to redeem the Series A Preferred Stock at that time and any accrued and unpaid dividends. In the event dividends on the Series A Preferred Stock are six or more quarters in arrears, holders voting as a class with holders of any other series of preferred stock also in arrears may vote to elect two directors. No arrearages currently exist.

Treasury Stock

The 1994 balance sheet of Avon Products, Inc., presented as Exhibit 16–6, shows 17,589,639 shares of treasury stock in the amount of $543,500,000. Treasury stock is stock that has been previously issued and then reacquired by the company. Companies reacquire their stock for many reasons, including: to fulfill the requirements of employee stock option plans; to exchange the shares for convertible securities; and to use in mergers and acquisitions. Treasury stock is sometimes acquired to prevent a takeover attempt by another company.

Treasury stock is never acquired for speculation. Speculation in a company's own stock is prohibited by the Securities and Exchange Commission. Because of this prohibition, the accounting profession does not permit companies to report the results of treasury stock transactions as gains or losses on their income statements; instead, these results are recorded as adjustments to paid-in capital or retained earnings. These "gains" and "losses" occur when the company sells shares of treasury stock for a price that differs from the purchase price of the treasury shares.

The purchase of treasury stock reduces total stockholders' equity because the number of shares outstanding and the investment of owners are reduced. The company normally uses cash to purchase the shares, which reduces total assets as well.

EXHIBIT 16–6

Avon Products, Inc., Consolidated Balance Sheet

(In millions, except share data)	December 31,	
	1994	1993
Assets		
Current assets:		
Cash, including cash equivalents of $132.5 and $159.7	$ 214.8	$ 223.9
Accounts receivable (less allowance for doubtful accounts of $27.3 and $22.0)	373.7	306.0
Inventories	412.8	360.5
Prepaid expenses and other	149.0	135.9
Net assets of discontinued operations	—	18.8
Total current assets	1,150.3	1,045.1
Property, plant, and equipment at cost:		
Land	54.3	41.7
Buildings and improvements	531.5	495.1
Equipment	560.9	524.7
	1,146.7	1,061.5
Less accumulated depreciation	618.3	585.3
	528.4	476.2
Net assets of discontinued operations	—	136.2
Other assets	299.6	261.2
Total assets	$1,978.3	$1,918.7
Liabilities and Shareholders' Equity		
Current liabilities:		
Debt maturing within one year	$ 61.2	$ 70.4
Accounts payable	408.0	365.4
Accrued compensation	100.0	62.7
Other accrued liabilities	222.3	203.3
Sales and other taxes	95.7	94.9
Income taxes	253.8	225.3
Total current liabilities	1,141.0	1,022.0
Long-term debt	116.5	123.7
Employee benefit plans	366.6	295.1
Deferred income taxes	32.2	30.5
Other liabilities (including minority interest of $48.9 and $43.2)	136.4	133.4
Commitments and contingencies		
Shareholders' equity:		
Common stock, par value $.50—authorized: 200,000,000 shares; issued 86,663,874 and 86,528,692 shares	43.3	43.3
Additional paid-in capital	660.5	652.3
Retained earnings	212.4	150.6
Translation adjustments	(187.1)	(175.3)
Treasury stock, at cost—17,589,639 and 14,430,073	(543.5)	(356.9)
Total shareholders' equity	185.6	314.0
Total liabilities and shareholders' equity	$1,978.3	$1,918.7

Treasury stock is a contra stockholders' equity account, not an asset. For this reason, Avon Products, Inc. has subtracted the cost of the treasury stock in arriving at total stockholders' equity (see Exhibit 16–6). Treasury stock does not carry voting privileges or receive cash dividends.

Donated Capital

Donated capital arises from donations to the company, usually by a governmental unit. For example, a city might donate a land site as an inducement to a company to locate in that city. The land would appear on the balance sheet of the company at its fair market value, and the account Donated Capital would appear in the stockholders' equity section of the balance sheet at that amount. Most often, the Donated Capital account is combined with other paid-in capital accounts when presented in published annual reports (See also Chapter 8).

Retained Earnings

Retained earnings is the portion of stockholders' equity representing assets in the company that were not distributed to stockholders as dividends. Retained earnings is increased by net income (which increases total net assets) and reduced by net losses and dividends paid to stockholders (which decreases total net assets). Retained earnings can also be affected by appropriations and prior-period adjustments. (These items are discussed later in the chapter.) Exhibit 16–7 is from the 1995 annual report of Interstate Bakeries Corporation. The company had a deficit for 1994 and 1993, even though it showed a profit for the preceding three years.

Dividends

Normally, dividend distributions are in cash, but sometimes other assets, such as marketable securities or inventories, are disbursed. The company's

EXHIBIT 16–7

Interstate Bakeries Corporation, Consolidated Balance Sheet and Consolidated Statement of Income

(In Thousands)	June 3, 1995	May 28, 1994
Assets		
Current assets:		
Cash and cash equivalents	$ 3,726	$ 5,046
Accounts receivable, less allowance for doubtful accounts of $1,792,000 ($1,645,000 in 1994)	75,184	71,734
Inventories	24,207	21,020
Other current assets	17,232	17,106
Total current assets	120,349	114,906
Property and equipment:		
Land and buildings	99,609	91,540
Machinery and equipment	246,800	224,922
	346,409	316,462
Less accumulated depreciation	(123,440)	(101,022)
Net property and equipment	222,969	215,440
Excess of purchase cost over net assets acquired	248,076	240,249
Other assets	7,047	4,196
	$ 598,441	$ 574,791
Liabilities and Stockholders' Equity		
Current liabilities:		
Long-term debt payable within one year	$ 1,030	$ 1,263
Accounts payable	48,979	47,848
Accrued expenses	59,145	58,182
Total current liabilities	109,154	107,293
Long-term debt:		
Related party	79,000	79,000
Other	133,205	122,235
Other liabilities	45,461	43,409
Deferred income taxes	33,584	35,413
Total long-term liabilities	291,250	280,057
Stockholders' equity:		
Preferred stock, par value $.01 per share: authorized—1,000,000 shares; issued—none	—	—
Common stock, par value $.01 per share: authorized—40,000,000 shares; issued—21,056,000 shares (21,050,000 in 1994)	211	211
Additional paid-in capital	261,065	261,064
Accumulated deficit	(42,213)	(53,091)
Treasury stock, at cost—1,421,000 shares (1,400,000 in 1994)	(21,026)	(20,743)
Total stockholders' equity	198,037	187,441
	$ 598,441	$ 574,791

EXHIBIT 16–7 *(Continued)*

(In Thousands, Except Per Share Data)	53 Weeks Ended June 3, 1995	52 Weeks Ended May 28, 1994	52 Weeks Ended May 29, 1993
Net sales	$1,222,779	$1,142,684	$1,165,588
Cost of products sold	630,884	581,226	590,004
Selling, delivery and administrative expenses	501,008	473,607	472,602
Other charges	—	9,400	—
Depreciation and amortization	33,594	31,568	31,638
	1,165,486	1,095,801	1,094,244
Operating income	57,293	46,883	71,344
Other income	(104)	(144)	(53)
Interest expense	17,745	14,745	17,388
	17,641	14,601	17,335
Income before income taxes	39,652	32,282	54,009
Provision for income taxes	18,955	16,528	23,225
Income before cumulative effect of accounting change	20,697	15,754	30,784
Cumulative effect of change in accounting forpostretirement benefits other than pensions	—	—	(14,121)
Net income	$ 20,697	$ 15,754	$ 16,663
Per share:			
Income before cumulative effect of accounting change	$ 1.05	$ .78	$ 1.46
Cumulative effect of accounting change	—	—	(.67)
Net income	$ 1.05	$ .78	$ .79

board of directors is usually responsible for assessing the financial desirability of the amount and timing of a dividend payment. For this reason, company dividend policies vary. Some well-established companies pay a stable or increasing dividend. Growth companies often pay no dividends; instead, they reinvest profits to finance growth or expansion.

Three dates are important in accounting for dividends:

1. *The declaration date*—the date when a dividend is formally declared by the board of directors. This is also the date when the date of record (a past date) and the payment date (a future date) are selected.

2. *The date of record*—owners of the company's stock as of this date are entitled to the dividend.

3. *The payment date*—the date the dividend payment is sent to stockholders of record.

Unpaid dividends are current liabilities if a balance sheet is prepared between the declaration date and the date of payment. All dividends that distribute assets reduce a company's retained earnings and total stockholders' equity.

Stock Dividends

A company might decide that, instead of paying a cash dividend to stockholders, it will preserve its cash for some objective, such as plant expansion. For this reason, a company might alternately decide to distribute additional shares of its own stock to its stockholders, based on the number of shares held by each stockholder. For example, if a stockholder owns 1,000 shares of stock and a 15 percent stock dividend is declared, the holder receives 150 additional shares. Although the total number of shares outstanding increases, the percentage of ownership of each stockholder is unchanged. Assume that the total number of shares of stock outstanding before the stock dividend was 100,000 shares. The company's board of directors now elects to issue a 15 percent stock dividend and issues 15,000 additional shares. A stockholder owning 1,000 shares has an ownership interest of 1 percent (1,000 shares divided by 100,000 shares) immediately prior to the distribution of the stock. After the 15 percent stock dividend, the total number of shares outstanding is 115,000, and the number held by the stockholder is 1,150. The ownership interest is still 1 percent (1,150 shares divided by 115,000 shares). The total market value of the company's stock is not altered, but the market value per share should decrease proportionately because of the increase in the number of shares. If the market value per share was $230 before the dividend, it should decrease to $200 immediately after the dividend:

Number of Shares × Market Price Per Share = Total Market Value

Before dividend

100,000 shares   × $230   = $23,000,000

After dividend

115,000 shares   × $200   = $23,000,000

Theoretically, the market value of the stock should decrease in direct proportion to the number of shares issued. However, because of other non-company-specific reasons, this is not always the case.

Cash dividends reduce both the company's total assets and its total stockholders' equity. However, because a stock dividend is not a transfer of assets but a distribution of stock, total assets and total stockholders' equity are unaffected. Instead, the company increases its common stock account and reduces retained earnings for the amount of the stock dividend. (Some states allow companies to reduce a paid-in capital account rather than retained earnings.)

The consolidated statements of shareholders' equity for Archer Daniels Midland Company appear in Exhibit 16–8. The company has issued a 5 percent stock dividend for the past three years. Archer Daniels Midland is in the business of procuring, transporting, storing, processing, and merchandising agricultural commodities.

Stock Splits

The board of directors may decide to reduce the market value of a company's stock by splitting the stock. A stock split increases the number of

EXHIBIT 16–8
Archer Daniels Midland Company, Consolidated
Statement of Shareholders' Equity

(In thousands)	Common Stock		Reinvested Earnings
	Shares	Amount	
Balance July 1, 1991	310,924	$2,637,129	$1,285,166
Net earnings			503,757
Cash dividends paid—$.09 per share			(30,789)
Acquisitions	2,636	72,764	
Treasury stock purchases	(3,329)	(85,889)	
5% stock dividend—September 1992	15,547	389,996	(389,996)
Foreign currency translation			93,879
Other	702	16,600	(264)
Balance June 30, 1992	326,480	3,030,600	1,461,753
Net earnings			567,527
Cash dividends paid—$.09 per share			(32,266)
Treasury stock purchases	(1,531)	(35,429)	
5% stock dividend—September 1993	16,300	348,927	(348,927)
Foreign currency translation			(131,153)
Other	1,050	22,524	(305)
Balance June 30, 1993	342,299	3,366,622	1,516,629
Net earnings			484,069
Cash dividends paid—$.09 per share			(32,586)
Acquisitions	19	422	
Treasury stock purchases	(15,597)	(355,226)	
5% stock dividend—declared July 1994	16,364	381,707	(381,707)
Foreign currency translation			43,363
Other	554	22,430	(302)
Balance June 30, 1994	343,639	$3,415,955	$1,629,466

shares outstanding by proportionately reducing the par or stated value of each share. The company calls in all the outstanding shares of stock and then issues new shares based on a stock multiple used for the split and the number of shares previously outstanding. The stock multiple is also called an exchange ratio.

For example, if a company splits its 20,000 outstanding shares of $20 par-value stock 2 for 1, the number of outstanding shares is doubled to 40,000, and each share's par value is halved to $10. The stock split has no effect on total stockholders' equity. In fact, the split does not affect the amount of any stockholders' equity account. The total par value of the company is still $400,000 (40,000 shares × $10), and each stockholder now has twice the number of shares held prior to the split. Only the change in the par or stated value and the call and issuance of the new shares of stock are reflected in the company's stockholder records. Also, the company will change the description of its stock in its balance sheet to indicate the new par or stated value and number of shares issued and outstanding. A stock split reduces the market value of the stock and makes it more appealing to a wider range of potential investors.

An illustration of a disclosure related to a stock split is presented in Exhibit 16–9, an excerpt from the 1995 annual report of Brown-Forman Corporation, a diversified producer and marketer of fine-quality consumer products. The company's consolidated statement of stockholders' equity indicates that, in fiscal year 1994, the company's common stock split 3 for 1.

Statement of Retained Earnings

Retained earnings is important because it represents the amount of earnings reinvested in a company to foster future growth. It also represents dividend distributions given up in the past in the hopes of greater dividend distributions in the future. Therefore, because retained earnings is a significant part of the stockholders' equity section of a balance sheet, companies prepare statements of retained earnings that disclose the changes in the account during the period. Exhibit 16–10 is a statement of retained earnings from the 1994 annual report of Pinnacle West Capital Corporation, a Phoenix-based holding company.

EXHIBIT 16–9
Brown-Forman Corporation, Consolidated
Statement of Stockholders' Equity

For the Years Ended April 30, 1995, 1994, and 1993 (Expressed in thousands, except share amounts)

	Total	Preferred Stock
Balance, April 30, 1992	$ 735,158	$11,779
Net income	156,190	
Cash dividends		
Preferred, per share $.40	(471)	
Common, per share $.86	(71,091)	
Foreign currency translation adjustment	(1,681)	
Other	18	
Balance, April 30, 1993	818,123	11,779
Net income	128,527	
Cash dividends		
Preferred, per share $.40	(471)	
Common, per share $.93	(73,367)	
Acquisition of treasury stock (Class A, 2,734,452 shares and Class B, 10,933,518 shares	(407,659)	
Retirement of treasury stock (Class A, 7,197,615 shares and Class B, 39,984,798 shares)	—	
Issuance of shares in connection with 3-for-1 stock split	—	
Foreign currency translation adjustment	(1,663)	
Other	197	
Balance, April 30, 1994	463,687	11,779
Net income	148,629	
Cash dividends		
Preferred, per share $.40	(471)	
Common, per share $.97	(66,885)	
Foreign currency translation adjustment	926	
Other	(39)	
Balance, April 30, 1995	$ 545,847	$11,779

| Common Stock | | Capital in | | Cumulative | |
Class A	Class B	Excess of Par Value	Retained Earnings	Translation Adjustment	Treasury Stock
$1,809	$ 4,000	$ 89,717	$ 972,833	$ (740)	$(344,240)
			156,190		
			(471)		
			(71,091)		
				(1,681)	
		18			
1,809	4,000	89,735	1,057,461	(2,421)	(344,240)
			128,527		
			(471)		
			(73,367)		
					(407,659)
(360)	(1,999)	(89,822)	(659,718)		751,899
2,899	4,000		(6,899)		
				(1,663)	
		87	110		
4,348	6,001	—	445,643	(4,084)	—
			148,629		
			(471)		
			(66,885)		
				926	
			(39)		
$4,348	$ 6,001	$ —	$ 526,877	$(3,158)	$ —

EXHIBIT 16–10
Pinnacle West Capital Corporation, Consolidated
Statements of Retained Earnings

(Thousands of dollars)	Year Ended December 31,		
	1994	1993	1992
Retained earnings (deficit) at beginning of year	$ 6,717	$(165,047)	$(321,487)
Net income	200,619	189,230	156,440
Common stock dividends	(72,115)	(17,466)	—
Retained earnings (deficit) at end of year	$135,221	$ 6,717	$(165,047)

Restrictions and Appropriations of Retained Earnings

Some companies have contingencies that may require a substantial amount of assets at a future date. These companies might decide to restrict the payment of dividends and, instead, accumulate assets to meet the contingencies. Examples of these types of contingencies include compliance with debt covenants, possible losses from lawsuits, and conservation of cash while completing a major plant expansion. Companies disclose the restriction of dividends in a footnote or as an appropriation of retained earnings in the body of the financial statements.

The effect of an appropriation is that a company cannot pay out dividends equal to its total balance in retained earnings. Total retained earnings does not change but is separated into two components: (1) the portion appropriated and (2) the portion not appropriated. For example, assume that a company has $10,000,000 in retained earnings and wishes to restrict dividend payments while expanding one of its plants. The cost of the plant is estimated to be $3,500,000 and the company appropriates $3,500,000 of retained earnings. After the appropriation, retained earnings will appear in the stockholders' equity section of the balance sheet as follows:

Retained Earnings:		
Unappropriated	$6,500,000	
Appropriated for Plant Expansion	3,500,000	$10,000,000

Many states limit the amount of dividend payments that can be paid to stockholders when a company holds treasury stock. An amount of retained earnings equal to the balance that the company holds as treasury stock is restricted, and only the excess over this amount is available for paying dividends.

Cash is not set aside by an appropriation of retained earnings. No asset account is affected; the appropriation represents nothing more than a paper procedure to segregate a portion of owners' property rights. In practice, restrictions on retained earnings are normally disclosed in the notes to the financial statements rather than by a formal appropriation of retained earnings.

Prior-Period Adjustments

Retained earnings may be adjusted for errors made in recording revenues and expenses. If these errors are discovered in the period in which they occur, an adjustment is made to correct the error prior to disseminating the financial statements. However, in some cases, an error might not be detected until a subsequent period, in which case the company would have issued erroneous financial statements for the prior period. Corrections of this type of error is called a prior-period adjustment. The adjustment does not appear in the income statement for the prior period in which the error was discovered; instead, it is reported as an adjustment to the beginning balance of retained earnings in the current period.

Other Items Appearing in the Stockholders' Equity Section of the Balance Sheet

In addition to the items previously discussed, five other items can be found in many, but not all, company annual reports. These items are required to be reported as either an addition or a subtraction, in arriving at total stockholders' equity. These adjustments are made for: (1) cumulative translation adjustments, (2) net unrealized holding gains and losses and adjustments for a company's pension plans, (3) employee stock option plans (ESOP), and (4) guarantees of unearned and deferred compensation relating to employee stock award (option) plans.

We discuss the first two adjustments in some detail because they are more commonly found in the annual reports of large companies. Because of the complexity surrounding the accounting for the other three adjustments, we provide only the disclosure relating to each item and a limited discussion.

Cumulative Translation Adjustments

Consolidated financial statements are the financial statements of a parent company and its subsidiary companies, combined as if they were a single economic entity (see Chapter 3). Quite often, consolidated statements include the financial results of foreign subsidiaries. Prior to combining the financial statements of a foreign subsidiary with those of its domestic parent, the financial statements of the subsidiary must be translated into U.S. dollars.

In the process of translating the accounts of a foreign subsidiary, a difference will normally occur between the total of the asset account balances and the total of the equity account balances (both liabilities and stockholders' equity) of the subsidiary. This difference is caused by two interrelated factors: (1) the exchange rate between two currencies is not stable over time, and (2) current accounting practice calls for some of a company's accounts to be translated at current exchange rates and for others to be translated at historical exchange rates. The mechanics are not important here. The point is that a difference will occur that requires an adjustment to balance the accounts of the foreign subsidiary. This difference will be either a negative (loss) or a positive (gain) amount. The adjustment (loss or gain) is needed to make the total assets equal total liabilities and stockholders' equity on the balance sheet of the subsidiary. The cumulative translation adjustment (the positive or negative amount accumulated over the years) is reported in the stockholders' equity section of the balance sheet.

EXHIBIT 16–11
Bristol-Meyers Squibb Company, Excerpt from
Consolidated Balance Sheet

	December 31,		
(Dollars in Millions)	1994	1993	1992
Stockholders' equity:			
Preferred stock, $2 convertible series: Authorized 10 million shares; issued and outstanding 21,857 in 1994, 25,798 in 1993 and 28,517 in 1992, liquidation value of $50 per share	$ —	$ —	$ —
Common stock, par value of $.10 per share: Authorized 1.5 billion shares; issued 540,173,669 in 1994, 532,688,458 in 1993 and 532,673,413 in 1992	54	53	53
Capital in excess of par value of stock	397	353	435
Cumulative translation adjustments	(301)	(332)	(208)
Retained earnings	7,600	7,243	6,769
	7,750	7,317	7,049
Less cost of treasury stock—32,887,848 common shares in 1994, 20,782,281 in 1993 and 14,689,052 in 1992	2,046	1,377	1,029
Total stockholders' equity	5,704	5,940	6,020
	$12,910	$12,101	$10,804

Referring to Exhibit 16–11, we see that Bristol-Meyers Squibb Company reported cumulative translation adjustments of $301,000,000, $332,000,000, and $208,000,000 in years 1994, 1993, and 1992, respectively.

The company discussed the adjustment in the following note to the financial statements:

NOTE 5 FOREIGN CURRENCY TRANSLATION

Cumulative translation adjustments, which represent the effect of translating assets and liabilities of the company's non-U.S. entities, except those in highly inflationary economies, were:

Dollars in Millions	1994	1993	1992
Balance, January 1	$332	$208	$ 90
Effect of balance sheet translations:			
Amount	(43)	141	151
Tax effect	12	(17)	(33)
Balance, December 31	$301	$332	$208

Included in net earnings were (losses) gains resulting from foreign currency transactions and translation adjustments related to non-U.S. entities operating in highly inflationary economies of $(44) million, $21 million and $(63) million in 1994, 1993 and 1992, respectively.

The reason for reporting the gain or loss as a separate component of stockholders' equity, rather than as a component of income, is that the amount can have a substantial impact on net income when there are extreme movements in exchange rates unrelated to company operations. Also, the gains and losses do not represent real changes in asset values because they are unrealized and may reverse in future periods.

Net Unrealized Holding Gains or Losses

Another item that might appear as a separate component in the stockholders' equity section is the net unrealized holding gains or losses on certain securities. This happens when the market value of available-for-sale debt or equity securities differs from their cost. (Available-for-sale securities are discussed in Chapters 4 and 7.) That is, the unrealized gains or losses relate to changes in the fair value of these securities, not to their sale. Changes in fair value are not reported as part of earnings until these securities are sold. A company will report a net unrealized holding gain (or loss) on the face of its balance sheet in the stockholders' equity section after comparing the cost and fair value of securities in this investment category. The object is to defer these unrealized gains and losses until the securities are sold. Exhibit 16–12 shows the disclosure of net unrealized holding gains on the balance sheet of Wm. Wrigley Jr. Company's 1994 annual report.

The company explained its policy relating to these securities in this note to the financial statements:

ACCOUNTING POLICIES AND NOTES TO CONSOLIDATED FINANCIAL STATEMENTS

Wm. Wrigley Jr. Company and Associated Companies

• • •

Investments in Debt & Equity Securities

Effective December 31, 1993, the Company adopted Statement of Financial Accounting Standards (SFAS) No. 115 "Accounting for Certain Investments in Debt and Equity Securities". The Company's investments in debt securities, which typically mature in one year or less, are held to maturity and valued at amortized cost, which approximates fair value. The aggregate fair values at December 31, 1994 and December 31, 1993 were, respectively, $69,287,000 and $82,881,000 for municipal securities, and $33,392,000 and $20,675,000 for other debt securities.

The Company's investments in marketable equity securities are held for an indefinite period. Application of SFAS No. 115 resulted in unrealized holding gains of $12,085,000 at December 31, 1994 and $28,171,000 at December 31, 1993. The aggregate fair value of the Company's marketable equity securities at December 31, 1994 and 1993 totaled $14,687,000 and $31,417,000 respectively. The unrealized holding gains, net of the related tax effect, added $7,855,000 and $18,312,000 to Stockholders' equity at December 31, 1994 and 1993, respectively. At the end of 1994, Section 170 (e)(5) of the U.S. Internal Revenue Code expired, greatly reducing the tax deductibility of appreciated securities contributed to private foundations. In anticipation of this change, a contribution of marketable equity securities having a fair value of $14,966,000 and an original cost of $624,000 was made to the Company's charitable foundation in 1994.

EXHIBIT 16–12
Wm. Wrigley Jr. Company and Associated Companies,
Excerpt from Consolidated Balance Sheet

	As of December 31,	
(In thousands of dollars and shares)	1994	1993
Liabilities and Stockholders' Equity		
Current liabilities:		
Accounts payable	$ 68,097	62,621
Accrued expenses	69,716	67,137
Dividends payable	16,269	11,640
Income and other taxes payable	55,178	17,127
Deferred income taxes—current	638	636
Total current liabilities	209,898	159,161
Deferred income taxes—noncurrent	15,760	22,716
Other noncurrent liabilities	64,706	58,265
Stockholders' equity:		
Preferred stock—no par value		
Authorized: 20,000 shares		
Issued: None		
Common stock—no par value		
Common stock		
Authorized: 400,000 shares		
Issued: 1994—91,326 shares; 1993—90,589		
shares	12,177	12,078
Class B common stock—convertible		
Authorized: 80,000 shares		
Issued and outstanding: 1994—25,075		
shares; 1993—25,812 shares	3,343	3,442
Additional paid-in capital	1,781	1,467
Retained earnings	685,850	564,640
Foreign currency translation adjustment	(13,502)	(24,757)
Unrealized holding gains on marketable equity		
securities	7,855	18,312
Common stock in treasury, at cost		
(1994—192 shares; 1993—0 shares)	(9,034)	—
Total stockholders' equity	688,470	575,182
Total liabilities and stockholders' equity	$978,834	815,324

EXHIBIT 16–13
State Street Boston Corporation, Excerpt from
Consolidated Statement of Condition

	December 31,	
(Dollars in thousands)	1994	1993
• • •		
Stockholders' equity—Notes H, I, J and Q:		
Preferred stock, no par: authorized 3,500,000; issued none		
Common stock, $1 par: authorized 112,000,000; issued 76,475,000 and 75,874,000	$ 76,475	$ 75,874
Surplus	30,468	19,253
Retained earnings	1,176,915	1,009,847
Net unrealized loss on available-for-sale securities	(52,568)	
Total stockholders' equity	$1,231,290	$1,104,974

Exhibit 16–13 is from the stockholders' equity section of the balance sheet of State Street Boston Corporation. The company had a net unrealized holding loss on available-for-sale securities in 1994.

Pension Plan Adjustment

Exhibit 16–14 is from the 1995 balance sheet of Standard Products Company. The shareholders' equity section displays an adjustment arising from the company's pension plan liability.

Unearned Compensation Relating to Stock Compensation Plans

Exhibit 16–15 contains an adjustment for unearned compensation relating to Colgate-Palmolive Company's stock option plan, as shown in its 1994 balance sheet. Unearned compensation relates to stock compensation plans that are used to pay and motivate employees.

EXHIBIT 16–14
Standard Products Company and Subsidiary Companies, Excerpt from Consolidated Balance Sheet

(Thousands of Dollars)	1995	1994
• • •		
Shareholders' equity:		
Serial preferred shares, without par value; authorized 6,000,000 voting shares and 6,000,000 non-voting shares, none issued	$ —	$ —
Common shares, par value $1 per share; authorized 50,000,000 shares, issued and outstanding 16,736,155 in 1995 and 16,674,016 in 1994	16,736	16,674
Paid-in capital	96,237	95,614
Retained earnings	151,492	142,871
Foreign currency translation adjustments	(496)	(10,359)
Minimum pension liability	(3,474)	(2,123)
Total shareholders' equity	$260,495	$242,677

EXHIBIT 16–15
Colgate-Palmolive Company, Excerpt from Consolidated Balance Sheet

(Dollars in Millions Except Per Share Amounts)	1994	1993
• • •		
Shareholders' equity:		
Preferred stock	$ 408.4	$ 414.3
Common stock, $1 par value (500,000,000 shares authorized, 183,213,295 shares issued)	183.2	183.2
Additional paid-in capital	1,020.4	1,000.9
Retained earnings	2,496.7	2,163.4
Cumulative translation adjustments	(439.3)	(372.9)
	3,669.4	3,388.9
Unearned compensation	(384.1)	(389.9)
Treasury stock, at cost	(1,462.4)	(1,124.0)
Total shareholders' equity	$ 1,822.9	$ 1,875.0

210

Adjustment Relating to ESOP Debt

The Stanley Works is a worldwide producer of tools, hardware, and specialty hardware for home improvement, consumer, industrial, and professional use. The company's 1994 annual report shows an account description relating to its guarantee of ESOP debt. Recall from the discussion earlier in this chapter that, in many cases, a trustee borrows funds from a financial institution to purchase stock for the company's employees. Normally, the company guarantees the liability of the ESOP. When the company does this, it records a liability and reduces stockholders' equity by an equal amount. As the ESOP makes payments on the debt that was guaranteed by

EXHIBIT 16–16
The Stanley Works and Subsidiaries, Excerpt from
Consolidated Balance Sheet

	December 31,	
(Millions of Dollars)	1994	1993

• • •

Shareholders' equity:		
Preferred stock, without par value:		
Authorized and unissued 10,000,000 shares		
Common stock, par value $2.50 per share:		
Authorized 110,000,000 shares;		
issued 46,171,705 shares in 1994 and 1993	$ 115.4	$ 115.4
Capital in excess of par value	70.1	73.1
Retained earnings	937.8	871.1
Foreign currency translation adjustment	(56.3)	(56.7)
ESOP debt	(253.7)	(261.5)
	813.3	741.4
Less: cost of common stock in treasury		
(1,722,330 shares in 1994 and 1,476,074		
shares in 1993)	69.1	60.5
Total shareholders' equity	$ 744.2	$ 680.9

the company, the liability is reduced and stockholders' equity is increased by reducing the ESOP guarantee appearing in the stockholders' equity section of the balance sheet. The Stanley Works stockholders' equity section from the 1994 report is reproduced in Exhibit 16–16.

Book Value per Share

The book value of a share of stock is a measure of the stockholders' equity of that share of stock in the assets of a corporation. Many corporations regularly report book value per share in their annual financial statements. If a corporation has only common stock, book value per share is simply the sum of common stock and paid-in capital and retained earnings, divided by the total number of shares of common stock outstanding. The divisor does not include treasury stock or unissued stock. If Western Company has 1,000 shares of $10 par value common stock, paid-in capital in excess of par of $20,000, and retained earnings of $45,000, then the book value per share is $75.00 ($10,000 + $20,000 + $45,000)/1,000 shares).

When a corporation issues both common and preferred stock, the book value of common stock is calculated by taking total stockholders' equity minus the equity of the preferred shareholders, divided by the number of common shares outstanding.

Most companies publish book value per share in their annual reports. Exhibit 16–17 is an excerpt from H. J. Heinz Company's eleven-year summary of operations and other related data, published in its 1995 annual report. Exhibit 16–18 shows the shareholders' equity section of Heinz's 1995 balance sheet.

The company's book value per common share for 1995 is $10.14. We can prove this figure by taking total shareholders' equity of $2,472,869,000, subtracting the amount for preferred stock ($358,000), and dividing the remainder ($2,472,511,000) by the number of shares of common stock outstanding at the end of 1995. The partial balance sheet shows that the number of shares of common stock issued at the end of 1995 is 287,401,000. Treasury shares are not outstanding and must be subtracted. Thus, the 43,724,933 treasury shares are subtracted from the total number

EXHIBIT 16–17
H. J. Heinz Company and Subsidiaries, Excerpt from
Summary of Operations and Other Related Data

(Dollars in thousands, except per share data)	1995	1994	1993	1992
Summary of operations:				
Sales	$8,086,794	$7,046,738	$7,103,374	$6,581,867
Cost of products sold	5,119,597	4,381,745	4,530,563	4,102,816
Interest expense	210,585	149,243	146,491	134,948
Provision for income taxes	346,982	319,442	185,838	346,050
Income before cumulative effect of accounting change	591,025	602,944	529,943	638,295
Cumulative effect of FAS No. 106 adoption	—	—	(133,630)	—
Net income	591,025	602,944	396,313	638,295
Income per common share before cumulative effect of accounting change	2.38	2.35	2.04	2.40
Cumulative effect of FAS No. 106 adoption	—	—	(0.51)	—
Net income per common share	2.38	2.35	1.53	2.40
Other related data:				
Dividends paid:				
Common	345,358	325,887	297,009	270,512
per share	1.41	1.29	1.17	1.05
Preferred	64	71	78	86
Average common shares outstanding	248,537,537	256,812,016	259,788,461	266,339,122
Number of employees	42,200	35,700	37,700	35,500
Capital expenditures	341,788	275,052	430,713	331,143
Depreciation and amortization	315,267	259,809	234,935	211,786
Total assets	8,247,188	6,381,146	6,821,321	5,931,901
Total debt	3,401,076	2,166,703	2,613,736	1,902,483
Shareholders' equity	2,472,869	2,338,551	2,320,996	2,367,398
Pretax return on average invested capital (%)	22.1	22.7	18.7	28.8
Return on average shareholders' equity before cumulative effect of accounting change (%)	24.6	25.9	22.0	27.5
Book value per common share	10.14	9.39	9.12	9.31
Price range of common stock:				
High	43	39⅞	45½	48⅝
Low	31⅝	30¾	35¼	35⅛

The 1994 results include pretax gains of $127.0 million relating to the divestiture of the confectionery and specialty rice businesses. The 1993 results include a pretax restructuring charge of $192.3 million. The 1992 results include a pretax gain of $221.5 million for the sale of The Hubinger Company, a pretax restructuring charge of $88.3 million and a pretax pension curtailment gain of $38.8 million.

EXHIBIT 16–18
H. J. Heinz Company and Subsidiaries, Excerpt from
Consolidated Balance Sheet

(Dollars in thousands)	May 3, 1995	April 27, 1994
• • •		
Shareholders' equity:		
Capital stock:		
Third cumulative preferred, $1.70 first		
series, $10 par value	$ 358	$ 398
Common stock, 287,401,000 shares		
issued, $.25 par value	71,850	71,850
	72,208	72,248
Additional capital	157,215	170,179
Retained earnings	3,878,988	3,633,385
Cumulative translation adjustments	(157,159)	(264,119)
	3,951,252	3,611,693
Less:		
Treasury shares, at cost (43,724,933		
shares at May 3, 1995 and		
38,359,744 shares at April 27, 1994)	1,450,724	1,239,177
Unearned compensation relating to the		
ESOP	27,659	33,965
Total shareholders' equity	$2,472,869	$2,338,551

of shares issued, to arrive at 243,676,067 shares of common stock outstanding. Dividing $2,472,511,000 by 243,676,067 results in a book value per share of $10.14.

Book value per share is not the same as either par or market value per share. In analyzing a company, book value loses much of its relevance if the fair value of a company's assets differs significantly from the balance sheet valuation of those assets.

17

DISCLOSURE, FOOTNOTES, AND THE AUDIT OPINION

*C*ertain supplemental schedules and other information are part of the financial statements. This material may be in the footnotes to the statements or presented separately. To understand a company's financial statements, one must study the footnotes. The financial statements contain a reminder: "The notes to the financial statements are an integral part of this statement," or "See the accompanying notes to the financial statements." This chapter discusses some of the note disclosures found in a typical company annual report.

There are two types of footnotes: (1) those that disclose the company's major accounting policies, and (2) those that provide information not given in the body of the financial statements. The first footnote (discussion to follow) deals with accounting policy disclosure. Among the supplementary disclosures will be information on pension plans and acquisitions, and a schedule of long-term debt showing interest rates and maturity dates. There is no limit to the number of footnotes a company can include in its annual report.

Note 1: Summary of Accounting Policies

Generally accepted accounting principles (GAAP) require disclosure of accounting policies in the first footnote to the financial statements. Here, a company reports its policies relating to such items as its principles of consolidation, inventory, income taxes, and depreciation. Disclosure of these policies is important. Where there are alternative policies, the financial statement reader obtains insight into management's philosophy through the accounting alternative chosen. Management may, for example, take a conservative or an aggressive approach to valuing assets or leveraging capital structure.

Exhibit 17–1 is Eaton Corporation's review of accounting policies, excerpted from the company's 1994 annual report.

Contingent Liabilities

Another item required by GAAP is the disclosure of contingent liabilities—liabilities subject to some future event that may or may not result in a payment, such as the settlement of a lawsuit or a tax court ruling stemming from a dispute. Sonoco Products Company provided this disclosure of a contingent liability relating to legal proceedings:

Commitments and Contingencies
The Company is a party to various legal proceedings incidental to its business and is subject to a variety of environmental and pollution control laws and regulations in all jurisdictions in which it operates. As is the case with other companies in similar industries, the Company faces exposure from actual or potential claims and legal proceedings. In 1994, a suit was

EXHIBIT 17–1
Eaton Corporation, Financial Review of Accounting Policies

Accounting Policies

Consolidation

The consolidated financial statements include accounts of the Company and all majority-owned subsidiaries. The equity method of accounting is used for investments where the Company has a 20% to 50% ownership interest.

Foreign Currency Translation

Financial statements for subsidiaries outside the United States, except those in highly inflationary economies, are translated into United States dollars at year-end exchange rates as to assets and liabilities and weighted average exchange rates as to revenues and expenses. The resulting translation adjustments are recorded in shareholders' equity. Financial statements for subsidiaries in highly inflationary economies are translated into United States dollars in the same manner except for inventories and property, plant, and equipment-net, and related expenses, which are translated at historical exchange rates. The resulting translation adjustments are included in net income.

Short-Term Investments

Short-term investments are not considered to be cash equivalents for purposes of classification in the statements of consolidated cash flows.

Inventories

Inventories are carried at lower of cost or market. Inventories in the United States are generally accounted for using the last-in, first-out (LIFO) method. The remaining United States and all other inventories are accounted for using the first-in, first-out (FIFO) method.

Depreciation and Amortization

Depreciation and amortization are computed by the straight-line method for financial statement purposes. The cost of plant and equipment is depreciated over the useful lives of the various classes of assets. Identified intangible assets, principally patents, trademarks and tradenames are amortized over the useful life of the respective asset. Excess of cost over net assets of businesses acquired is amortized principally over forty years (accumulated amortization in millions was $102 and $78 at the end of 1994 and 1993, respectively). Excess of cost over net assets of businesses acquired is assessed for impairment when operating profit from the related business indicates that the carrying amount may not be recoverable.

EXHIBIT 17–1 *(Continued)*

Financial Instruments

The Company uses various financial instruments, including foreign exchange contracts and options, and interest rate swaps and caps, as part of foreign exchange and interest rate risk management programs. The Company does not buy and sell financial instruments solely for the purpose of earning a profit due to changes in the market price of the instruments, except for nominal amounts authorized under limited, controlled circumstances.

The Company has subsidiaries operating in Canada, Europe, Latin America and the Pacific region. In the normal course of business, these operations are exposed to fluctuations in related foreign currencies. The Company seeks to reduce exposure to foreign currency fluctuations, primarily the European and Canadian currencies, through the use of foreign currency forward exchange contracts and options.

Gains or losses on foreign currency forward exchange contracts and options which hedge net investments in consolidated subsidiaries outside the United States are accrued in shareholders' equity. Gains or losses on foreign currency forward exchange contracts and options which hedge specific transactions are recognized in net income, offsetting the underlying foreign currency transaction gains or losses. Premiums and discounts related to foreign currency forward exchange contracts and options are amortized to other income—net over the lives of the agreements.

In the normal course of business, the Company's operations are also exposed to fluctuations in interest rates. The Company seeks to reduce the cost of and exposure to interest rate fluctuations through the use of interest rate swaps and caps. Gains or losses on interest rate swaps and caps are included in interest expense since they hedge interest on debt. Premiums related to interest rate caps are amortized to interest expense over the lives of the agreements.

Counterparties to various hedging instruments are many major international financial institutions. While the Company may be exposed to credit losses in the event of nonperformance by these counterparties, no losses are anticipated due to control over the limit of positions entered into with any one party and the strong credit ratings of these institutions.

Net Income Per Common Share

Net income per Common Share is computed by dividing net income by the average month-end number of shares outstanding during each period. The dilutive effect of common stock equivalents, comprised solely of employee options for Common Shares, is not material.

filed against the Company in the U.S. District Court for the District of Massachusetts for alleged patent infringement involving grocery bag packs. The suit also seeks to have a patent involving plastic bag loading systems owned by the Company declared invalid. The Company believes this lawsuit is without merit. The Company will vigorously defend its position and expects to prevail.

Subsequent Events

A company must disclose events that occur after the balance sheet date, but before the company issues its financial statements, and which may make the financial statements misleading if not disclosed. Examples of subsequent events include settlement of lawsuits and casualty losses to fire or flood after year end.

Segment Reporting

A business segment is a product line, territory, department, division, or subsidiary company. Because the results of operations of those segments may differ, GAAP requires companies to disclose, on a segmented basis, information about sales, operating income, identifiable assets, depreciation, amortization, depletion, and capital expenditures. Exhibit 17–2 shows segment information for SCANA Corporation. Though not required, a separate disclosure of its operating profit, net assets, and other information relating to its foreign operations is provided by Sonoco Products. This disclosure, done in addition to Sonoco's required disclosure of business segments, is shown in Exhibit 17–3.

Operating Lease Liabilities

Future rental payments are important in assessing future cash outflows for a company, even though those amounts are not liabilities on the balance

EXHIBIT 17-2
Scana Corporation, Segment Information

(Thousands of Dollars)	December 31, 1994			
	Electric	Gas	Transit	Total
Operating revenues	$ 975,388	$342,672	$ 4,002	$1,322,062
Operating expenses, excluding depreciation and amortization	640,528	292,227	10,577	943,332
Depreciation and amortization	102,647	16,304	226	119,177
Total operating expenses	743,175	308,531	10,803	1,062,509
Operating income (loss)	$ 232,213	$ 34,141	$ (6,801)	259,553
Add—Other income, net				5,998
Less—Interest charges				108,397
—Preferred stock dividends				5,955
Net income				$ 151,199
Capital expenditures: Identifiable	$ 364,007	$ 20,079	$ 347	$ 384,433
Utilized for overall Company operations				20,167
Total				$ 404,600
Identifiable assets at December 31, 1994:				
Utility plant, net	$2,897,954	$315,746	$ 1,791	$3,215,491
Inventories	98,669	17,026	495	116,190
Total	$2,996,623	$332,772	$ 2,286	3,331,681
Other assets				1,061,447
Total assets				$4,393,128

sheet. Rental expense and future minimum rental commitments are required disclosures. Eaton Corporation gave this lease commitments disclosure:

LEASE COMMITMENTS
Future minimum rental commitments as of December 31, 1994, under noncancelable operating leases, which expire at various dates and in most

EXHIBIT 17-3
Sonoco Products Corporation, International Operations Disclosure

The operating profit, net assets and dividends received by the Company from operations outside the United States are as follows:

	1994	1993
Operating profit	$ 15,675	$ 11,923
Net assets	245,423	185,723
Dividends	194	2,087

The aggregate foreign currency transaction gain/loss recognized in net income was immaterial for 1994, 1993 and 1992.

Information regarding the Company's significant foreign geographic area in Europe is as follows:

	1994	1993	1992*
Sales to unaffiliated customers	$184,247	$180,044	$226,127
Operating loss	(2,085)	(890)	(20,325)
Total assets	215,981	171,073	222,164

* Restructuring costs of $28,200 are included in 1992 results.

cases contain renewal options, are as follows (in millions): 1995, $42; 1996, $31; 1997, $24; 1998, $15; 1999, $12; and after 1999, $97.

Rental expense in 1994, 1993 and 1992 (in millions) was $65, $43 and $45, respectively.

Retirement Plan Liabilities

Employee pension plans result in significant liabilities for most companies, but the size of the liability and the assets that will be used to satisfy that liability are disclosed in the notes, rather than the body of the financial statements. The pension liability is called the Projected Benefit Obligation, and the assets to be used to pay retirees are called Plan Assets at Fair Value.

Pension accounting is complicated, but we can easily see whether pension assets are equal to pension liabilities. Exhibit 17–4 shows that, for Sonoco Products, the total Plan Assets in Excess of (Less Than) Projected Benefit Obligation is positive at the end of 1994. The plan is fully funded, and additional cash contributions are not necessary. This information is essential in assessing a company's cash flow and dividend prospects.

Five-Year Financial Summary of Financial and Statistical Data

Five-year (and sometimes ten-year) summaries of financial and statistical information normally appear in the back of the annual report or in a footnote. The data generally include total assets, liabilities, operating revenues and expenses, net income, earnings and dividends per share, and other types of information. Exhibit 17–5 is the five-year consolidated financial summary for Eaton Corporation.

The Auditor's Report

Published annual reports are audited by independent certified public accountants (CPAs). In a short report addressed to the stockholders and board of directors of the company, the CPA expresses an opinion on the financial statements prepared by management. The auditor can give one of three opinions or may disclaim an opinion. Auditors disclaim an opinion when they are unable to satisfy themselves as to whether the financial statements are presented fairly or not. The three types of audit opinion are:

1. *Unqualified or "clean" opinion.* When expressing this type of opinion, the auditor believes that the financial statements are "fair" representations of the company's financial position, results of operations, and cash flows, in conformity with generally accepted accounting principles (GAAP). This is the most common type of opinion.

EXHIBIT 17–4
Sonoco Products, Note on Retirement Benefit Plans

Non-contributory defined benefit pension plans cover substantially all U.S. employees. Under the plans, retirement benefits are based either on both years of service and compensation or on service only. It is the Company's policy to fund these plans, at a minimum, in amounts required under ERISA. Plan assets consist primarily of common stocks, bonds and real estate.

The Company also maintains a plan to supplement executive benefits limited through qualified plans. Benefits are based on years of service and compensation. The plan is partially funded through a grantor trust as defined under Section 671 of the Internal Revenue Service Code of 1986.

The Company's subsidiaries in the United Kingdom have contributory pension plans covering about 75% of the groups' employees. The acquisition of M. Harland and Son, Ltd. of the U.K. is included in 1994. Pension benefits are based either on the employee's salary in the year of retirement or the average of the final three years. The funding policy is to contribute annually at actuarially determined rates that are intended to remain a level percentage of salary.

Net pension cost for the domestic and United Kingdom plans included the following components:

	Combined Plans		
	1994	1993	1992
Service cost-benefits earned during year	$ 13,716	$ 9,555	$ 9,074
Interest cost on projected benefit obligation	27,160	23,881	22,196
Actual return on plan assets	(1,205)	(32,165)	(19,510)
Net amortization and deferral	(33,209)	2,031	(9,581)
	$ 6,462	$ 3,302	$ 2,179

EXHIBIT 17-4 *(Continued)*

The following table sets forth the funded status of the plans at December 31:

	Over-Funded Plans		Under-Funded Plans	
	1994	1993	1994	1993
Projected benefit obligation				
Vested benefits	$273,601	$271,733	$	$
Non-vested benefits	8,043	9,757	14,521	14,473
Accumulated benefit obligation	281,644	281,490	14,521	14,473
Effect of assumed increase in compensation levels	45,523	35,768	2,442	1,369
Projected benefit obligation	327,167	317,258	16,963	15,842
Plan assets at fair value	365,802	341,669	12,965	12,502
Plan assets in excess of (less than) projected benefit obligation	38,635	24,411	(3,998)	(3,340)
Unrecognized net loss	20,376	26,729	1,997	1,142
Unrecognized prior service cost	2,192	3,333	1,803	2,235
Unrecognized net transition (asset) obligation	(2,671)	(6,150)	1,370	1,599
Adjustment required to recognize minimum liability			(2,728)	(3,607)
Prepaid (accrued pension) cost	$ 58,532	$ 48,323	$(1,556)	$(1,971)

EXHIBIT 17–5
Eaton Corporation, Five Year Consolidated Financial Summary

(Millions except for per share data)	1994	1993	1992	1991	1990
For the year					
Net sales	$6,052	$4,401	$4,101	$3,659	$4,083
Income before extraordinary item and cumulative effect of accounting changes	333	180	140	74	179
Extraordinary item		(7)			
Cumulative effect of accounting changes					
Postretirement benefits other than pensions			(274)		
Income taxes			6		
Net income (loss)	333	173	(128)	74	179
Per Common Share					
Income before extraordinary item and cumulative effect of accounting changes	$ 4.40	$ 2.57	$ 2.03	$ 1.09	$ 2.53
Extraordinary item		(.10)			
Cumulative effect of accounting changes					
Postretirement benefits other than pensions			(3.97)		
Income taxes			.09		
Net income (loss)	4.40	2.47	(1.85)	1.09	2.53
Cash dividends paid	1.20	1.15	1.10	1.10	1.05
At the year-end					
Total assets	$4,682	$3,268	$3,220	$3,184	$3,140
Long-term debt	1,053	649	833	795	755
Total debt	1,089	773	882	927	815
Shareholders' equity	1,680	1,105	948	1,153	1,140

Results for 1994 reflect the acquisition of DCBU on January 31, 1994.

Income in 1993 was reduced by a $55 million acquisition integration charge related to the purchase of DCBU ($34 million after income tax credits, or $.49 per Common Share).

Income in 1993 was reduced by an extraordinary loss of $11 million for the redemption of debentures ($7 million after income tax credits, or $.10 per Common Share).

Income in 1991 was reduced by a restructuring charge of $39 million ($25 million after income tax credits, or $.38 per Common Share).

2. **Qualified opinion.** When expressing this type of opinion, the auditor takes exception to the "fair presentation" of a particular financial statement item or disclosure in conformity with GAAP. A qualified opinion contains the words "except for" preceding the item to which the auditor is taking exception. In a qualified opinion, the auditor believes that the remaining statements are "fairly presented."

3. **Adverse opinion.** When expressing an adverse opinion, the auditor believes that the statements are not "fairly presented" in conformity with GAAP. An adverse opinion is given by the auditor when the departure from GAAP is so pervasive that the financial statements are misleading to users of those statements.

Exhibit 17–6 is an auditor's report containing an unqualified audit opinion of Ernst & Young, LLP, an international accounting firm, on the financial statements of Eaton Corporation.

The first paragraph of the auditors' report says that the financial statements are the responsibility of management, not the auditors. The second paragraph explains what an audit is and that the auditor tests the accounting records and supporting documentation to support the opinion rendered. This is important because some financial statement users are under the mistaken impression that the auditor checks every transaction that occurred during the year. The third paragraph contains the auditors' opinion and states that the financial statements are "presented fairly" in accordance with GAAP.

EXHIBIT 17–6
Eaton Corporation, Auditors' Report

To the Shareholders
Eaton Corporation

We have audited the consolidated balance sheets of Eaton Corporation as of December 31, 1994 and 1993, and the related statements of consolidated income, shareholders' equity, and cash flows for each of the three years in the period ended December 31, 1994, appearing on pages 20 to 32. These financial statements are the responsibility of the Company's management. Our responsibility is to express an opinion on these financial statements based on our audits.

We conducted our audits in accordance with generally accepted auditing standards. Those standards require that we plan and perform the audit to obtain reasonable assurance about whether the financial statements are free of material misstatement. An audit includes examining, on a test basis, evidence supporting the amounts and disclosures in the financial statements. An audit also includes assessing the accounting principles used and significant estimates made by management, as well as evaluating the overall financial statement presentation. We believe that our audits provide a reasonable basis for our opinion.

In our opinion, the financial statements referred to above present fairly, in all material respects, the consolidated financial position of Eaton Corporation at December 31, 1994 and 1993, and the consolidated results of its operations and its cash flows for each of the three years in the period ended December 31, 1994 in conformity with generally accepted accounting principles.

As described under "Accounting Changes" on page 25 in the Financial Review, in 1992 the Company changed its methods of accounting for postretirement benefits other than pensions and for income taxes.

Ernst & Young LLP

Cleveland, Ohio
January 27, 1995

18

FINANCIAL LEVERAGE

*T*wo types of leverage are used to increase a company's performance: (1) financial leverage and (2) operating leverage. Financial leverage is used to increase a company's return on equity (ROE), calculated as earnings divided by common stockholders' equity. Operating leverage is used to increase a company's return on investment (ROI), calculated as earnings divided by investment in assets.

Both types of business leverage are similar to physical leverage, which uses a lever to gain a mechanical advantage. If a lever is placed off-center across a fulcrum (see Exhibit 18–1), a force applied to the longer end of the lever results in an increased force at the shorter end. A small person pressing down on the longer end will provide sufficient force to lift a car, if the lever is long enough and is positioned correctly. Physical leverage gives a person a mechanical advantage. Financial leverage and operating leverage give a company a business advantage. Financial leverage is discussed in this chapter; operating leverage is covered in Chapter 19. Characteristics of all three types of leverage are shown in Exhibit 18–2.

EXHIBIT 18–1
Using Leverage to Lift a Weight

150 pounds		1,000 pounds

EXHIBIT 18–2
Three Types of Leverage

Type of Leverage	Nature of the Advantage	Use
Physical leverage	Mechanical	To increase strength in lifting
Financial leverage	Capital structure	To increase return on equity*
Operating leverage	Asset mix	To increase return on investment**

$$* \text{ ROE} = \frac{\text{Earnings}}{\text{Common Stockholders' Equity}}$$

$$** \text{ ROI} = \frac{\text{Earnings}}{\text{Investment in Assets}}$$

Financial Leverage

Companies use financial leverage when they borrow at an interest rate below the return they can generate on the borrowed funds. Suppose, for example, Ted and Lou form a company with an investment in assets of $10,000. Using the equation in Chapter 1:

Assets = Liabilities + Owners' Equity

$10,000 = -0- + $10,000

If the company earns $1,000 per year, ROE and ROI are both 10 percent.

$$\text{ROE} = \frac{\text{Net Income}}{\text{Owners' Equity}} = \frac{\$1,000}{\$10,000} = 10 \text{ percent}$$

$$\text{ROI} = \frac{\text{Net Income}}{\text{Assets}} = \frac{\$1,000}{\$10,000} = 10 \text{ percent}$$

But suppose Ted and Lou purchase their $10,000 in assets to start the business by borrowing $2,500 at 8 percent and investing $7,500.

Assets = Liabilities + Owners' Equity

$10,000 = $2,500 + $7,500

The earnings of $1,000 per year will be reduced to $800 because $200 interest ($2,500 × .08) must be paid on the $2,500 debt. The lower earnings amount decreases ROI to 8 percent but ROE is increased to 10.67 percent. Ted and Lou have leveraged their investment by borrowing funds at a lower rate (8 percent) than they earn before interest on the invested funds (10 percent).

$$\text{ROE} = \frac{\text{Net Income}}{\text{Owners' Equity}} = \frac{\$800}{\$7,500} = 10.67 \text{ percent}$$

$$\text{ROI} = \frac{\text{Net Income}}{\text{Assets}} = \frac{\$800}{\$10,000} = 8 \text{ percent}$$

Exhibits 18–3 and 18–4 show how ROE and ROI change when Ted and Lou use 0 percent, 25 percent, 50 percent, and 75 percent debt financing in their capital structure. ROE increases from 10 percent at zero debt to 16 percent at 75 percent debt (Exhibit 18–3). ROI decreases from 10 percent to 4 percent (Exhibit 18–4). Greater leverage yields greater returns for owners but, because of the increased interest burden, yields lower return on assets. Financial leverage increases owners' wealth but it increases the owners' risk of loss as well.

EXHIBIT 18–3
Return on Equity

Interest rate = 8%

CAPITAL STRUCTURE

Debt	$ —	$ 2,500.00	$ 5,000.00	$ 7,500.00
Equity	$10,000.00	$ 7,500.00	$ 5,000.00	$ 2,500.00
Total	$10,000.00	$10,000.00	$10,000.00	$10,000.00

NET INCOME

Operating profit	8% Interest on debt	Net income				
$1,000.00	$ —	$1,000.00	10.00%			
$1,000.00	$200.00	$ 800.00		10.67%		
$1,000.00	$400.00	$ 600.00			12.00%	
$1,000.00	$600.00	$ 400.00				16.00%

EXHIBIT 18–4
Return on Investment

Interest rate = 8%

CAPITAL STRUCTURE

Debt	$ —	$ 2,500.00	$ 5,000.00	$ 7,500.00
Equity	$10,000.00	$ 7,500.00	$ 5,000.00	$ 2,500.00
Total	$10,000.00	$10,000.00	$10,000.00	$10,000.00

NET INCOME

Operating profit	8% Interest on debt	Net income				
$1,000.00	$ —	$1,000.00	10.00%			
$1,000.00	$200.00	$ 800.00		8.00%		
$1,000.00	$400.00	$ 600.00			6.00%	
$1,000.00	$600.00	$ 400.00				4.00%

Financial Leverage and Risk

When owners borrow to leverage their investment, they also increase the risk of loss because earnings might not be sufficient to cover the fixed interest charge. Exhibit 18–5 shows the ROE results of a range of operating incomes (before interest is subtracted), from $600 to $1,200. The interest rate is again 8 percent. With no debt, $600 of operating income results in an ROE of 6 percent (Exhibit 18–5). When operating earnings are $600 and debt is $2,500, net income is $400 ($600 − $200 interest expense) and leverage is negative, reducing ROE to 5.33 percent. When operating earnings are $600, greater proportions of debt yield lower returns to owners.

Continuing with Exhibit 18–5, with $800 in operating earnings, the interest rate and the ROI are both 8 percent, and debt does not change the return to owners. When operating earnings are greater than $800, leverage is positive and debt increases the return to owners.

Exhibits 18–6 through 18–8 show the same range of operating earnings with interest rates of 6 percent, 10 percent, and 12 percent, respectively. In each case, leverage is negative, thereby decreasing returns to owners, when

EXHIBIT 18–5
Return on Equity

Interest rate = 8%

CAPITAL STRUCTURE				
Debt	$ —	$ 2,500.00	$ 5,000.00	$ 7,500.00
Equity	$10,000.00	$ 7,500.00	$ 5,000.00	$ 2,500.00
Total	$10,000.00	$10,000.00	$10,000.00	$10,000.00

NET INCOME				
Operating profit				
$ 600.00	6.00%	5.33%	4.00%	0.00%
$ 800.00	8.00%	8.00%	8.00%	8.00%
$1,000.00	10.00%	10.67%	12.00%	16.00%
$1,200.00	12.00%	13.33%	16.00%	24.00%

EXHIBIT 18–6
Return on Equity

Interest rate = 6%

CAPITAL STRUCTURE

Debt	$ —	$ 2,500.00	$ 5,000.00	$ 7,500.00
Equity	$10,000.00	$ 7,500.00	$ 5,000.00	$ 2,500.00
Total	$10,000.00	$10,000.00	$10,000.00	$10,000.00

NET INCOME

Operating
profit

$ 600.00	6.00%	6.00%	6.00%	6.00%
$ 800.00	8.00%	8.67%	10.00%	14.00%
$1,000.00	10.00%	11.33%	14.00%	22.00%
$1,200.00	12.00%	14.00%	18.00%	30.00%

EXHIBIT 18–7
Return on Equity

Interest rate = 10%

CAPITAL STRUCTURE

Debt	$ —	$ 2,500.00	$ 5,000.00	$ 7,500.00
Equity	$10,000.00	$ 7,500.00	$ 5,000.00	$ 2,500.00
Total	$10,000.00	$10,000.00	$10,000.00	$10,000.00

NET INCOME

Operating
profit

$ 600.00	6.00%	4.67%	2.00%	−6.00%
$ 800.00	8.00%	7.33%	6.00%	2.00%
$1,000.00	10.00%	10.00%	10.00%	10.00%
$1,200.00	12.00%	12.67%	14.00%	18.00%

EXHIBIT 18–8
Return on Equity

Interest rate = 12%				
CAPITAL STRUCTURE				
Debt	$ —	$ 2,500.00	$ 5,000.00	$ 7,500.00
Equity	$10,000.00	$ 7,500.00	$ 5,000.00	$ 2,500.00
Total	$10,000.00	$10,000.00	$10,000.00	$10,000.00
NET INCOME				
Operating profit				
$ 600.00	6.00%	4.00%	0.00%	−12.00%
$ 800.00	8.00%	6.67%	4.00%	−4.00%
$1,000.00	10.00%	9.33%	8.00%	4.00%
$1,200.00	12.00%	12.00%	12.00%	12.00%

the interest rate is higher than the return earned on the borrowed funds. When interest rates are high or earnings are low, financial leverage can be dangerous.

Measuring Financial Leverage

The degree of financial leverage is the percentage change in earnings available to owners that accompanies a certain change in earnings before interest and taxes. To illustrate, refer to Exhibit 18–5 and a capital structure containing 50 percent debt at 8 percent interest. Because the degree of financial leverage must be measured at a specific level of activity, we examine operating earnings of $1,000 and measure the percentage change in net income available to owners after interest is paid, when operating earnings are increased 20 percent. Net income, not shown in Exhibit 18–5, is calculated as follows:

	Base	*Increased*	*Change (%)*
Operating income	$1,000	$1,200	20.0%
Less interest ($5,000 × .08)	400	400	—
Net income	$ 600	$ 800	33.3%

$$\text{Degree of financial leverage } \frac{33.3}{20.0} = 1.67$$

The same calculation result can be achieved from the financial statements of a single year (a single level of activity), using the following formula:

$$\text{Degree of financial leverage} = \frac{\text{Operating income}}{\text{Operating Income} - \text{Interest Expense}}$$

Using the figures for an operating income of $1,000 above, we get

$$\text{Degree of financial leverage} = \frac{\$1,000}{\$1,000 - \$400} = 1.67$$

This equation is handy because it lets us calculate the degree of financial leverage in a company's capital structure from one year of its earnings. Exhibit 18–9 shows the 1994 income statement of Deluxe Corporation. Deluxe's degree of financial leverage is 1.05 for both 1994 and 1993:

For 1994:

$$\text{Degree of financial leverage} = \frac{\text{Operating income}}{\text{Operating Income} - \text{Interest Expense}}$$

$$\text{Degree of financial leverage} = \frac{\$243,659}{\$243,659 - \$11,305}$$

$$\text{Degree of financial leverage} = 1.049$$

For 1993:

$$\text{Degree of financial leverage} = \frac{\$231,827}{\$231,827 - \$10,276}$$

$$\text{Degree of financial leverage} = 1.046$$

EXHIBIT 18–9
Deluxe Corporation, 1994 Consolidated Income Statement

(Dollars in Thousands Except per Share Amounts)	Years Ended December 31,		
	1994	1993	1992
Net Sales	$1,747,920)	$1,581,767)	$1,534,351)
Operating expenses			
Cost of sales	801,884	730,436	702,969
Selling, general, and administrative	630,531	489,127	423,362
Employee profit sharing and pension	59,668	61,162	60,307
Employee bonus and stock purchase discount	22,178	20,215	25,494
Restructuring charge (credit)	(10,000)	49,000	
Total	1,504,261	1,349,940	1,212,132
Income from operations	243,659	231,827	322,219
Other income (expense)			
Investment and other income	8,532	14,362	17,935
Interest expense	(11,305)	(10,276)	(15,371)
Income before income taxes	240,886	235,913	324,783
Provision for Income Taxes	100,020	94,052	121,999
Net Income	$ 140,866	$ 141,861	$ 202,784
Net Income per Common Share— Based on average number of shares outstanding	$ 1.71	$ 1.71	$ 2.42
Cash Dividends per Common Share	$ 1.46	$ 1.42	$ 1.34

19

OPERATING LEVERAGE

Operating leverage is the second type of business leverage used to increase a company's performance. Financial leverage, discussed in Chapter 18, is used to increase a company's return on equity (ROE) by adjusting the proportion of debt and equity in a company's capital structure. Operating leverage is used to increase a company's return on investment (ROI) by selecting operating expenditures and capital assets that give the optimal mix of costs. The calculation of ROE and ROI is discussed in Chapter 18.

Two Types of Costs

Accountants categorize costs simplistically as following two general behavior patterns: (1) a variable pattern, where the total cost changes in direct proportion to changes in some company activity; and (2) a fixed pattern, where the total cost remains the same during normal changes in company activities. Costs varying with activity are called *variable costs;*

costs remaining the same are called *fixed costs.* Examples of variable costs include the costs of sales commissions, energy, raw materials, supplies, maintenance, and assembly-line labor. Examples of fixed costs include the cost of insurance, property taxes, equipment leases, and salaried workers.

Exhibit 19–1 is a graph of energy cost for a factory, generally considered largely a variable cost. Exhibit 19–2 graphs the cost of salaried employees in a data processing department, a typical fixed cost.

A company obtains benefits from operating leverage by adjusting the mix of fixed and variable costs that compose the total cost of its operations. Assume Bendox Company manufactures a product that it sells for $50. Assume further that Bendox's production process is labor-intensive and that its labor, materials, and sales costs for each unit of product manufactured total $35. Because each unit of product requires $35 to produce and sell, $35 is the product's variable cost. By leasing its building and

EXHIBIT 19–1
A Variable Cost: Energy Cost in a Shoe Factory

Activity Is Measured by the Number of Pairs of Shoes Produced

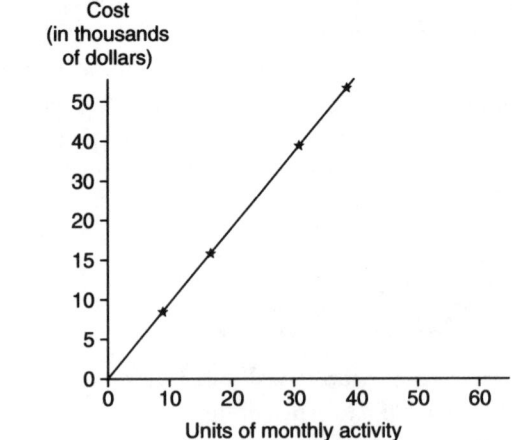

Units of monthly activity
(in thousands)

EXHIBIT 19–2
A Fixed Cost: Salaried Employees in Data Processing

Activity Is Measured by the Number of Units Produced in the Plant

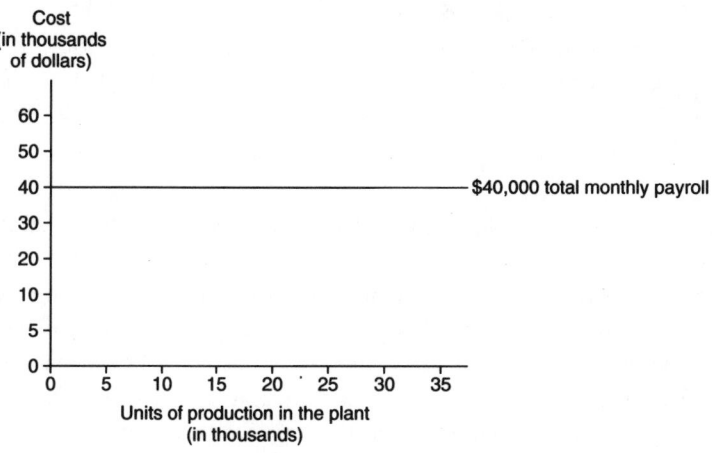

equipment, Bendox incurs annually $100,000 in lease and other fixed costs that do not vary as production and sales activity change.

This mix of fixed and variable costs causes each unit produced and sold to contribute $15 toward covering Bendox's fixed costs and building profit.

Selling price	$50
Variable costs (labor, materials, and sales cost)	35
Contribution margin per unit	$15

If Bendox produces and sells 7,000 units, its total contribution margin is $105,000 ($15 × 7,000 units). After its $100,000 fixed costs are covered, its profit is $5,000 ($105,000 − $100,000). Bendox's contribution margin formatted income statement will be:

Bendox Company
Income Statement
For the year ended December 31, 2000

Sales ($50 × 7,000 units)	$350,000
Variable costs ($35 × 7,000)	245,000
Contribution margin	105,000
Fixed costs	100,000
Profit	$ 5,000

Profit results for other levels of production (from 3,000 to 9,000 units) are shown in Exhibit 19–3.

If Bendox converts its production line from labor-consuming (using people) to automated (using robots), some portion of the variable cost of assembly labor will be replaced by the fixed cost of robotic machinery. Assume Bendox's annual fixed costs are increased to $150,000, and the variable cost of labor, materials, and sales is reduced to $20 per unit. Each unit then contributes $30 to covering fixed costs and building profit, as follows:

Selling price	$50
Variable costs (labor, materials, and sales costs)	20
Contribution per unit	$30

If Bendox now produces and sells 7,000 units, its contribution margin is $230,000 and its profit is $80,000:

Bendox Company
Income Statement
For the year ended December 31, 2001

Sales ($50 × 7,000 units)	$370,000
Variable costs ($20 × 7,000)	140,000
Contribution margin	230,000
Fixed costs	150,000
Profit	$ 80,000

EXHIBIT 19–3
Bendox Company, Profit Using Labor-Intensive Cost Structure

Operating Leverage—Manual

Selling price per unit	$ 50.00
Variable cost per unit	$ 35.00
Fixed cost (in total)	$100,000.00

Units	3,000	5,000	7,000	9,000
Sales	$150,000.00	$250,000.00	$350,000.00	$450,000.00
Variable costs	105,000.00	175,000.00	245,000.00	315,000.00
Contribution margin	45,000.00	75,000.00	105,000.00	135,000.00
Fixed costs	100,000.00	100,000.00	100,000.00	100,000.00
Profit	$ (55,000.00)	$ (25,000.00)	$ 5,000.00	$ 35,000.00

Profit results with the new cost structure, for other levels of production, are shown in Exhibit 19–4. The company has moved from labor-intensive (with low leverage) to capital-intensive (with high leverage). Trading the variable labor cost of production for the fixed machinery cost has increased the contribution to profit of a 1,000-unit sale from $15,000

EXHIBIT 19–4
Bendox Company, Profit Using the New
Capital-Intensive Cost Structure

Operating Leverage—Automated

Selling price per unit	$ 50.00
Variable cost per unit	$ 20.00
Fixed cost (in total)	$150,000.00

Units	3,000	5,000	7,000	9,000
Sales	$150,000.00	$250,000.00	$350,000.00	$450,000.00
Variable costs	60,000.00	100,000.00	140,000.00	180,000.00
Contribution margin	90,000.00	150,000.00	210,000.00	270,000.00
Fixed costs	150,000.00	150,000.00	150,000.00	150,000.00
Profit	$ (60,000.00)	$ —	$ 60,000.00	$120,000.00

to $30,000. Automation has "leveraged" the effect of a change in sales on company profit:

Manual operation:

1,000 units × $15 contribution/unit = $15,000 impact on profit

Automated operation:

1,000 units × $30 contribution/unit = $30,000 impact on profit

But this is a two-edged sword.

Operating Leverage and Risk

One way to define and measure the risk of an undertaking is to consider the potential *variability of the outcome*. The greater the variability of the outcome, the greater the risk involved in the undertaking. As an example, a company with $10,000 to invest for one year has three alternative investments:

Alternative 1 returns 5 percent interest and is federally insured.

Alternative 2 will either gain $3,000 or lose $2,000.

Alternative 3 will either gain $11,000 or lose all the money invested.

High and low outcomes are equally likely.

Principal		Outcome	Weighted Average Outcome
Alternative 1	$10,000 will yield	$10,500	$10,500
Alternative 2	$10,000 will yield	$13,000 (high)	$10,500
		$ 8,000 (low)	
Alternative 3	$10,000 will yield	$21,000 (high)	$10,500
		$–0– (low)	

All three investments have the same expected value, or weighted average outcome (meaning, if repeated large numbers of times, the three investments would all create the same return). Alternative 1 has no risk to the investor because there is zero variability of outcome. The investor knows with certainty that the return will be 5 percent. Alternative 3 is riskier than alternative 2 because the outcome for a single investment in alternative 3 varies by $21,000, high to low, versus only $5,000, high to low, for alternative 2.

Notice in Exhibit 19–3 that Bendox's outcome for production and sale of 3,000 to 9,000 units varies from a low of a $55,000 loss to a high of a $35,000 profit. This is a variation of $90,000, high to low.

But in Exhibit 19–4, Bendox has changed its mix of fixed and variable costs to leverage its earnings, and, in so doing, has increased its riskiness as measured by variability of outcome. Now, Bendox's outcome for production and sale of 3,000 to 9,000 units varies from a low of a $60,000 loss to a high of a $120,000 profit, a variation of $180,000, high to low.

With the automated production system, Bendox will have a greater increase in its profit for an increase in production and sales, but it will also have a greater decrease in profit when activity decreases. An automated Bendox Company is better able to capitalize on opportunity, but it also faces much more risk. Operating leverage improves Bendox's profitability at high sales levels, but to receive this benefit, Bendox must endure the risk associated with higher variability of profit.

Measuring Operating Leverage

The degree of operating leverage is measured at a particular activity level. It is the percentage change in operating earnings (that is, before interest and taxes) that accompanies a percentage change in contribution margin, when sales volume is changed. To illustrate, refer to Exhibit 19–3 and sales of 7,000 units. When sales are increased to 9,000 units, we measure the degree of operating leverage as shown below. (Note that when variable cost and selling price remain the same, the percentage change in sales and contribution margin is the same.) We have no taxes or interest, so operating income is the same as the final profit in Exhibit 19–3.

	Base	*Increased*	*Change (%)*
Sales in units	7,000	9,000	28.57
Sales in dollars	$350,000	$450,000	28.57
Contribution margin	$105,000	$135,000	28.57
Operating income	$ 5,000	$ 35,000	600.00

$$\text{Degree of operating leverage} = \frac{\text{Percentage Change in Operating Income}}{\text{Percentage Change in Sales}}$$

$$\text{Degree of operating leverage} = \frac{600\%}{28.57\%} = 21$$

This means that a certain percentage change in sales (X) will result in 21 times as large a percentage change in operating earnings (21X). Each $1,000 increase in sales will result in a $21,000 increase in operating earnings.

The same calculation result can be achieved from the financial statements for a single year (a single activity level), using the following formula:

$$\text{Degree of operating leverage} = \frac{\text{Contribution Margin}}{\text{Operating Income}}$$

At 7,000 units of sales and assuming the cost structure and operating leverage shown in Exhibit 19–3, the degree of operating leverage is:

$$\text{Degree of operating leverage} = \frac{\$105,000}{\$5,000} = 21$$

The equation is useful because it lets us calculate the degree of operating leverage in a company's cost structure from one year of its earnings. Still, its usefulness is limited to companies examining their own operations; published financial statements do not show costs separated by behavior (and hence do not show contribution margin) in either the income statement or the balance sheet.

The income statement of Deluxe Corporation is shown in Exhibit 18–9. If we wish to calculate Deluxe's degree of operating leverage, we must use two years' data (because contribution margin is not shown in Deluxe's financial statements) and we must use change in sales rather than the contribution margin. Deluxe's degree of operating leverage is negligible at 1.0009, calculated as follows:

	Base Year: 1993	Year of Increase: 1994	Change (%)
Sales in dollars	$1,581,767	$1,747,920	10.50
Operating income	$ 231,827	$ 243,659	10.51

$$\text{Degree of operating leverage} = \frac{\text{Percentage Change in Operating Income}}{\text{Percentage Change in Sales}}$$

Degree of operating leverage = 1.0009

Measuring Total Leverage

A company levers its sales to produce increased operating income by adjusting its mix of fixed and variable costs. It also levers its operating income to yield increased earnings by adjusting the debt-to-equity mix in its capital structure. Operating leverage is sometimes called first-stage leverage, and financial leverage is sometimes called second-stage leverage.

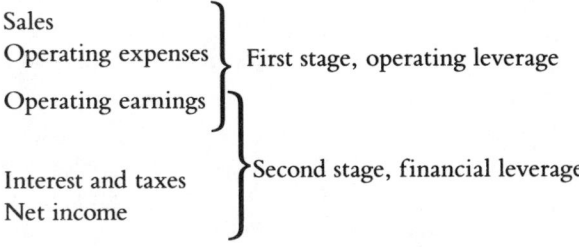

A company's total leverage is the product of its financial and operating leverage. For Deluxe, taking the financial leverage calculated in Chapter 18 for 1993 and the operating leverage for the same year calculated here, total leverage is 1.047:

Financial leverage × Operating leverage = Total leverage

  1.046   ×   1.0009   =   1.047

The formula for calculating total leverage directly is:

$$\frac{\text{Degree of}}{\text{operating leverage}} = \frac{\text{Contribution Margin}}{\text{Operating Income} - \text{Interest}}$$

or

$$\frac{\text{Degree of}}{\text{operating leverage}} = \frac{\text{Percentage Change in Operating Income} - \text{Interest}}{\text{Percentage Change in Sales}}$$

20

RATIO ANALYSIS

Ratios in and of themselves have little information value unless they are compared to norms such as average ratios for the industry the company operates in, or values for the same company in previous years. Ratios are generally classified into four areas of interest:

1. *Liquidity* relates to a company's short-term ability to meet its maturing obligations.

2. *Activity* refers to how efficiently a company is employing its assets.

3. *Profitability* refers to how successful a company is in generating profits.

4. *Solvency* refers to a company's ability to meet its long-term obligations.

Computing ratios is only a starting point in analyzing a company. Ratios do not give answers, but they do provide clues as to what might be expected.

Also, ratios often give conflicting signals. For instance, one might presume that the more cash a company has, the better it is able to pay its debts. But accumulating a lot of cash is not necessarily a good strategy, because idle cash earns little or no return. The company might have higher net income if it invested its cash. This type of inconsistency is pervasive throughout financial statement analysis.

Financial statement users make various types of financial decisions. Creditors, such as banks or vendors, are generally concerned about a company's current condition and its ability to pay currently maturing obligations. Long-term creditors, such as bondholders, are more interested in long-term indicators of financial strength and the likelihood of future earnings. Current and prospective stockholders are concerned with profitability, earnings, dividends, and increases in the market price of a company's shares; and, because they make long-term commitments, they are also interested in some of the same attributes that are the focus of long-term creditors. Even if a company pays its current obligations and repays its bonds and other long-term debts, its earnings may not be high enough to justify the purchase of its stock.

Illustrative Financial Statements

Although this book is about the balance sheet, we would be remiss if we only presented ratios that resulted in calculations using balance sheet information. Ratio analysis is normally performed using all of the information contained in the financial statements and related footnotes. Important ratios often result by using data from the income statement or statement of cash flows in conjunction with information obtained from the balance sheet. For this purpose, we present comparative financial statements and additional information from the annual report of Minnesota Mining and Manufacturing Company and Subsidiaries (3M), for 1994 and 1993 (Exhibits 20–1 through 20–4). All amounts shown in the financial statements and in the textual material are in millions.

EXHIBIT 20-1
Minnesota Mining and Manufacturing Company and Subsidiaries, Consolidated Balance Sheet

	At December 31,	
(Dollars in millions)	1994	1993
Assets		
Current assets:		
Cash and cash equivalents	$ 297	$ 274
Other securities	194	382
Accounts receivable—net	2,948	2,610
Inventories	2,763	2,401
Other current assets	726	696
Total current assets	6,928	6,363
Investments	536	455
Property, plant, and equipment—net	5,054	4,830
Other assets	978	549
Total	$13,496	$12,197
Liabilities and Stockholders' Equity		
Current liabilities:		
Accounts payable	$ 996	$ 878
Payroll	328	331
Income taxes	110	290
Short-term debt	917	697
Other current liabilities	1,254	1,086
Total current liabilities	3,605	3,282
Other liabilities	2,126	1,607
Long-term debt	1,031	796
Stockholders' Equity—net	6,734	6,512
Shares outstanding—1994: 419,793,702		
1993: 429,478,638		
Total	$13,496	$12,197

Share data reflect a two-for-one stock split effective March 15, 1994.

EXHIBIT 20–2
Minnesota Mining and Manufacturing Company and Subsidiaries,
Consolidated Statement of Income

(Amounts in millions, except per-share amounts)	For the Years Ended December 31,		
	1994	1993	1992
Net Sales	$15,079	$14,020	$13,883
Operating expenses:			
Cost of goods sold	8,995	8,529	8,346
Selling, general and administrative expenses	3,833	3,535	3,557
Legal settlement	—	—	(129)
Special charges	—	—	115
Total	12,828	12,064	11,889
Operating Income	2,251	1,956	1,994
Other income and expense:			
Interest expense	87	50	76
Investment and other income—net	(25)	(96)	(29)
Implant litigation—net	35	—	—
Total	97	(46)	47
Income before income taxes, minority interest, and cumulative effect of accounting changes	2,154	2,002	1,947
Provision for income taxes	771	707	687
Minority interest	61	32	24
Income before cumulative effect of accounting changes	1,322	1,263	1,236
Cumulative effect of accounting changes	—	—	(3)
Net income	$ 1,322	$ 1,263	$ 1,233
Per-share amounts:			
Income before cumulative effect of accounting changes	$ 3.13	$ 2.91	$ 2.82
Cumulative effect of accounting changes	—	—	(0.01)
Net income	$ 3.13	$ 2.91	$ 2.81
Average shares outstanding	423.0	434.3	438.2

All share and per-share data reflect a two-for-one stock split effective March 15, 1994.

EXHIBIT 20-3
Minnesota Mining and Manufacturing Company and Subsidiaries,
Consolidated Statement of Cash Flows

	For the Years Ended December 31,		
(Dollars in millions)	1994	1993	1992*
Cash Flows from Operating Activities			
Net income	$ 1,322	$ 1,263	$ 1,233
Adjustments to reconcile net income to net cash provided by operating activities:			
Legal settlement	—	129	(129)
Special charges	—	(29)	115
Cumulative effect of accounting changes	—	—	103
Depreciation	1,003	976	1,004
Amortization	98	100	83
Accounts receivable	(243)	(327)	(142)
Inventories	(302)	(161)	(78)
Working capital and other changes	51	140	88
Net cash provided by operating activities	1,929	2,091	2,277
Cash Flows from Investing Activities			
Capital expenditures	(1,148)	(1,112)	(1,318)
Proceeds from sale of property, plant, and equipment	45	53	78
Acquisitions and other investments	(93)	(71)	(59)
Proceeds from divestitures and investments	25	38	63
Net cash used in investing activities	(1,171)	(1,092)	(1,236)
Cash Flows from Financing Activities			
Net change in short-term debt	216	48	(83)
Repayment of long-term debt	(62)	(80)	(187)
Proceeds from long-term debt	401	150	139
Purchases of treasury stock	(689)	(706)	(247)
Reissuances of treasury stock	138	181	177
Payment of dividends	(744)	(721)	(701)
Net cash used in financing activities	(740)	(1,128)	(902)
Effect of exchange rate changes on cash	5	21	(15)
Net increase (decrease) in cash and cash equivalents	23	(108)	124
Cash and cash equivalents at beginning of year	274	382	258
Cash and cash equivalents at end of year	$ 297	$ 274	$ 382

* Includes cash flows of international companies for a 14-month period from November 1, 1991, to December 31, 1992. See note on page 37 for details.

EXHIBIT 20–4
Minnesota Mining and Manufacturing Company and Subsidiaries,
Additional Information

Short-Term Debt (Millions)	Effective Interest Rate*		1994	1993
Commercial paper	6.03%		$ 593	$193
Long-term debt—				
current portion	8.13%		174	79
Other borrowings	7.93%		150	425
Total short-term debt			$ 917	$697

Long-Term Debt (Millions)	Effective Interest Rate*	Maturity Date	1994	1993
ESOP debt guarantee	8.21%	1996–2004	$ 444	$469
U.S. 6.375% Eurobond	6.52%	1997	200	—
Canadian 6.5% Eurobond	4.81%	1998	114	114
Medium-term 6.25% note	6.61%	1999	100	75
Swiss Franc 5.5% note	5.73%	1997	98	—
Other borrowings	7.50%	1996–2025	75	138
Total long-term debt			$1,031	$796

* Weighted-average effective interest rates, which reflect the effects of interest rate and currency swaps, at December 31, 1994.

Other borrowings consist primarily of borrowings of 3M's international companies and industrial bond issues in the United States.

On January 10, 1995, the company completed a two-year, $200 million 7.75 percent Eurobond offering. The company entered into an interest rate swap, which resulted in an all-in borrowing cost of the 30-day commercial paper rate less 30 basis points for two years.

Maturities of long-term debt for the next five years are as follows: 1995, $174 million; 1996, $45 million; 1997, $340 million; 1998, $160 million; and 1999, $146 million.

Interest payments included in the Consolidated Statement of Cash Flows totaled $89 million in 1994, $53 million in 1993 and $88 million in 1992. The

EXHIBIT 20–4 *(Continued)*

$88 million in 1992 included cash flows of international companies for a 14-month period from November 1, 1991, to December 31, 1992. For the calendar year 1992, interest payments were $79 million. The ESOP debt is being serviced by dividends on stock held by the ESOP and by Company contributions. These contributions are reported as a benefit expense.

The company estimates that the fair value of short-term and long-term debt approximates the carrying amount of this debt. Payment of dividends is not restricted by debt covenants.

Income Before Income Taxes (Millions)	1994	1993	1992
U.S.	$1,435	$1,390	$1,301
International	719	612	646
Total	$2,154	$2,002	$1,947

Provision for Income Taxes (Millions)	1994	1993	1992
Currently payable			
Federal	$ 338	$ 430	$ 371
State	67	74	78
International	297	292	339
Deferred			
Federal	52	(66)	(63)
State	5	(5)	(6)
International	12	(18)	(32)
Total	$ 771	$ 707	$ 687

Deferred taxes in 1994 and 1993 include benefit costs not currently deductible of $293 million and $336 million, respectively, and accelerated depreciation for tax purposes of $362 million in both 1994 and 1993.

Income tax payments included in the Consolidated Statement of Cash Flows totaled $895 million in 1994, $802 million in 1993 and $743 million in 1992. The $743 million in 1992 includes cash flows of international companies for a 14-month period from November 1, 1991, to December 31, 1992. For calendar year 1992, income tax payments were $714 million.

EXHIBIT 20–4 *(Continued)*

At December 31, 1994, there were approximately $3.060 billion of retained earnings attributable to international companies that are considered to be permanently invested. No provision has been made for taxes that might be payable if these earnings were remitted to the United States. It is not practical to determine the amount of incremental tax that might arise were these earnings to be remitted.

Reconciliation of Effective Income Tax Rate	1994	1993	1992
Statutory U.S. tax rate	35.0 %	35.0 %	34.0 %
State income taxes—net	2.2	2.2	2.5
International taxes	2.7	3.0	4.4
Adjusted prior years' export sales benefit	(1.9)	—	—
All other—net	(2.2)	(4.9)	(5.6)
Effective worldwide tax rate	35.8 %	35.3 %	35.3 %

Other Information

Cash dividends paid	1994	1993
Per share	1.76	1.66
Stock price at year end	53.38	54.38

All share and per-share data reflect a two-for-one stock split effective March 15, 1994.

Liquidity Ratios

A company exhibits high liquidity when (1) the amount of its current assets is large in relation to the amount of its current liabilities, and (2) it has a high proportion of current assets in cash, securities, and receivables, as opposed to inventory or prepaid expenses. Liquidity ratios indicate whether a company has sufficient liquid current assets to meet currently maturing or short-term obligations.

Working Capital

Working capital is the difference between current assets and current liabilities and is a crude measure of liquidity. Exhibit 20–1 shows that 3M had the following amounts of working capital at the end of 1994 and 1993:

	1994	*1993*
Current assets	$6,928	$6,363
Current liabilities	3,605	3,282
Working capital	$3,323	$3,081

An increase in working capital does not always result in increased liquidity because working capital is a dollar amount, not a ratio. Amounts by themselves can be difficult to evaluate. Two better measures of liquidity include the current ratio and the quick ratio. The use of different inventory cost flow methods (such as FIFO or LIFO), resulting in different inventory amounts on the balance sheet, can make intercompany comparisons of working capital and liquidity somewhat difficult.

Current Ratio

The current ratio is calculated by dividing current assets by current liabilities. The ratio indicates whether a company can meet its short-term obligations with current assets. Because it is a ratio and not an amount, it can be used to compare companies of different sizes or the same company at different balance sheet dates.

3M's current ratios are:

$$1994: \frac{\$6,928}{\$3,605} = 1.92 \qquad 1993: \frac{\$6,363}{\$3,283} = 1.94$$

On the basis of the current ratio, 3M appears to be slightly less liquid at the end of 1994. However, the ratio needs to be interpreted with respect to an industry norm and as part of a trend.

A major problem with the current ratio (and other ratios) is one of composition; that is, the use of a total, such as total current assets (or current liabilities), might mask information about individual components of the ratio. A user must look at the balance sheet to see the extent to which current assets are composed of relatively liquid items, such as cash and receivables. In 3M's case, 50 percent of its current assets consist of inventories and other current assets. Additionally, the current ratio does not provide any information regarding how quickly current assets will be converted into cash and liabilities paid.

Quick Ratio (Acid-Test Ratio)

As stated above, the composition of current assets can result in varying degrees of liquidity. To avoid this problem, another ratio can be calculated that more directly takes into consideration the degrees of liquidity of current assets. The quick ratio, or acid-test ratio, is quick assets (cash, temporary investments, and accounts receivable) divided by current liabilities. The quick ratio is a stricter test of liquidity (the "acid test") than the current ratio because it indicates whether a company could extinguish its current liabilities if they came due within a fairly short period of time.

$$\text{Quick Ratio} = \frac{\text{Cash} + \text{Temporary Investments} + \text{Receivables}}{\text{Current Liabilities}}$$

3M describes temporary investments as "Other securities" on its balance sheet. 3M's quick ratios are as follows:

$$1994: \frac{\$297 + \$194 + \$2,948}{\$3,605} = .95 \quad 1993: \frac{\$274 + \$382 + \$2,620}{\$3,282} = 1.00$$

3M's liquidity has decreased slightly because its quick ratio decreased. The company is in approximately the same position to meet current liabilities as it was in 1993. In examining the balance sheets of 3M for 1994 and 1993 (Exhibit 20–1), we can see that the cause of the decrease in the ratio is that accounts payable, short-term debt, and other current liabilities have increased by a greater amount than the company's quick assets. Excluding inventories and other similar nonliquid assets from the numerator of the quick ratio can give users more information about a company's liquidity than the current ratio provides.

Current Asset Activity (Turnover) Ratios

Activity ratios, also called turnover ratios, are used to measure how efficiently a company uses its assets. They generally take the following form:

$$\text{Activity Ratio} = \frac{\text{Best Measure of Asset Activity}}{\text{Asset}}$$

Accounts Receivable Turnover

Accounts receivable turnover measures how rapidly receivables are collected (turned over). The ratio is net sales divided by average net accounts receivable:

$$\text{Accounts Receivable Turnover} = \frac{\text{Net Sales}}{\text{Average Net Accounts Receivable}}$$

The numerator *should be* net credit sales because cash sales do not create accounts receivable; in most cases, net sales is used as the numerator because companies do not normally report credit sales separately. The information provided by the ratio should not be negatively affected by using net sales, as long as the relationship between cash and credit sales remains constant. Average net accounts receivable is normally the beginning balance of accounts receivable plus the ending balance, divided by 2. Or, the end-of-year figure could be used instead of the average. One must be careful in using averages or year-end balances because these amounts might not be representative of the year and could lead to erroneous conclusions.

The ratio shows the number of times during the year that the average accounts receivable balance was converted into cash. Normally, the higher the turnover is, the better, because receivables are being collected rapidly. This reduces the amount of sales dollars tied up in accounts receivable and makes more cash available for other purposes. However, a high turnover ratio might also indicate that the company's credit policies are too stringent, resulting in lost sales and reduced profitability. The accounts receivable turnover ratio for 3M for 1994 is calculated as:

$$\frac{\$15,079}{(\$2,948 + \$2,610)/2} = 5.43$$

The numerator is the revenues figure from the income statement in Exhibit 20–2, and the denominator is the accounts receivable figures from the balance sheets in Exhibit 20–1.

Days' Sales in Accounts Receivable

Another related ratio, called days' sales in accounts receivable, is used to assess the efficiency of accounts receivable management. This figure represents the average age of accounts receivable and is calculated as follows:

$$\text{Days' Sales in Accounts Receivable} = \frac{\text{Ending Accounts Receivable}}{\text{Average Daily Sales}}$$

Average daily sales is the annual net credit sales divided by 365. (Net sales are normally used because net credit sales are unavailable.) This ratio has the same problem as the accounts receivable turnover ratio in that the ending balance might not be representative of the year.

3M has average daily sales of $41.3 million ($15,079/365) for 1994 and $38.4 million ($14,020/365) for 1993. Hence, days' sales in accounts receivable are:

$$1994: \frac{\$2,948}{\$41.3} = 71 \text{ days} \qquad 1993: \frac{\$2,610}{\$38.4} = 68 \text{ days}$$

On average, 3M's accounts receivable were 71 days old at the end of 1994, and 68 days old at the end of 1993. The collection period has increased, perhaps due to a loosening of credit policies. The number of days' sales in accounts receivable should be viewed as part of a trend rather than simply a single number.

Normally, the faster customers pay, the better; but a company must consider the fact that there are trade-offs. If sales are lost because of tight credit policies, the advantage of faster collection might be more than offset by the loss of profits.

Inventory Turnover

The faster the inventory is sold, the quicker the company turns its investment in inventory into cash. Inventory turnover is calculated as follows:

$$\text{Inventory Turnover} = \frac{\text{Cost of Goods Sold}}{\text{Average Inventory}}$$

Again, average inventory is usually the beginning balance plus the ending balance divided by 2; the year-end balance could be used instead. The problem of representativeness applies here as with accounts receivable.

The costs of carrying inventory are high; they must be balanced against the costs of a stockout. Generally, the higher the turnover, the better, although high turnover can also mean that the company is experiencing stockouts by not maintaining enough inventory, and is turning away disgruntled customers. Low turnover may also indicate that the company is carrying too much inventory or has a lack of sales. Therefore, a company attempts to maintain a turnover rate that balances inventory carrying costs and stockouts. This results in the most profitable turnover rate, not necessarily the highest rate.

3M's inventory turnover for 1994 is about 3.5 times, calculated as follows:

$$\frac{\$8,995}{(\$2,763 + \$2,401)/2} = 3.5$$

Because inventory turnover rates vary widely and are related to a company's profit margin, the turnover rate should be compared to industry norms and also viewed as a trend over time.

Days' Sales in Inventory

Like accounts receivable turnover, inventory turnover has a counterpart, days' sales in inventory, calculated as follows:

$$\text{Days' Sales in Inventory} = \frac{\text{Ending Inventory}}{\text{Average Daily Cost of Goods Sold}}$$

Average daily cost of goods sold is simply cost of goods sold for the year, divided by 365. For 3M, this figure is $24.6 million ($8,995/365) for 1994 and $23.4 million ($8,529/365) for 1993. The days' sales in inventory are:

$$1994: \frac{\$2,763}{\$24.6} = 112.0 \text{ days} \qquad 1993: \frac{\$2,401}{\$23.4} = 103.0 \text{ days}$$

The increase in days' sales in inventory could be caused by a number of factors. For example, the company may have changed its policy on how much inventory to carry. Or, the increase might be temporary, caused by purchases made near the end of the year.

Profitability Ratios

The income statement has at least three important ratios relating to profitability:

1. Gross Profit Ratio: $\dfrac{\text{Gross Profit (Net Sales} - \text{Cost of Goods Sold)}}{\text{Net Sales}}$

2. Operating Ratio: $\dfrac{\text{Operating Income}}{\text{Net Sales}}$

3. Return on Sales: $\dfrac{\text{Net Income}}{\text{Net Sales}}$

These ratios for 3M in 1994 are 40.3 percent, 14.9 percent, and 8.8 percent, respectively. The gross profit ratio and the operating ratio increased slightly in 1994 over 1993, but return on sales declined.

These ratios can provide information as to how well the company's managers were able to turn each dollar of sales into gross profit, operating profit, and net income. Other profitability measures use information from the income statement and the balance sheet, the most common of which is return on investment (ROI). This group of ratios has the following general form:

$$\text{Return on Investment} = \frac{\text{Income}}{\text{Investment}}$$

Most measures relate an income statement item (such as net income) to a balance sheet item (such as stockholders' equity). Company managers are concerned with earning satisfactory returns on the investments they control, as are current and potential stockholders. There are different forms of the ratio, based on the different definitions of income and investment.

Return on Assets

Return on assets (ROA) is a better measure of profitability than the gross profit ratio, operating ratio, or return on sales because it measures operating efficiency. The ratio indicates the company's effectiveness at using the assets under its control to generate income. The most common calculation of the ratio is:

$$\text{Return on Assets} = \frac{\text{Operating Income}}{\text{Average Total Assets}}$$

For 3M, ROA was 17.5 for 1994, calculated as:

$$\frac{\$2,251}{(\$13,496 + \$12,197)/2} = 17.5 \text{ percent}$$

Because the ratio relates to operations, we use operating income, thereby excluding interest and income taxes, which depend on how the company finances assets. Other variations of operating income are used, such as including interest in the numerator but not taxes. There are arguments to support several measures of the numerator and denominator in the ROA calculation, so the choice is one of personal preference.

The most common measure of average total assets is the sum of the beginning and ending balance sheet amounts divided by 2. Average total assets is used in the calculation, because income, the numerator, is earned during the entire period. The balance of total assets at the end of the year might also be used as the denominator.

Return on Common Equity (ROE)

Return on investment depends on profitable operations as well as the amount of debt and preferred stock in the company's capital structure.

Return on common equity (ROE) is computed as follows:

$$\text{Return on Common Equity} = \frac{\text{Net Income} - \text{Preferred Dividends}}{\text{Average Common Stockholders' Equity}}$$

For a company without preferred stock, average common stockholders' equity is the sum of the beginning and ending amounts of total stockholders' equity divided by 2. If the company has preferred stock, preferred dividends must be subtracted from net income in the numerator because only net income minus preferred dividends is available for distribution to common stockholders. The equity attributable to preferred stock must also be subtracted from total stockholders' equity in the denominator. 3M does not have any outstanding preferred stock. ROE for 3M in 1994 is 20 percent.

$$\frac{\$1,322}{(\$6,734 + \$6,512)/2} = 20.0 \text{ percent}$$

When 3M's return on common equity is compared to its operating ratio, return on sales, and return on assets, we see that return on common equity is greater than all of these other measures of profitability. This is an indication that the company's management has performed reasonably well; however, the return may still not be satisfactory and must be compared to some other benchmark or norm.

Creditors receive a fixed amount of interest. Companies can therefore increase ROE by using debt, provided that ROA is greater than the interest rate it pays to creditors. Using debt (or preferred stock) to increase ROE is called leverage. Leverage increases risk but it provides the potential for greater return. (Financial leverage is discussed in Chapter 18.)

Earnings per Share

Earnings per share (EPS) is the most widely reported statistic in the financial press and, in the absence of complicating factors, is calculated as follows:

$$\text{Earnings per Share} = \frac{\text{Net Income Available for Common Stockholders}}{\text{Weighted-Average Common Shares Outstanding}}$$

(Complicating factors relating to earnings per share are beyond the scope of this book.) In computing EPS, the denominator is the weighted-average number of shares outstanding during the year and not the number of shares outstanding at year end, because the weighted-average is the best measure of the number of shares outstanding throughout the period. Preferred stock dividends are subtracted from net income to arrive at earnings available to the common stockholders, because preferred stockholders are paid dividends before common stockholders. Exhibit 20–4 indicates that

3M had 423.0 million shares outstanding at the end of 1994 and 434.3 million shares outstanding at the end of 1993, resulting in EPS figures of

$$1994: \frac{\$1,322}{423.0 \text{ shares}} = \$3.13 \qquad 1993: \frac{\$1,263}{434.3 \text{ shares}} = \$2.91$$

Growth Rate of EPS

Earnings per share were $0.22 higher than in 1993, almost an 8 percent growth rate, calculated as follows:

$$\text{Growth Rate of EPS} = \frac{\text{EPS in Current Year} - \text{EPS in Prior Year}}{\text{EPS in Prior Year}}$$

$$\frac{\$3.13 - \$2.91}{\$2.91} = 7.6 \text{ percent}$$

All things equal, the higher the company's EPS growth rate, the more investors will pay for the company's stock. Like other ratios, the growth rate should be viewed over a number of years, rather than for a single year, because, to be significant, growth must be sustained.

Price–Earnings Ratio

The price–earnings (PE) ratio is the market price of a share of common stock divided by its EPS (earnings per share).

$$\text{Price–Earnings Ratio} = \frac{\text{Market Price per Share}}{\text{Earnings per Share}}$$

Price–earnings ratios are reported in the financial press; they represent the amount an investor pays for a dollar of earnings. The trend of a company's PE ratio is an indication of its long-term growth potential. High-growth companies usually have high PE ratios; low-growth, stable, or declining companies have low PE ratios. In Exhibit 20–4, we see that 3M's common stock sold at $53.38 per share at the end of 1994 and $54.38 at the end of 1993. The PE ratios are as follows:

$$1994: \frac{\$53.38}{\$3.13} = 17.1 \qquad 1993: \frac{\$54.38}{\$2.91} = 18.7$$

The PE ratio decreased during the year, possibly indicating that investors were slightly less willing to pay more for each dollar of earnings. The decrease also could have occurred because the company's earnings prospects were less optimistic or because PE ratios in general sagged, reflecting investors' sentiment regarding the economic climate.

Dividend Yield

Investors benefit from dividends and increases in the market value of their shares of stock. The dividend yield measures the percentage of market value that is paid annually in dividends to stockholders.

$$\text{Dividend Yield} = \frac{\text{Dividend per Share}}{\text{Market Price per Share}}$$

3M's annual report indicates that the company had dividends per share of $1.76 and $1.66 for 1994 and 1993, respectively. With the share prices of $53.38 and $54.38 at the end of 1994 and 1993, dividend yields are as follows.

$$1994: \frac{\$1.76}{\$58.38} = 3.3 \text{ percent} \qquad 1993: \frac{\$1.66}{\$54.38} = 3.1 \text{ percent}$$

Investors compare dividend yields to other investment options. Adding the dividend yield to the percentage change in share price for the period results in an estimate of a stockholders' return for that period, which can also be compared to other investment alternatives.

Dividend yields vary widely. Older, more established companies can have a dividend yield of 4 to 8 percent; growth companies, which reinvest earnings, can have a dividend yield of 0 to 3 percent.

Dividend Payout Ratio

The dividend payout ratio is the ratio of dividends per share to earnings per share. For 3M, the payout ratio was 56 percent ($1.76/$3.13) in 1994 and 57 percent ($1.66/$2.91) in 1993. Companies with high growth rates generally have relatively low dividend yields and payout ratios because they reinvest the cash that could be used to pay dividends.

Solvency Ratios

Investors and long-term creditors are both concerned with solvency. Long-term creditors are interested in receiving interest payments and re-payment of the principal amount of debt. Investors are interested in solvency because if the company cannot pay its long-term liabilities, the company cannot pay dividends, and its share price will not increase. Solvency relates to whether a company is able to pay its long-term liabilities and how the company uses debt in its capital structure. A solvency problem signals uncertainty regarding debt repayment to long-term creditors and return on investment to stockholders.

Debt Ratio

A very common measure of solvency is the debt ratio. The debt ratio is computed as:

$$\text{Debt Ratio} = \frac{\text{Total Liabilities}}{\text{Total Assets}}$$

This ratio measures the percentage of debt in the capital structure. Like other ratios, it has several variations, including the debt-to-equity ratio:

$$\frac{\text{Total Liabilities}}{\text{Total Stockholders' Equity}}$$

All forms of the ratio attempt to measure the debt burden of a company to determine whether the company is too highly leveraged. In general, the higher the debt ratio, the riskier the company.

3M's debt ratios for 1994 and 1993 are as follows:

$$1994: \frac{\$6,762}{\$13,496} = 50.1 \text{ percent} \qquad 1993: \frac{\$5,685}{\$12,197} = 46.6 \text{ percent}$$

Total liabilities for 3M consist of the sum of current liabilities plus other liabilities plus long-term debt. The debt ratio increased during the period, resulting in a greater portion of the assets being financed by the creditors rather than by the owners. This situation increased the pressure on 3M to make principal and interest payments on its debts.

Times Interest Earned

Additional information on a company's debt burden is obtained by calculating times interest earned. Times interest earned, or interest coverage, measures the extent to which operations cover interest expense. The higher the ratio, the more likely the company will be able to continue meeting the interest payments. This ratio also indicates the amount that income can decline before a company has a problem in meeting its interest payments.

$$\text{Times Interest Earned} = \frac{\text{Net Income Before Interest and Income Taxes}}{\text{Interest Expense}}$$

3M had interest coverage of 25.1 times in 1994 and 40.4 times in 1993, which indicates a deterioration in this ratio.

$$1994: \frac{\$1,322 + \$771 + \$87}{\$30,665} = 25.1 \qquad 1993: \frac{\$1,263 + \$707 + \$50}{\$25,739} = 40.4$$

Because cash, not earnings, is used to pay interest, another ratio that can be used to measure interest coverage is the cash flows to interest coverage. The ratio is expressed as

$$\frac{\text{Net Cash Provide by}}{\text{Operating Activities} + \text{Interest Paid} + \text{Income Taxes Paid}}{\text{Interest Paid}}$$

Net cash provided by operating activities is found in Exhibit 20–3, 3M's statement of cash flows. Exhibit 20–4, from the notes to the financial statements, indicates the amounts paid in 1994 for interest and income taxes. The calculations for the ratio are:

$$1994: \frac{\$1,929 + \$89 + \$895}{\$89} = 32.7 \qquad 1993: \frac{\$2,091 + \$53 + \$802}{\$53} = 55.6$$

The reduction in the ratio from 1993 to 1994 is consistent with our findings regarding the times interest earned ratio.

Cash flow ratios are used to examine solvency in terms of a company's cash flows. Two other cash flow ratios can also be used to assess solvency:

$$1. \quad \frac{\text{Cash Flow to}}{\text{Net Income}} = \frac{\text{Net Cash Provided by Operating Activities}}{\text{Net Income}}$$

$$2. \quad \frac{\text{Cash Return}}{\text{on Sales}} = \frac{\text{Net Cash Provided by Operating Activities}}{\text{Sales}}$$

Cash flow to net income is used to determine how closely a company's operating cash flows are correlated with its income. All things being equal, the higher the correlation, the better. A ratio of less than 1 indicates that a company had more success in generating earnings rather than cash.

Cash return on sales is very similar to the conventional return on sales figure, that is, net income divided by sales. The ratio reveals the percentage of each sales dollar that can be spent for operating purposes.

Cash Flow to Net Income

$$1994: \frac{\$1,929}{\$1,322} = \$1.46 \qquad 1993: \frac{\$2,091}{\$1,263} = \$1.66$$

Cash Return on Sales

$$1994: \frac{\$1,929}{\$15,079} = \$.13 \qquad 1993: \frac{\$2,091}{\$14,020} = \$.15$$

In 1994, the company generated $1.46 in cash flows from net income, but only 13 cents from sales. As with all other ratios, in order to assess 3M's cash flow ratios, we would need to make comparisons to a norm, such as industry averages, or view the ratios over time.

Exhibit 20–5 provides a summary of the ratios discussed in this chapter.

EXHIBIT 20–5
Summary of Ratios and Analytical Measurements

Liquidity

1. Working Capital = Current Assets − Current Liabilities

2. Current Ratio = $\dfrac{\text{Current Assets}}{\text{Current Liabilities}}$

3. Quick Ratio = $\dfrac{\text{Cash + Temporary Investments + Receivables}}{\text{Current Liabilities}}$

Activity

4. Accounts Receivable Turnover = $\dfrac{\text{Net Sales}}{\text{Average Net Accounts Receivable}}$

5. Days' Sales in Accounts Receivable = $\dfrac{\text{Ending Accounts Receivable}}{\text{Average Daily Sales}}$

6. Inventory Turnover = $\dfrac{\text{Cost of Goods Sold}}{\text{Average Inventory}}$

7. Days' Sales in Inventory = $\dfrac{\text{Ending Inventory}}{\text{Average Daily Cost of Goods Sold}}$

Profitability

8. Gross Profit = $\dfrac{\text{Gross Profit}}{\text{Net Sales}}$

9. Operating Ratio = $\dfrac{\text{Operating Income}}{\text{Net Sales}}$

10. Return on Sales = $\dfrac{\text{Net Income}}{\text{Net Sales}}$

11. Return on Investment = $\dfrac{\text{Income}}{\text{Investment}}$

12. Return on Assets = $\dfrac{\text{Operating Income}}{\text{Average Total Assets}}$

13. Return on Common Equity (ROE) = $\dfrac{\text{Net Income}}{\text{Average Common Stockholders' Equity}}$

14. Earnings per Share = $\dfrac{\text{Net Income Available for Common Stockholders}}{\text{Weighted-Average Common Shares Outstanding}}$

15. Growth Rate of EPS = $\dfrac{\text{EPS Current Year − EPS Prior Year}}{\text{EPS Prior Year}}$

16. Price–Earnings Ratio = $\dfrac{\text{Market Price per Share}}{\text{Earnings per Share}}$

EXHIBIT 20-5 *(Continued)*

17. Dividend Yield $= \dfrac{\text{Dividend per Share}}{\text{Market Price per Share}}$

18. Dividend Payout Ratio $= \dfrac{\text{Dividend per Share}}{\text{Earnings per Share}}$

Solvency

19. Debt Ratio $= \dfrac{\text{Total Liabilities}}{\text{Total Assets}}$

20. Debt-to-Equity Ratio $= \dfrac{\text{Total Liabilities}}{\text{Total Stockholders' Equity}}$

21. Times Interest Earned $= \dfrac{\text{Net Income Before Interest and Income Taxes}}{\text{Interest Expense}}$

22. Cash Flow Interest Coverage $= \dfrac{\text{Net Cash Provided from Operating Activities + Interest Paid + Income Taxes Paid}}{\text{Interest Paid}}$

23. Cash Flow to Net Income $= \dfrac{\text{Net Cash Provided by Operating Activities}}{\text{Net Income}}$

24. Cash Return on Sales $= \dfrac{\text{Net Cash Provided by Operating Activities}}{\text{Sales}}$

Index